Pro Processing for Images and Computer Vision with OpenCV

Solutions for Media Artists and Creative Coders

Bryan WC Chung

Apress®

Pro Processing for Images and Computer Vision with OpenCV

Bryan WC Chung
Academy of Visual Arts, Kowloon Tong, Hong Kong

ISBN-13 (pbk): 978-1-4842-2774-9   ISBN-13 (electronic): 978-1-4842-2775-6
DOI 10.1007/978-1-4842-2775-6

Library of Congress Control Number: 2017951872

Copyright © 2017 by Bryan WC Chung

This work is subject to copyright. All rights are reserved by the Publisher, whether the whole or part of the material is concerned, specifically the rights of translation, reprinting, reuse of illustrations, recitation, broadcasting, reproduction on microfilms or in any other physical way, and transmission or information storage and retrieval, electronic adaptation, computer software, or by similar or dissimilar methodology now known or hereafter developed.

Trademarked names, logos, and images may appear in this book. Rather than use a trademark symbol with every occurrence of a trademarked name, logo, or image we use the names, logos, and images only in an editorial fashion and to the benefit of the trademark owner, with no intention of infringement of the trademark.

The use in this publication of trade names, trademarks, service marks, and similar terms, even if they are not identified as such, is not to be taken as an expression of opinion as to whether or not they are subject to proprietary rights.

While the advice and information in this book are believed to be true and accurate at the date of publication, neither the authors nor the editors nor the publisher can accept any legal responsibility for any errors or omissions that may be made. The publisher makes no warranty, express or implied, with respect to the material contained herein.

Cover image by Freepik (www.freepik.com).

Managing Director: Welmoed Spahr
Editorial Director: Todd Green
Acquisitions Editor: Jonathan Gennick
Development Editor: Laura Berendson
Technical Reviewer: Kathleen Sullivan
Coordinating Editor: Jill Balzano
Copy Editor: Kim Wimpsett

Distributed to the book trade worldwide by Springer Science+Business Media New York, 233 Spring Street, 6th Floor, New York, NY 10013. Phone 1-800-SPRINGER, fax (201) 348-4505, e-mail orders-ny@springer-sbm.com, or visit www.springeronline.com. Apress Media, LLC is a California LLC and the sole member (owner) is Springer Science + Business Media Finance Inc (SSBM Finance Inc). SSBM Finance Inc is a **Delaware** corporation.

For information on translations, please e-mail rights@apress.com, or visit www.apress.com/rights-permissions.

Apress titles may be purchased in bulk for academic, corporate, or promotional use. eBook versions and licenses are also available for most titles. For more information, reference our Print and eBook Bulk Sales web page at www.apress.com/bulk-sales.

Any source code or other supplementary material referenced by the author in this book is available to readers on GitHub via the book's product page, located at www.apress.com/9781484227749. For more detailed information, please visit www.apress.com/source-code.

Printed on acid-free paper

Contents at a Glance

Contents

About the Author

Bryan WC Chung is an interactive media artist and design consultant. He was the grand prize winner of the 19th Japan Media Arts Festival, Art Division, 2015. In 2009, his consultation work on the Coca-Cola Happy Whistling Machine won the Media Kam Fan Advertising Award. Bryan's works have been exhibited at the World Wide Video Festival, Multimedia Art Asia Pacific, Stuttgart Film Winter Festival, Microwave International New Media Arts Festival, and China Media Art Festival. In the Shanghai Expo 2010, he provided interactive design consultancy to industry leaders in Hong Kong. Bryan also develops software libraries for the open source programming language Processing. He is the author of the book *Multimedia Programming with Pure Data*. Currently, he is an associate professor in the Academy of Visual Arts at Hong Kong Baptist University, where he teaches classes on interactive art, computer graphics, and multimedia. His personal website can be found at http://www.magicandlove.com.

About the Technical Reviewer

Kat Sullivan lives somewhere in the intersection between movement and technology. After double majoring in computer science and dance at Skidmore College, she worked for several years as a software engineer and freelanced as a dancer. Not wanting to compartmentalize her life, she went to the Interactive Telecommunications Program (ITP) and began creating work involving creative coding, live performance, machine learning, and more. Upon completing her master's degree at ITP, she was invited to stay an additional year as a research resident. Her work has been presented at Lincoln Center, National Sawdust, Pioneer Works, Flux Factory, South by Southwest, and the Liberty Science Center. She is currently teaching a motion capture course at NYU.

Acknowledgments

I would like to express my gratitude to my wife, Kimburley, for her support and patience throughout the writing and creative process.

Thanks to my father for introducing me to the world of arts and craft at an early age.

Thanks to my late brother, Percy, for sharing his inspiration in illustration and graphic design.

Thanks to my mother and sister for their continuous support and caring.

Thanks to my boss, Professor John Aiken, for providing me with a beautiful place to work.

CHAPTER 1

Getting Started with Processing and OpenCV

The chapter introduces you to Processing and OpenCV and how to install them. By the end of the chapter, you will have a general understanding about the types of applications you can build by following the examples in this book. You will also be able to write a "Hello World" program to display version information for OpenCV within the Processing programming environment.

Processing

Ben Fry and Casey Reas from the former Aesthetic + Computation Group of the MIT Media Lab initiated the Processing project (`http://processing.org`) in 2001 to create a programming environment for artists and designers to learn the fundamentals of computer programming within the context of electronic arts. Based on the Java programming language, Processing is modeled as an electronic sketchbook for artists and designers to generate their creative ideas. Processing comes with an integrated development environment (IDE). Users can directly code in the environment and execute the code to see the visual results in real time. Processing is equipped with a comprehensive set of frameworks and libraries to provide simple access to functions for creating 2D and 3D graphics and building animation. Java was chosen as the programming language to cater to cross-platform compatibility. At the moment, it supports macOS, Windows, and the major Linux operating systems. Recently, Processing has evolved to include other programming languages such as JavaScript and Python.

Besides the core functions of the Processing language and the vast number of native Java libraries, Processing supports user-contributed libraries (`https://processing.org/reference/libraries/`) from the community. A lot of the libraries were built to hide the technical details of implementing complex software such as physics engines and machine-learning algorithms or to support additional hardware devices such as the Kinect camera. For example, I have developed a wrapper library called `Kinect4WinSDK` to support the Kinect version 1 camera with the official Kinect for Windows software development kit (SDK).

In the area of computer graphics, Processing is capable of producing both vector graphics and raster graphics. In creative applications, algorithmic art and generative art (Figure 1-1) will often make use of vector graphics. In this book, the focus is on image processing and computer vision. In this case, raster graphics will be the primary approach to generate images.

© Bryan WC Chung 2017
B. WC. Chung, *Pro Processing for Images and Computer Vision with OpenCV*,
DOI 10.1007/978-1-4842-2775-6_1

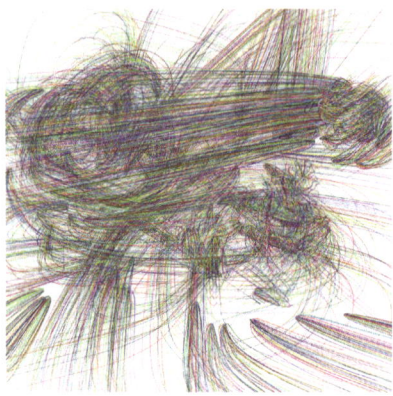

Figure 1-1. *Algorithmic art example*

OpenCV

Open Source Computer Vision Library (OpenCV, http://opencv.org/) started as an Intel research initiative around 1999. Now, it is the most popular open source software library for computer vision and machine learning. In the beginning, it was a set of C library functions for image processing and computer vision. Now, it has C++, Python, Java, and MATLAB bindings and works on macOS, Windows, Linux, Android, and iOS, with acceleration support from CUDA and OpenCL. The OpenCV library comes with a collection of modules. Each of the modules handles a specific group of applications under the umbrella of image processing, computer vision, and machine learning. The following are the common modules:

- `core`: Core OpenCV data structures and functionalities
- `imgproc`: Image processing
- `imgcodecs`: Image file reading and writing
- `videoio`: Media input/output routines
- `highgui`: High-level graphical user interface
- `video`: Video analysis
- `calib3d`: Camera calibration and 3D reconstruction
- `features2d`: Working with 2D features description and matching
- `objdetect`: Object detection such as faces
- `ml`: Machine learning
- `flann`: Clustering and searching in higher-dimensional spaces
- `photo`: Computational photography
- `stitching`: Stitching images together
- `shape`: Shape matching
- `superres`: Super-resolution enhancement
- `videostab`: Video stabilization
- `viz`: 3D visualization

OpenCV includes several extra modules that provide additional functionalities, such as text recognition, surface matching, and 3D depth processing. This book also covers the module optflow, which performs optical flow analysis.

Processing Installation

This section explains the procedures to download and install the Processing programming environment. At the time of writing, the latest version of Processing is 3.2.3. It is advised that you use version 3, rather than previous versions, of Processing for compatibility reasons. Each distribution of Processing also includes with the Java runtime code. The installation processes for the three platforms are straightforward and similar.

Install Processing

Download the Processing code from https://processing.org/download/. In this book, I will use the 64-bit versions. If you want to take a look at the Processing source code, you can download it from the GitHub distribution (https://github.com/processing/processing). The following are the three files for the macOS, Windows, and Linux platforms:

- processing-3.2.3-macosx.zip

- processing-3.2.3-windows64.zip

- processing-3.2.3-linux64.tgz

Processing does not assume any particular location to install the software. For macOS, you can download and expand the file into a macOS program named Processing. Copy the program to the Applications folder similar to other applications you install for macOS. For Windows and Linux, the compressed file will be expanded into a folder named processing-3.2.3. You can download and expand the compressed file into any folder you want to maintain the Processing software. In this book, we expand the folder processing-3.2.3 into the user's Documents folder. Figure 1-2 shows the contents of the folder. To run Processing, simply double-click the Processing icon.

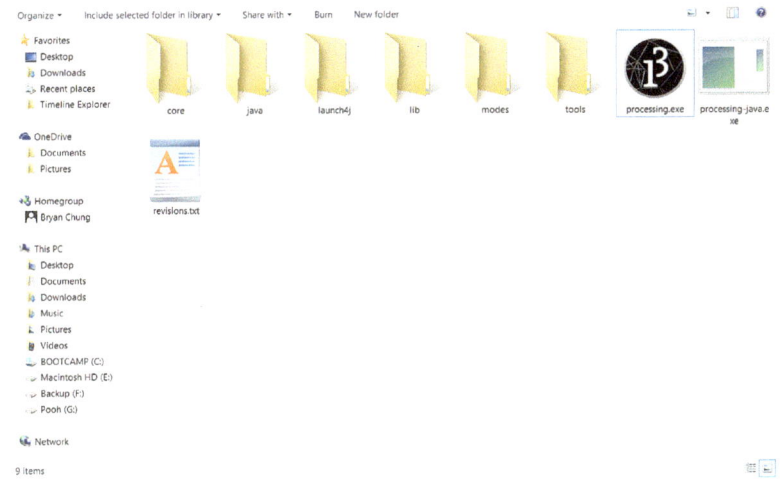

Figure 1-2. *Processing folder for Windows*

Figure 1-3 shows the default screen layout of the Processing IDE. The code in the window will be the first Processing program you are going to test.

```
void setup() {
  size(800, 600);
}

void draw() {
  background(100, 100, 100);
}
```

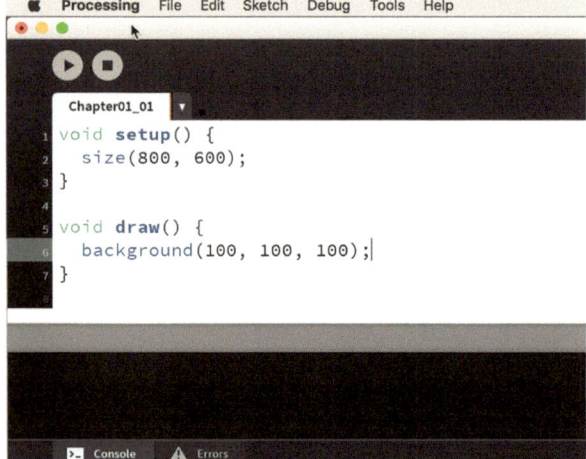

Figure 1-3. *Processing IDE screen*

After you have started Processing, it will automatically create a folder in your personal Documents folder in which it maintains all the Processing programs. For macOS, its name is /Users/bryan/Documents/Processing. In Windows, the folder name is C:\Users\chung_000\Documents\Processing. In Linux, it is /home/bryan/sketchbook. (In the example, the username is bryan or chung_000.) Figure 1-4 shows an example view of the folder contents.

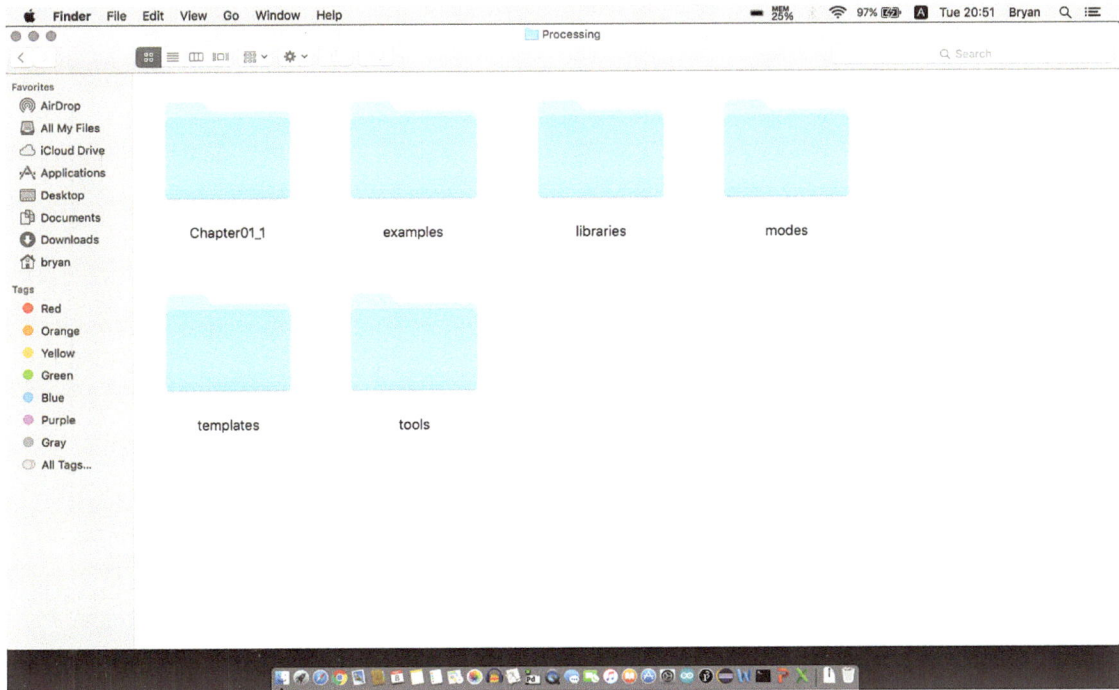

Figure 1-4. *Processing sketchbook folder contents*

Each Processing program is maintained in its own folder within the `Processing` folder. In addition to each program, the folder contains other subfolders, such as the `libraries` folder for downloading external libraries from the Processing distribution and the `modes` folder for implementing other languages in Processing such as Python and JavaScript.

Run Processing

In the top-left corner of the Processing IDE, there are two buttons, Play and Stop. Clicking the Play button will start the compilation and execution of the program. Figure 1-5 shows the blank screen created with your first program. Clicking the Stop button at this moment will stop the execution and close the window.

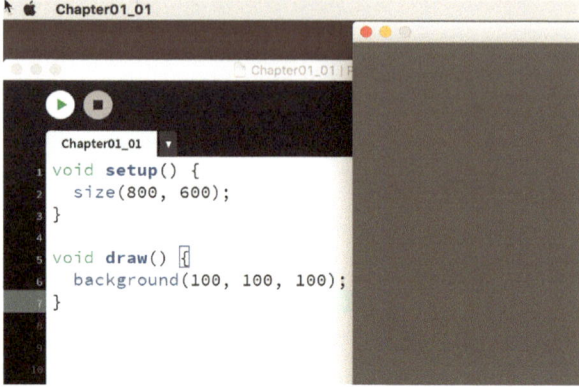

Figure 1-5. *First Processing program*

You need to install an additional library for the exercises in this book. It is the `video` library that is built on top of the open source multimedia framework GStreamer (`https://gstreamer.freedesktop.org/`). Processing will use it for playing back digital videos such as MP4 files and capturing live video with a webcam. To install the library (Figure 1-6), choose Sketch ➤ Import Library ➤ Add Library from the main menu. From the Contribution Manager window, choose the Video library and click the Install button. The library will then be downloaded to the `libraries` subfolder of your Processing folder.

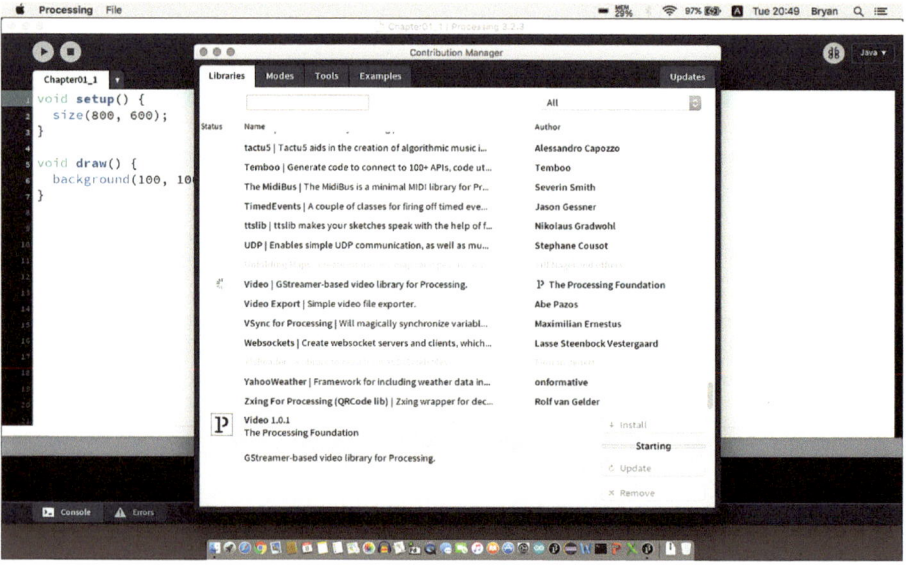

Figure 1-6. *Installing the video library*

In Chapter 2, you will use this library for loading external digital video and capturing live video streams from webcams. After you have installed the Processing programming environment, you can proceed to install OpenCV on your system.

OpenCV Installation

The installation for OpenCV is a bit complicated because you are going to build the OpenCV library from source. The library you are going to build is different from the existing OpenCV for Processing library written by Greg Borenstein (`https://github.com/atduskgreg/opencv-processing`). It is better for you to remove the existing OpenCV for Processing library before proceeding with this installation process. The OpenCV distribution includes all the core functions. To use other functions for motion analysis, you also need to build the extra modules that are maintained in the contributed libraries. You are going to download both of them from the GitHub repositories. The original OpenCV source is at `https://github.com/opencv/opencv`, and the source for the extra modules is at `https://github.com/opencv/opencv_contrib`. Note that the master branch in the OpenCV repository contains only version 2.4. To use version 3.1, which you want to do for this book, you need to select the 3.1.0 tag, as shown in Figure 1-7. After choosing the right version tag, you can download the OpenCV source by clicking the "Clone or download" button and then the Download ZIP button, as shown in Figure 1-8.

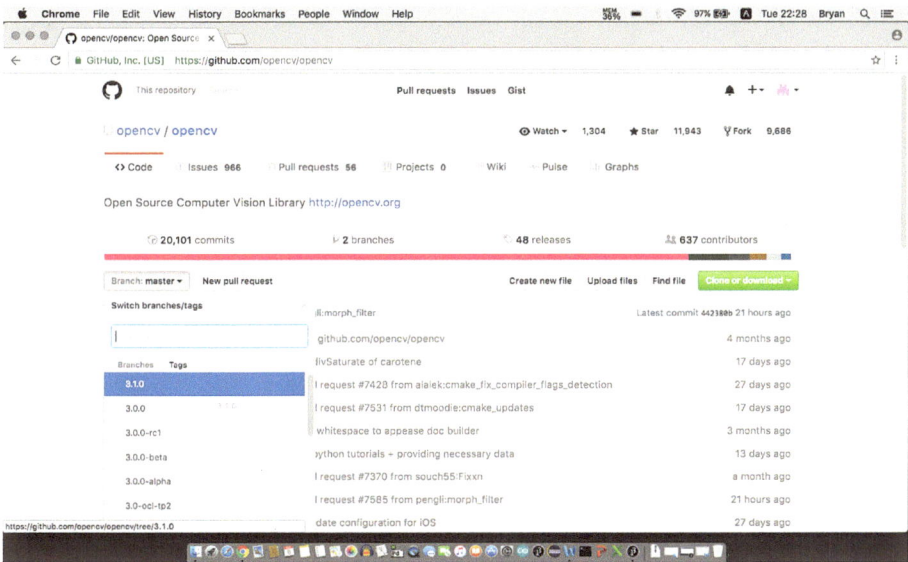

Figure 1-7. *Selecting the tag 3.1.0*

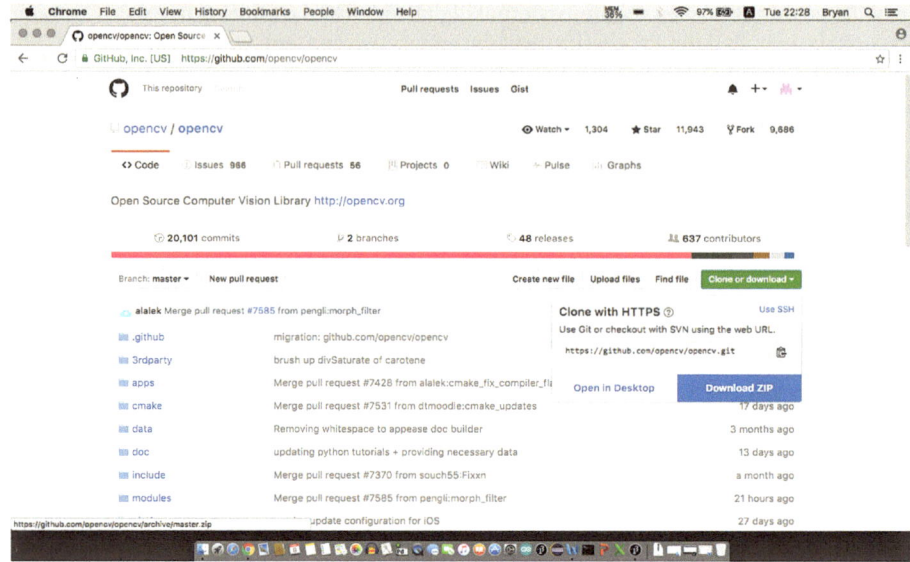

Figure 1-8. *Downloading the OpenCV source*

After you download and extract the OpenCV source, the process will create the opencv-3.1.0 folder. For the opencv_contrib source, follow the same procedure to select the 3.1.0 tag, download the zip file, and extract it into your opencv-3.1.0 folder. Figure 1-9 shows the contents of the opencv-3.1.0 folder.

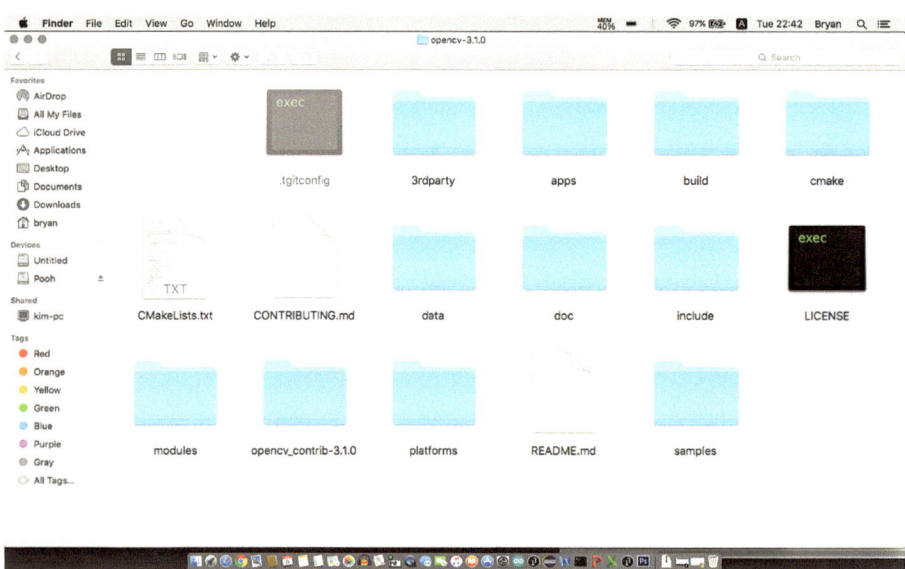

Figure 1-9. *Contents of the opencv-3.1.0 folder*

After you successfully download the OpenCV 3.1.0 source and the extra modules library, you can create a subfolder named build inside the opencv-3.1.0 folder. All OpenCV libraries will be built into this folder. Before you start the build process, there is one more step you have to take care of. To build the Java library that includes the extra module optflow, which you will use for motion analysis, you have to edit its CMakeLists.txt file. From the opencv_contrib-3.1.0 folder, go into the modules folder and then the optflow folder. Use any text editor to modify the CMakeLists.txt file in the optflow folder. In the second line, the original code is as follows:

```
ocv_define_module(optflow opencv_core opencv_imgproc opencv_video opencv_highgui
opencv_ximgproc WRAP python)
```

Insert the token java between the two keywords WRAP and python. The new line will be as follows:

```
ocv_define_module(optflow opencv_core opencv_imgproc opencv_video opencv_highgui
opencv_ximgproc WRAP java python)
```

The new file will enable the build process to include the optflow module into the Java library that was built. The following sections describe the different build processes depending on the platform you are using. Since you are going to build the OpenCV Java library, you should also download and install the Java Development Kit (JDK) from the Oracle web site at www.oracle.com/technetwork/java/javase/downloads/jdk8-downloads-2133151.html. To check whether you already have installed the JDK, you can go to a Terminal or command-line session and type the following:

```
javac -version
```

macOS

You are going to use Homebrew to install the necessary dependent software. The installation process will be executed from a command-line Terminal session. The Terminal tool is in the /Applications/Utilities folder. The Homebrew installation instructions are on the official web site at http://brew.sh/. After you have installed the Homebrew package manager, you can start to install the software required for the OpenCV build process. In a Terminal session, enter the following:

```
brew install cmake
brew install ant
```

These two commands install the software cmake and ant. The cmake tool (http://cmake.org) is an open source tool to build, test, and package software. The Apache ant tool (http://ant.apache.org) is a utility to build Java applications. The next step is to start the configuration process with the ccmake interactive tool. First, navigate to the build folder of the original OpenCV folder, opencv-3.1.0, and issue the ccmake command, as shown in Figure 1-10.

```
ccmake ..
```

```
apples-MacBook-Pro:build bryan$ java -version
java version "1.8.0_112"
Java(TM) SE Runtime Environment (build 1.8.0_112-b16)
Java HotSpot(TM) 64-Bit Server VM (build 25.112-b16, mixed mode)
apples-MacBook-Pro:build bryan$ javac -version
javac 1.8.0_112
apples-MacBook-Pro:build bryan$ ant -version
Apache Ant(TM) version 1.10.1 compiled on February 2 2017
apples-MacBook-Pro:build bryan$ ccmake ..█
```

Figure 1-10. *ccmake command to configure the build process*

In the ccmake panel, type c to configure the installation process. Select the appropriate options, as shown in Figure 1-11. Please note that you should first turn off most of the options on the first page, including the BUILD_SHARED_LIBS option. Next turn on the BUILD_opencv_java option, as shown in Figure 1-12 and Figure 1-13.

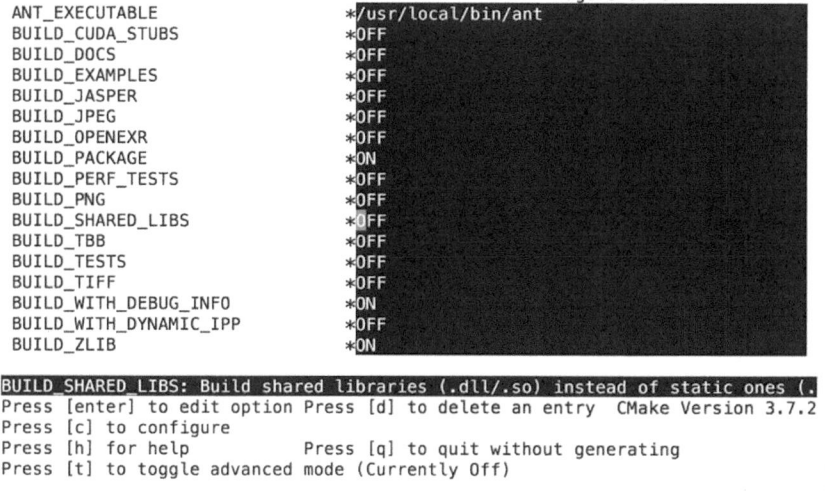

Figure 1-11. *BUILD_SHARED_LIBS and other options*

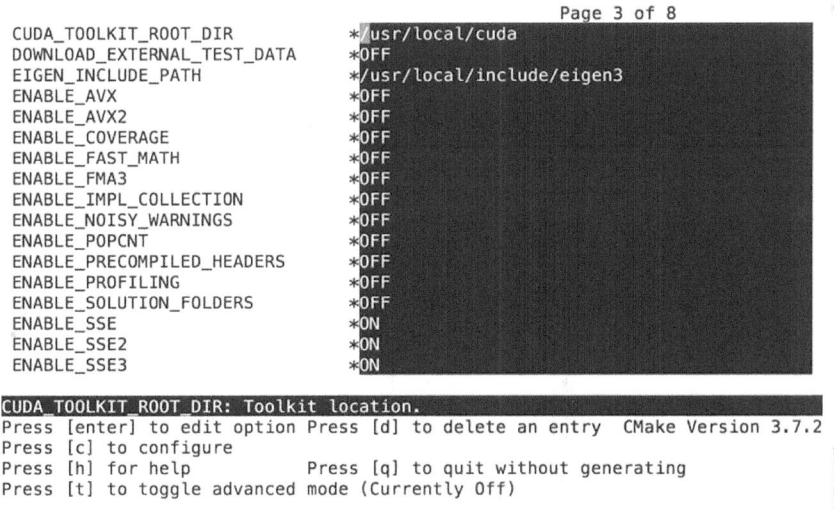

```
                                        Page 2 of 8
BUILD_opencv_apps                    *OFF
CLAMDBLAS_INCLUDE_DIR                 *CLAMDBLAS_INCLUDE_DIR-NOTFOUND
CLAMDBLAS_ROOT_DIR                    *CLAMDBLAS_ROOT_DIR-NOTFOUND
CLAMDFFT_INCLUDE_DIR                  *CLAMDFFT_INCLUDE_DIR-NOTFOUND
CLAMDFFT_ROOT_DIR                     *CLAMDFFT_ROOT_DIR-NOTFOUND
CMAKE_BUILD_TYPE                      *
CMAKE_CONFIGURATION_TYPES             *Debug;Release
CMAKE_INSTALL_PREFIX                  */usr/local
CMAKE_OSX_ARCHITECTURES               *
CMAKE_OSX_DEPLOYMENT_TARGET           *
CMAKE_OSX_SYSROOT                     *
CUDA_ARCH_BIN                         *2.0 2.1(2.0) 3.0 3.5
CUDA_ARCH_PTX                         *3.0
CUDA_FAST_MATH                        *OFF
CUDA_GENERATION                       *
CUDA_HOST_COMPILER                    */Applications/Xcode.app/Contents/Developer/
CUDA_SEPARABLE_COMPILATION            *OFF

BUILD_opencv_apps: Build utility applications (used for example to train class
Press [enter] to edit option Press [d] to delete an entry   CMake Version 3.7.2
Press [c] to configure
Press [h] for help           Press [q] to quit without generating
Press [t] to toggle advanced mode (Currently Off)
```

Figure 1-12. *Second page of the build options*

```
                                        Page 3 of 8
CUDA_TOOLKIT_ROOT_DIR                 */usr/local/cuda
DOWNLOAD_EXTERNAL_TEST_DATA           *OFF
EIGEN_INCLUDE_PATH                    */usr/local/include/eigen3
ENABLE_AVX                            *OFF
ENABLE_AVX2                           *OFF
ENABLE_COVERAGE                       *OFF
ENABLE_FAST_MATH                      *OFF
ENABLE_FMA3                           *OFF
ENABLE_IMPL_COLLECTION                *OFF
ENABLE_NOISY_WARNINGS                 *OFF
ENABLE_POPCNT                         *OFF
ENABLE_PRECOMPILED_HEADERS            *OFF
ENABLE_PROFILING                      *OFF
ENABLE_SOLUTION_FOLDERS               *OFF
ENABLE_SSE                            *ON
ENABLE_SSE2                           *ON
ENABLE_SSE3                           *ON

CUDA_TOOLKIT_ROOT_DIR: Toolkit location.
Press [enter] to edit option Press [d] to delete an entry   CMake Version 3.7.2
Press [c] to configure
Press [h] for help           Press [q] to quit without generating
Press [t] to toggle advanced mode (Currently Off)
```

Figure 1-13. *Third page of the build options*

The next important option is OPENCV_EXTRA_MODULES_PATH, which should be set to the path name of the OpenCV extra modules. Specifically, it should be the folder opencv_contrib-3.1.0/modules, inside your original opencv-3.1.0 folder, as shown in Figure 1-14.

```
                                    Page 4 of 8                           ■
ENABLE_SSE41                  *OFF
ENABLE_SSE42                  *OFF
ENABLE_SSSE3                  *OFF
EXECUTABLE_OUTPUT_PATH        */Users/bryan/Documents/opencv-3.1.0/build/b
FFMPEG_INCLUDE_DIR            *FFMPEG_INCLUDE_DIR-NOTFOUND
GENERATE_ABI_DESCRIPTOR       *OFF
GIGEAPI_INCLUDE_PATH          *GIGEAPI_INCLUDE_PATH-NOTFOUND
GIGEAPI_LIBRARIES             *GIGEAPI_LIBRARIES-NOTFOUND
INSTALL_CREATE_DISTRIB        *OFF
INSTALL_C_EXAMPLES            *OFF
INSTALL_PYTHON_EXAMPLES       *OFF
INSTALL_TESTS                 *OFF
INSTALL_TO_MANGLED_PATHS      *OFF
M_LIBRARY                     */usr/lib/libm.dylib
OPENCV_CONFIG_FILE_INCLUDE_DIR */Users/bryan/Documents/opencv-3.1.0/build
OPENCV_EXTRA_MODULES_PATH     */Users/bryan/Documents/opencv-3.1.0/opencv_
OPENCV_WARNINGS_ARE_ERRORS    *OFF


OPENCV_EXTRA_MODULES_PATH: Where to look for additional OpenCV modules
Press [enter] to edit option Press [d] to delete an entry  CMake Version 3.7.2
Press [c] to configure
Press [h] for help          Press [q] to quit without generating
Press [t] to toggle advanced mode (Currently Off)
```

Figure 1-14. *OPENCV_EXTRA_MODULES_PATH option*

The rest of the build options are shown in the following images: Figure 1-15, Figure 1-16, Figure 1-17, and Figure 1-18.

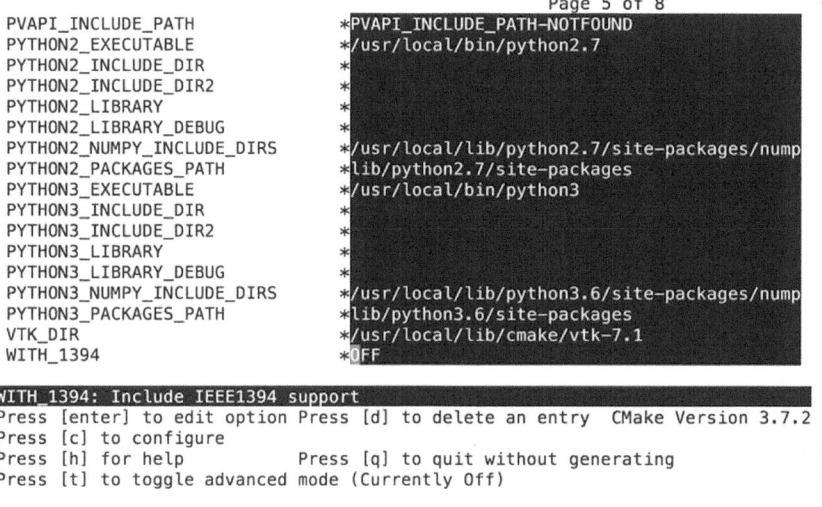

```
                                    Page 5 of 8                           ■
PVAPI_INCLUDE_PATH            *PVAPI_INCLUDE_PATH-NOTFOUND
PYTHON2_EXECUTABLE            */usr/local/bin/python2.7
PYTHON2_INCLUDE_DIR           *
PYTHON2_INCLUDE_DIR2          *
PYTHON2_LIBRARY               *
PYTHON2_LIBRARY_DEBUG         *
PYTHON2_NUMPY_INCLUDE_DIRS    */usr/local/lib/python2.7/site-packages/nump
PYTHON2_PACKAGES_PATH         *lib/python2.7/site-packages
PYTHON3_EXECUTABLE            */usr/local/bin/python3
PYTHON3_INCLUDE_DIR           *
PYTHON3_INCLUDE_DIR2          *
PYTHON3_LIBRARY               *
PYTHON3_LIBRARY_DEBUG         *
PYTHON3_NUMPY_INCLUDE_DIRS    */usr/local/lib/python3.6/site-packages/nump
PYTHON3_PACKAGES_PATH         *lib/python3.6/site-packages
VTK_DIR                       */usr/local/lib/cmake/vtk-7.1
WITH_1394                     *OFF


WITH_1394: Include IEEE1394 support
Press [enter] to edit option Press [d] to delete an entry  CMake Version 3.7.2
Press [c] to configure
Press [h] for help          Press [q] to quit without generating
Press [t] to toggle advanced mode (Currently Off)
```

Figure 1-15. *OpenCV build options*

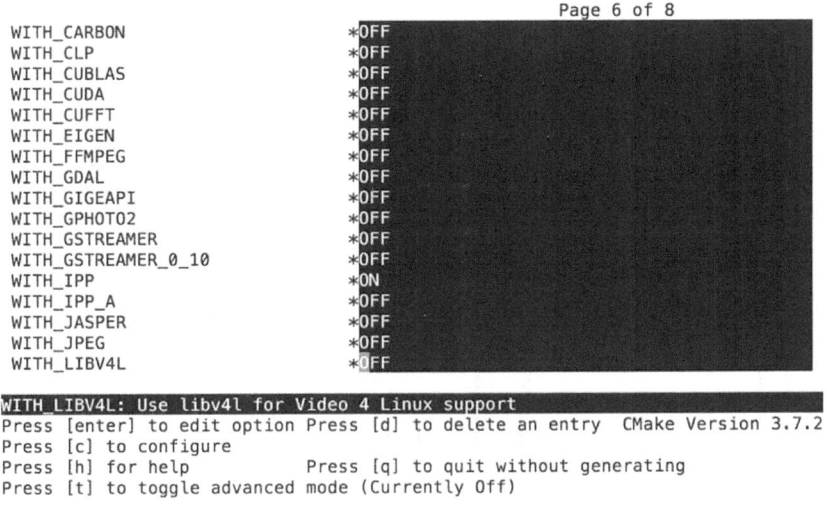

Figure 1-16. *OpenCV build options, continued*

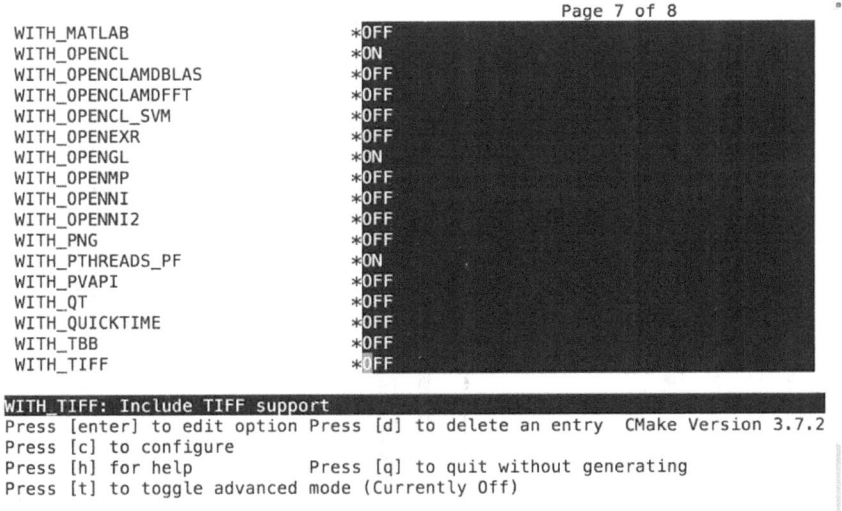

Figure 1-17. *OpenCV build options, continued*

```
                                          Page 8 of 8                    ·
WITH_V4L                        *OFF
WITH_VA                         *OFF
WITH_VA_INTEL                   *OFF
WITH_VTK                        *OFF
WITH_WEBP                       *OFF
WITH_XIMEA                      *OFF
```

```
WITH_XIMEA: Include XIMEA cameras support
Press [enter] to edit option Press [d] to delete an entry   CMake Version 3.7.2
Press [c] to configure
Press [h] for help           Press [q] to quit without generating
Press [t] to toggle advanced mode (Currently Off)
```

Figure 1-18. *Last page of OpenCV build options*

After filling in the first round of build options, type c again to configure the extra modules. First, turn off the BUILD_FAT_JAVA_LIB option, as shown in Figure 1-19.

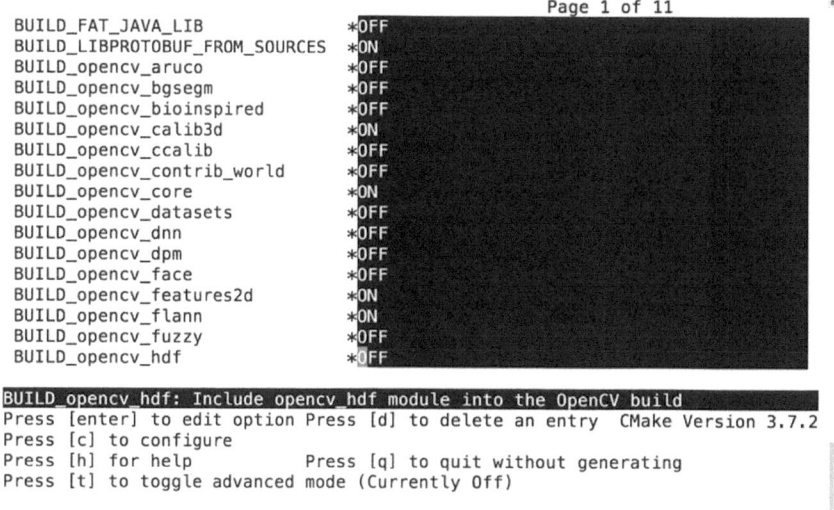

```
                                          Page 1 of 11                   ·
BUILD_FAT_JAVA_LIB                   *OFF
BUILD_LIBPROTOBUF_FROM_SOURCES       *ON
BUILD_opencv_aruco                   *OFF
BUILD_opencv_bgsegm                  *OFF
BUILD_opencv_bioinspired             *OFF
BUILD_opencv_calib3d                 *ON
BUILD_opencv_ccalib                  *OFF
BUILD_opencv_contrib_world           *OFF
BUILD_opencv_core                    *ON
BUILD_opencv_datasets                *OFF
BUILD_opencv_dnn                     *OFF
BUILD_opencv_dpm                     *OFF
BUILD_opencv_face                    *OFF
BUILD_opencv_features2d              *ON
BUILD_opencv_flann                   *ON
BUILD_opencv_fuzzy                   *OFF
BUILD_opencv_hdf                     *OFF
```

```
BUILD_opencv_hdf: Include opencv_hdf module into the OpenCV build
Press [enter] to edit option Press [d] to delete an entry   CMake Version 3.7.2
Press [c] to configure
Press [h] for help           Press [q] to quit without generating
Press [t] to toggle advanced mode (Currently Off)
```

Figure 1-19. *OpenCV extra modules build options*

To work on with the optical flow examples later in the book, you also should turn on the options for BUILD_opencv_optflow, BUILD_opencv_ximgproc, and BUILD_opencv_java, as shown in Figure 1-20 and Figure 1-21.

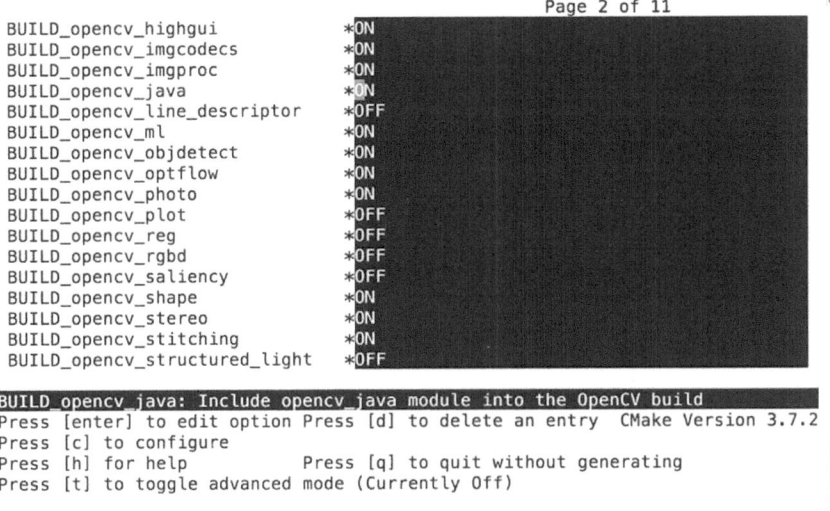

Figure 1-20. *Turning on options for Java and optflow*

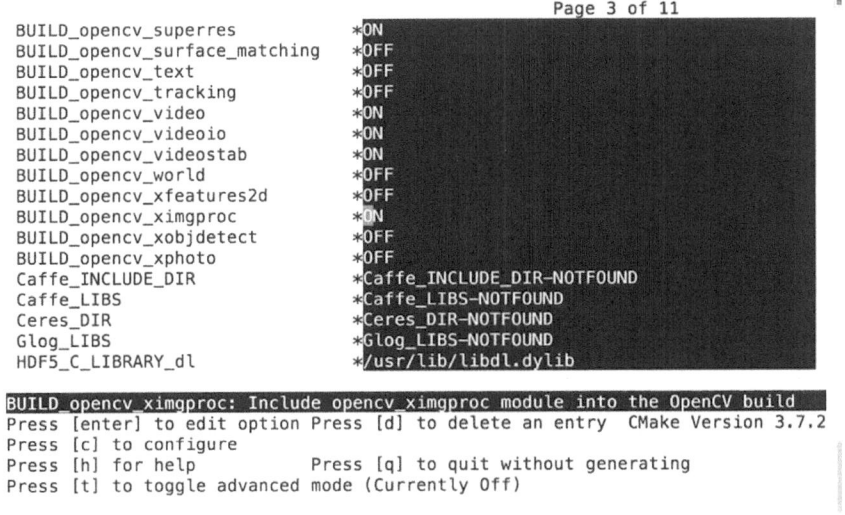

Figure 1-21. *Turning on the option for ximgproc*

Complete the rest of the extra modules options, as shown in Figure 1-22.

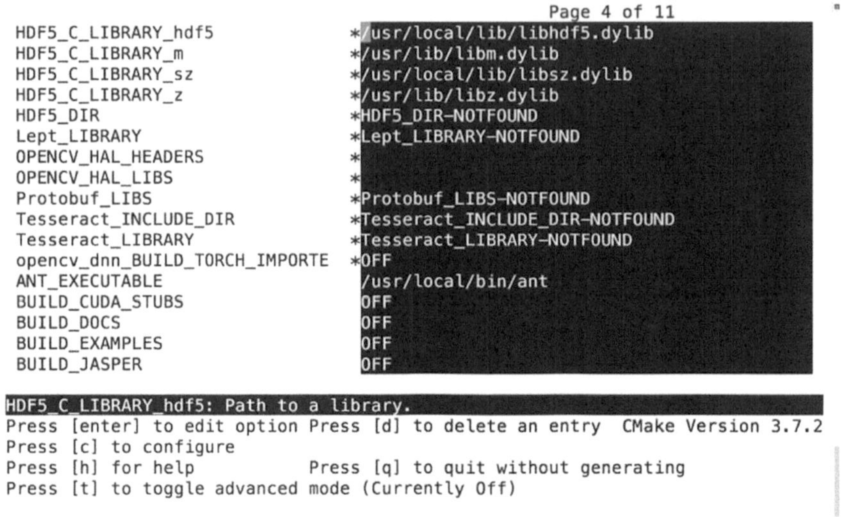

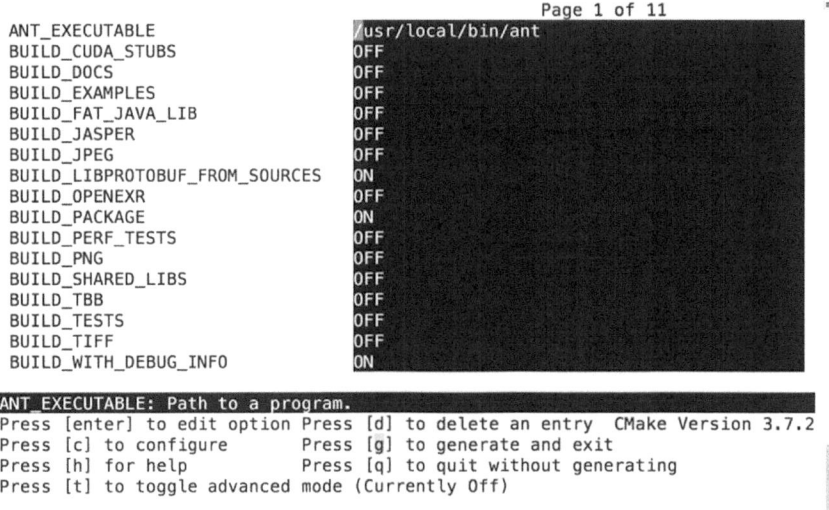

Figure 1-22. *Extra module options*

After setting all the options, type c again to finish the last configuration task. Type the option g to generate the configuration files (Figure 1-23). The ccmake program will quit and take you back to the Terminal window.

Figure 1-23. *Generating the configuration file*

Enter the following command to start the build process:

```
make -j4
```

When the build process completes successfully, navigate into the bin folder within the build folder. Locate the opencv-310.jar file. Then navigate into the lib folder within the build folder. Locate the libopencv_java310.so file. Rename it to libopencv_java310.dylib. Copy the two files into a separate folder. You are going to prepare the Windows and Linux versions and copy them to the same folder to create the multiplatform library. The author has tested building the OpenCV 3.1 in the macOS 10.11, El Capitan. For readers using the new macOS 10.12 Sierra, the building of OpenCV 3.1 will fail due to the removal of QTKit. In this case, it is better to use OpenCV 3.2 together with macOS 10.12. Please refer to the building note in `http://www.magicandlove.com/blog/2017/03/02/opencv-3-2-java-build/` to generate the `optflow` module properly with OpenCV 3.2.

Windows

On a Windows system, you use the graphical version of `cmake` to configure the installation process. I have tested the installation in Windows 8.1 and Windows 10. Download and install the following software packages for the OpenCV build process:

- Microsoft Visual Studio Community 2015 at `https://www.visualstudio.com/downloads/`

- CMake at `https://cmake.org/download/`

- Apache Ant at `http://ant.apache.org/bindownload.cgi`

- Oracle JDK 8 at `www.oracle.com/technetwork/java/javase/downloads/jdk8-downloads-2133151.html`

- Python at `https://www.python.org/downloads/`

After the successful installation of the software package dependencies, run the CMake (`cmake-gui`) program to start the configuration process. Fill in the source folder name for the OpenCV distribution and the build folder name, as shown in Figure 1-24. Remember that you need to create the build folder inside the OpenCV distribution folder.

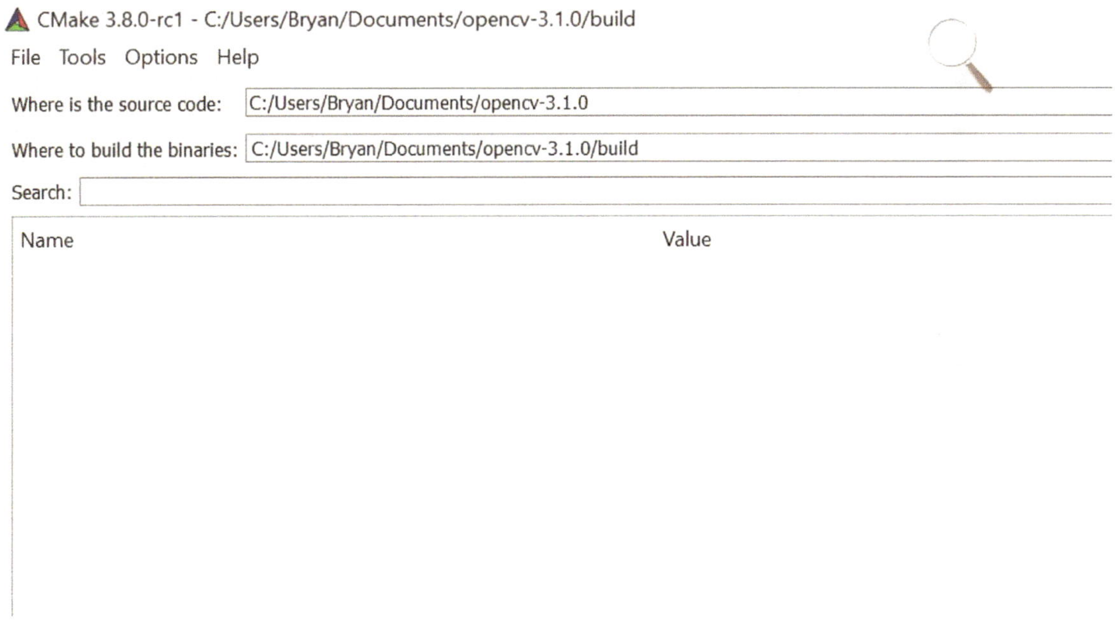

Figure 1-24. *Folder names of OpenCV distribution in the CMake window*

Click the Configure button to start the configuration. For the first generator panel, choose Visual Studio 14 2015 Win64 from the pull-down menu and select the "Use default native compilers" radio button, as shown in Figure 1-25. Click the Finish button to proceed.

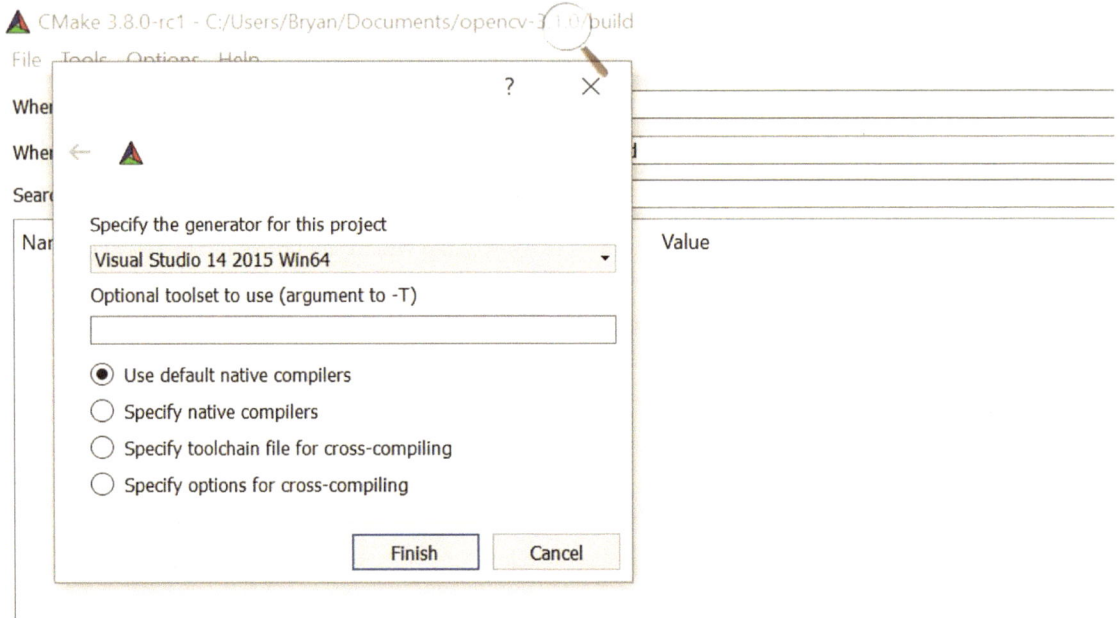

Figure 1-25. *Choosing the default compiler*

Follow Figure 1-26 through Figure 1-33 to enter the build options. Make sure to first turn off the BUILD_SHARED_LIBS option, and enter the path name for ant.bat for the ANT_EXECUTABLE option.

Name	Value
ANT_EXECUTABLE	C:/Users/Bryan/Documents/apache-ant-1.10.1/bin
BUILD_CUDA_STUBS	☐
BUILD_DOCS	☐
BUILD_EXAMPLES	☐
BUILD_JASPER	☐
BUILD_JPEG	☐
BUILD_OPENEXR	☐
BUILD_PACKAGE	☑
BUILD_PERF_TESTS	☐
BUILD_PNG	☐
BUILD_SHARED_LIBS	☐
BUILD_TBB	☐
BUILD_TESTS	☐
BUILD_TIFF	☐
BUILD_WITH_DEBUG_INFO	☑
BUILD_WITH_DYNAMIC_IPP	☐
BUILD_WITH_STATIC_CRT	☑
BUILD_ZLIB	☑
BUILD_opencv_apps	☑
BUILD_opencv_calib3d	☑

Figure 1-26. *Turning off the BUILD_SHARED_LIBS option*

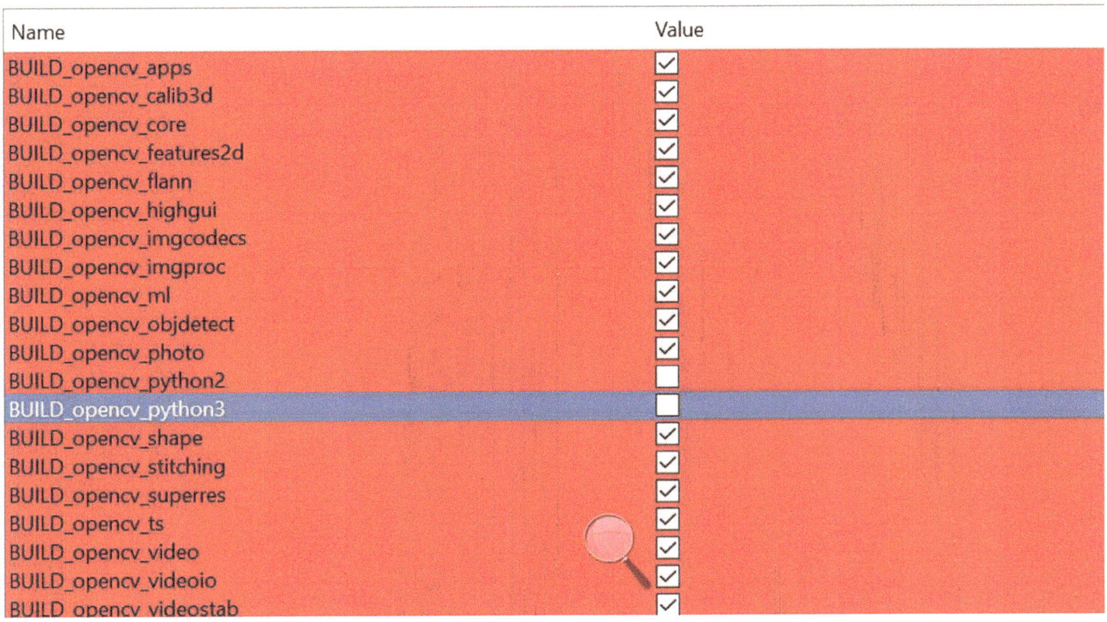

Figure 1-27. *Second page of OpenCV build options*

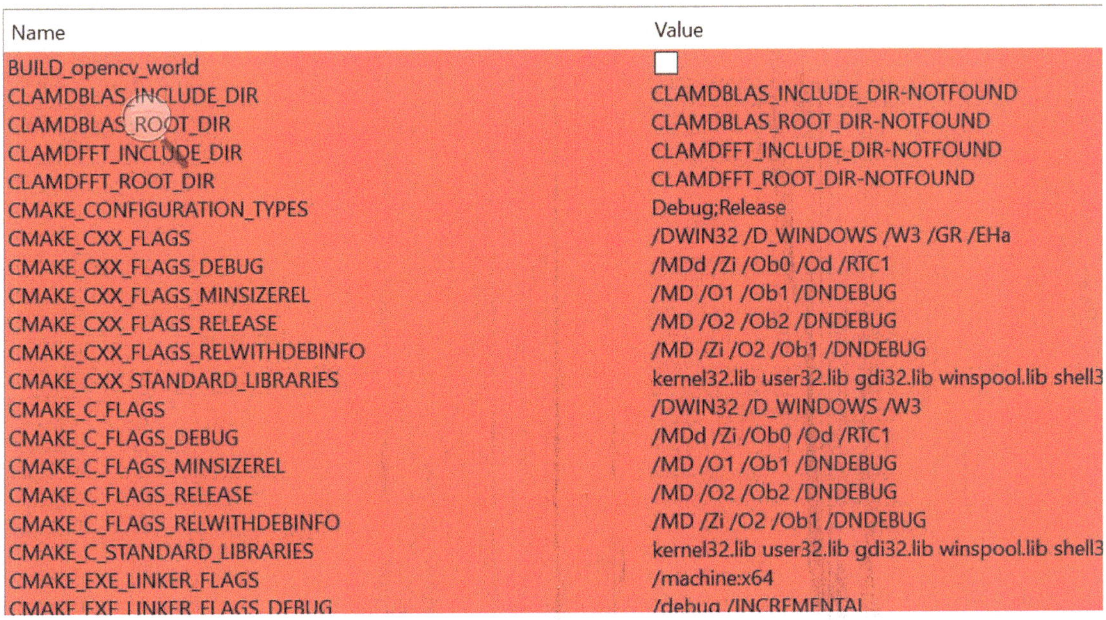

Figure 1-28. *Third page of OpenCV build options*

Name	Value
CMAKE_EXE_LINKER_FLAGS_RELEASE	/INCREMENTAL:NO
CMAKE_EXE_LINKER_FLAGS_RELWITHDEBINFO	/debug /INCREMENTAL
CMAKE_INSTALL_PREFIX	C:/Users/Bryan/Documents/opencv-3.1.0/build/in
CMAKE_LINKER	C:/Program Files (x86)/Microsoft Visual Studio 14.
CMAKE_MODULE_LINKER_FLAGS	/machine:x64
CMAKE_MODULE_LINKER_FLAGS_DEBUG	/debug /INCREMENTAL
CMAKE_MODULE_LINKER_FLAGS_MINSIZEREL	/INCREMENTAL:NO
CMAKE_MODULE_LINKER_FLAGS_RELEASE	/INCREMENTAL:NO
CMAKE_MODULE_LINKER_FLAGS_RELWITHDEBINFO	/debug /INCREMENTAL
CMAKE_RC_COMPILER	rc
CMAKE_RC_FLAGS	/DWIN32
CMAKE_SHARED_LINKER_FLAGS	/machine:x64
CMAKE_SHARED_LINKER_FLAGS_DEBUG	/debug /INCREMENTAL
CMAKE_SHARED_LINKER_FLAGS_MINSIZEREL	/INCREMENTAL:NO
CMAKE_SHARED_LINKER_FLAGS_RELEASE	/INCREMENTAL:NO
CMAKE_SHARED_LINKER_FLAGS_RELWITHDEBINFO	/debug /INCREMENTAL
CMAKE_SKIP_INSTALL_RPATH	☐
CMAKE_SKIP_RPATH	☐
CMAKE_STATIC_LINKER_FLAGS	/machine:x64
CMAKE_STATIC_LINKER_FLAGS_DEBUG	

Figure 1-29. *Fourth page of OpenCV build options*

Name	Value
CMAKE_STATIC_LINKER_FLAGS_MINSIZEREL	
CMAKE_STATIC_LINKER_FLAGS_RELEASE	
CMAKE_STATIC_LINKER_FLAGS_RELWITHDEBINFO	
CMAKE_VERBOSE_MAKEFILE	☐
CPACK_BINARY_7Z	☐
CPACK_BINARY_IFW	☐
CPACK_BINARY_NSIS	☑
CPACK_BINARY_WIX	☐
CPACK_BINARY_ZIP	☐
CPACK_SOURCE_7Z	☑
CPACK_SOURCE_ZIP	☑
CUDA_64_BIT_DEVICE_CODE	☑
CUDA_ATTACH_VS_BUILD_RULE_TO_CUDA_FILE	☑
CUDA_BUILD_CUBIN	☐
CUDA_BUILD_EMULATION	☐
CUDA_CUDART_LIBRARY	CUDA_CUDART_LIBRARY-NOTFOUND
CUDA_CUDA_LIBRARY	CUDA_CUDA_LIBRARY-NOTFOUND
CUDA_GENERATED_OUTPUT_DIR	
CUDA_HOST_COMPILATION_CPP	☑
CUDA_HOST_COMPILER	$(VCInstallDir)bin

Figure 1-30. *Fifth page of OpenCV build options*

Name	Value
CUDA_NVCC_EXECUTABLE	CUDA_NVCC_EXECUTABLE-NOTFOUND
CUDA_NVCC_FLAGS	
CUDA_NVCC_FLAGS_DEBUG	
CUDA_NVCC_FLAGS_MINSIZEREL	
CUDA_NVCC_FLAGS_RELEASE	
CUDA_NVCC_FLAGS_RELWITHDEBINFO	
CUDA_PROPAGATE_HOST_FLAGS	☑
CUDA_SDK_ROOT_DIR	CUDA_SDK_ROOT_DIR-NOTFOUND
CUDA_SEPARABLE_COMPILATION	☐
CUDA_TARGET_CPU_ARCH	
CUDA_TARGET_OS_VARIANT	
CUDA_TARGET_TRIPLET	
CUDA_TOOLKIT_INCLUDE	CUDA_TOOLKIT_INCLUDE-NOTFOUND
CUDA_TOOLKIT_ROOT_DIR	CUDA_TOOLKIT_ROOT_DIR-NOTFOUND
CUDA_VERBOSE_BUILD	☐
CUDA_cublas_LIBRARY	CUDA_cublas_LIBRARY-NOTFOUND
CUDA_cublasemu_LIBRARY	CUDA_cublasemu_LIBRARY-NOTFOUND
CUDA_cufft_LIBRARY	CUDA_cufft_LIBRARY-NOTFOUND
CUDA_cufftemu_LIBRARY	CUDA_cufftemu_LIBRARY-NOTFOUND
DOWNLOAD_EXTERNAL_TEST_DATA	☐

Figure 1-31. *Sixth page of OpenCV build options*

Name	Value
DOXYGEN_DOT_EXECUTABLE	DOXYGEN_DOT_EXECUTABLE-NOTFOUND
DOXYGEN_EXECUTABLE	DOXYGEN_EXECUTABLE-NOTFOUND
EIGEN_INCLUDE_PATH	EIGEN_INCLUDE_PATH-NOTFOUND
ENABLE_AVX	☐
ENABLE_AVX2	☐
ENABLE_FMA3	☐
ENABLE_IMPL_COLLECTION	☐
ENABLE_NOISY_WARNINGS	☐
ENABLE_POPCNT	☐
ENABLE_PRECOMPILED_HEADERS	☑
ENABLE_SOLUTION_FOLDERS	☑
ENABLE_SSE	☑
ENABLE_SSE2	☑
ENABLE_SSE3	☑
ENABLE_SSE41	☐
ENABLE_SSE42	☐
ENABLE_SSSE3	☐
EXECUTABLE_OUTPUT_PATH	C:/Users/Bryan/Documents/opencv-3.1.0/build/bi
GIGEAPI_INCLUDE_PATH	GIGEAPI_INCLUDE_PATH-NOTFOUND
GIGEAPI_LIBRARIES	GIGEAPI_LIBRARIES-NOTFOUND

Figure 1-32. *Seventh page of OpenCV build options*

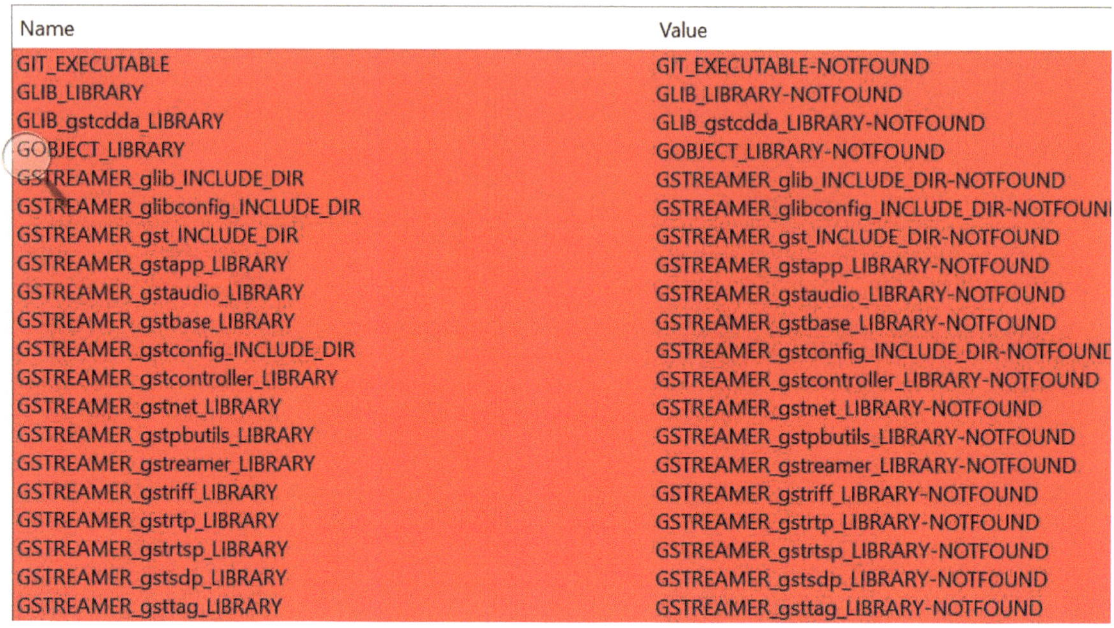

Name	Value
GIT_EXECUTABLE	GIT_EXECUTABLE-NOTFOUND
GLIB_LIBRARY	GLIB_LIBRARY-NOTFOUND
GLIB_gstcdda_LIBRARY	GLIB_gstcdda_LIBRARY-NOTFOUND
GOBJECT_LIBRARY	GOBJECT_LIBRARY-NOTFOUND
GSTREAMER_glib_INCLUDE_DIR	GSTREAMER_glib_INCLUDE_DIR-NOTFOUND
GSTREAMER_glibconfig_INCLUDE_DIR	GSTREAMER_glibconfig_INCLUDE_DIR-NOTFOUN
GSTREAMER_gst_INCLUDE_DIR	GSTREAMER_gst_INCLUDE_DIR-NOTFOUND
GSTREAMER_gstapp_LIBRARY	GSTREAMER_gstapp_LIBRARY-NOTFOUND
GSTREAMER_gstaudio_LIBRARY	GSTREAMER_gstaudio_LIBRARY-NOTFOUND
GSTREAMER_gstbase_LIBRARY	GSTREAMER_gstbase_LIBRARY-NOTFOUND
GSTREAMER_gstconfig_INCLUDE_DIR	GSTREAMER_gstconfig_INCLUDE_DIR-NOTFOUND
GSTREAMER_gstcontroller_LIBRARY	GSTREAMER_gstcontroller_LIBRARY-NOTFOUND
GSTREAMER_gstnet_LIBRARY	GSTREAMER_gstnet_LIBRARY-NOTFOUND
GSTREAMER_gstpbutils_LIBRARY	GSTREAMER_gstpbutils_LIBRARY-NOTFOUND
GSTREAMER_gstreamer_LIBRARY	GSTREAMER_gstreamer_LIBRARY-NOTFOUND
GSTREAMER_gstriff_LIBRARY	GSTREAMER_gstriff_LIBRARY-NOTFOUND
GSTREAMER_gstrtp_LIBRARY	GSTREAMER_gstrtp_LIBRARY-NOTFOUND
GSTREAMER_gstrtsp_LIBRARY	GSTREAMER_gstrtsp_LIBRARY-NOTFOUND
GSTREAMER_gstsdp_LIBRARY	GSTREAMER_gstsdp_LIBRARY-NOTFOUND
GSTREAMER_gsttag_LIBRARY	GSTREAMER_gsttag_LIBRARY-NOTFOUND

Figure 1-33. *Eighth page of OpenCV build options*

In the next screen (Figure 1-34), enter the path name of the opencv_contrib extra modules for the OPENCV_EXTRA_MODULES_PATH option. Figures 1-35 through 1-37 show the rest of the settings.

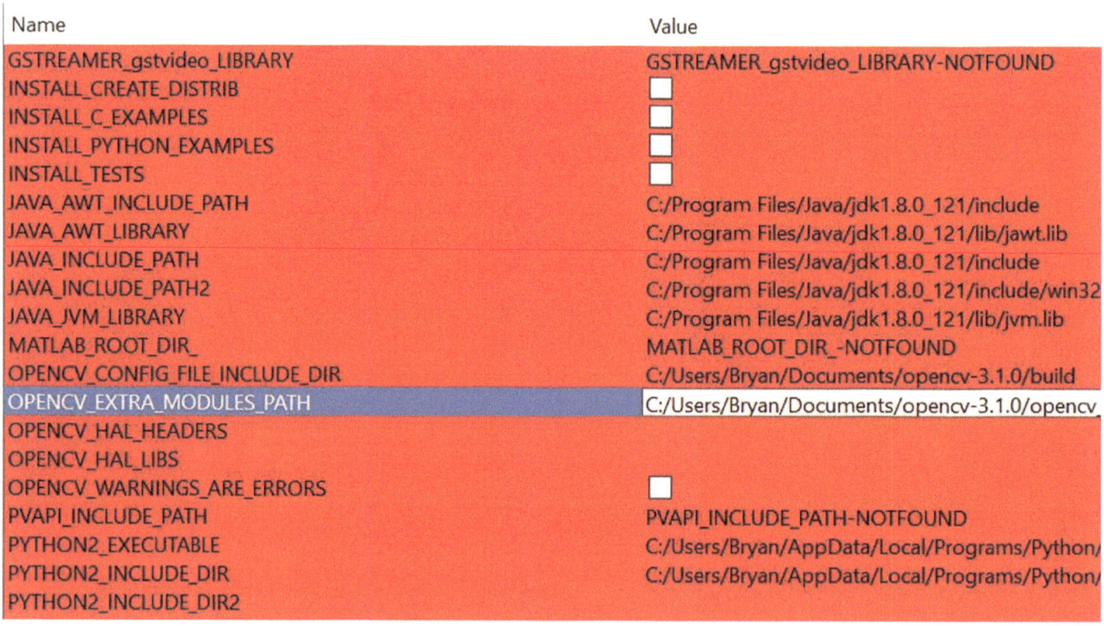

Name	Value
GSTREAMER_gstvideo_LIBRARY	GSTREAMER_gstvideo_LIBRARY-NOTFOUND
INSTALL_CREATE_DISTRIB	☐
INSTALL_C_EXAMPLES	☐
INSTALL_PYTHON_EXAMPLES	☐
INSTALL_TESTS	☐
JAVA_AWT_INCLUDE_PATH	C:/Program Files/Java/jdk1.8.0_121/include
JAVA_AWT_LIBRARY	C:/Program Files/Java/jdk1.8.0_121/lib/jawt.lib
JAVA_INCLUDE_PATH	C:/Program Files/Java/jdk1.8.0_121/include
JAVA_INCLUDE_PATH2	C:/Program Files/Java/jdk1.8.0_121/include/win32
JAVA_JVM_LIBRARY	C:/Program Files/Java/jdk1.8.0_121/lib/jvm.lib
MATLAB_ROOT_DIR_	MATLAB_ROOT_DIR_-NOTFOUND
OPENCV_CONFIG_FILE_INCLUDE_DIR	C:/Users/Bryan/Documents/opencv-3.1.0/build
OPENCV_EXTRA_MODULES_PATH	C:/Users/Bryan/Documents/opencv-3.1.0/opencv
OPENCV_HAL_HEADERS	
OPENCV_HAL_LIBS	
OPENCV_WARNINGS_ARE_ERRORS	☐
PVAPI_INCLUDE_PATH	PVAPI_INCLUDE_PATH-NOTFOUND
PYTHON2_EXECUTABLE	C:/Users/Bryan/AppData/Local/Programs/Python/
PYTHON2_INCLUDE_DIR	C:/Users/Bryan/AppData/Local/Programs/Python/
PYTHON2_INCLUDE_DIR2	

Figure 1-34. *OPENCV_EXTRA_MODULES_PATH option*

Name	Value
PYTHON2_LIBRARY	C:/Users/Bryan/AppData/Local/Programs/Python/
PYTHON2_LIBRARY_DEBUG	PYTHON_DEBUG_LIBRARY-NOTFOUND
PYTHON2_NUMPY_INCLUDE_DIRS	C:/Users/Bryan/AppData/Local/Programs/Python/
PYTHON2_PACKAGES_PATH	C:/Users/Bryan/AppData/Local/Programs/Python/
PYTHON3_EXECUTABLE	C:/Users/Bryan/AppData/Local/Programs/Python/
PYTHON3_INCLUDE_DIR	C:/Users/Bryan/AppData/Local/Programs/Python/
PYTHON3_INCLUDE_DIR2	
PYTHON3_LIBRARY	C:/Users/Bryan/AppData/Local/Programs/Python/
PYTHON3_LIBRARY_DEBUG	PYTHON_DEBUG_LIBRARY-NOTFOUND
PYTHON3_NUMPY_INCLUDE_DIRS	C:/Users/Bryan/AppData/Local/Programs/Python/
PYTHON3_PACKAGES_PATH	C:/Users/Bryan/AppData/Local/Programs/Python/
VTK_DIR	VTK_DIR-NOTFOUND
WEBP_INCLUDE_DIR	WEBP_INCLUDE_DIR-NOTFOUND
WITH_1394	☐
WITH_CLP	☐
WITH_CSTRIPES	☐
WITH_CUBLAS	☐
WITH_CUDA	☐
WITH_CUFFT	☐
WITH_DIRECTX	☑

Figure 1-35. *Tenth page of OpenCV build options*

Name	Value
WITH_DSHOW	☑
WITH_EIGEN	☐
WITH_FFMPEG	☐
WITH_GDAL	☐
WITH_GIGEAPI	☐
WITH_GSTREAMER	☐
WITH_GSTREAMER_0_10	☐
WITH_INTELPERC	☐
WITH_IPP	☑
WITH_IPP_A	☐
WITH_JASPER	☐
WITH_JPEG	☐
WITH_MATLAB	☐
WITH_MSMF	☐
WITH_NVCUVID	☐
WITH_OPENCL	☑
WITH_OPENCLAMDBLAS	☐
WITH_OPENCLAMDFFT	☐
WITH_OPENCL_SVM	☐
WITH_OPENEXR	☐

Figure 1-36. *Eleventh page of OpenCV build options*

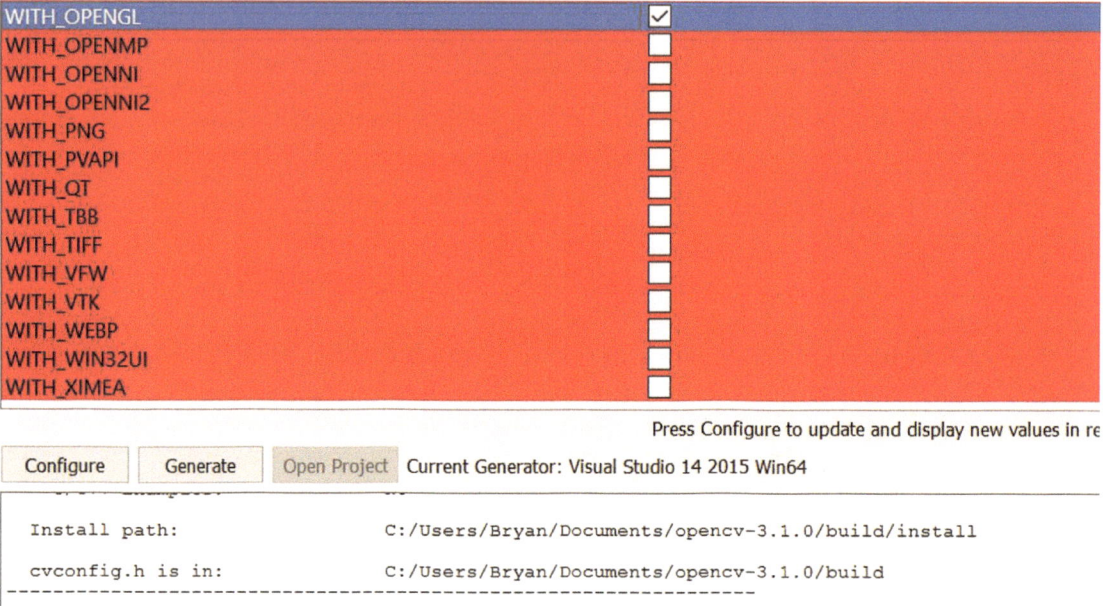

Figure 1-37. *The last page of OpenCV build options*

Click the Configure button to create the configuration details. In the red areas, be sure to enable the options BUILD_opencv_java, BUILD_opencv_optflow, and BUILD_opencv_ximgproc (Figures 1-38 and 1-39). Leave the rest of the extra modules with the empty option.

Name	Value
BUILD_LIBPROTOBUF_FROM_SOURCES	☑
BUILD_opencv_aruco	☐
BUILD_opencv_bgsegm	☐
BUILD_opencv_bioinspired	☐
BUILD_opencv_ccalib	☐
BUILD_opencv_contrib_world	☐
BUILD_opencv_datasets	☐
BUILD_opencv_dnn	☐
BUILD_opencv_dpm	☐
BUILD_opencv_face	☐
BUILD_opencv_fuzzy	☐
BUILD_opencv_java	☑
BUILD_opencv_line_descriptor	☐
BUILD_opencv_optflow	☑
BUILD_opencv_plot	☐
BUILD_opencv_reg	☐
BUILD_opencv_rgbd	☐
BUILD_opencv_saliency	☐
BUILD_opencv_stereo	☐
BUILD_opencv_structured_light	☐

Figure 1-38. *BUILD_opencv_java and BUILD_opencv_optflow options*

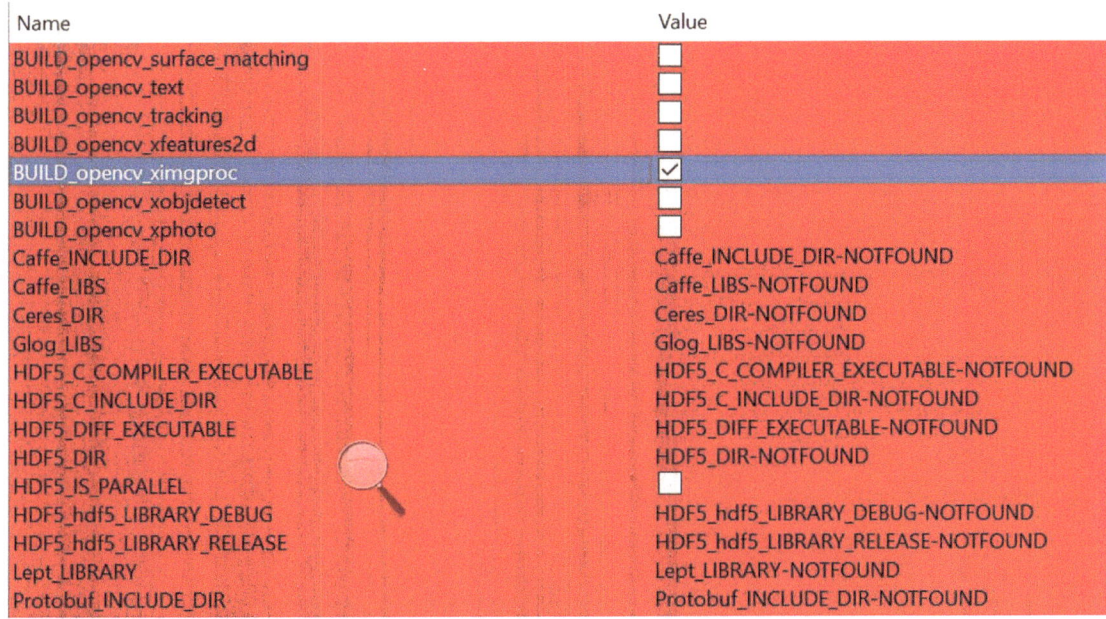

Figure 1-39. BUILD_opencv_ximgproc option

Click the Configure button again to complete the configuration process. After all the configuration options are set, click the Generate button to create the Visual Studio solution file. When it finishes, quit the CMake program. In the build folder, start the Visual Studio solution OpenCV.sln (Figure 1-40).

INSTALL.vcxproj	9/4/2017 11:49 AM	VC++ Project
INSTALL.vcxproj.filters	9/4/2017 11:49 AM	VC++ Project Filters F...
OpenCV.sln	9/4/2017 11:49 AM	Microsoft Visual Stud...
opencv_modules.vcxproj	9/4/2017 11:49 AM	VC++ Project
opencv_modules.vcxproj.filters	9/4/2017 11:49 AM	VC++ Project Filters F...
OpenCVConfig.cmake	9/4/2017 11:48 AM	CMAKE File
OpenCVConfig-version.cmake	9/4/2017 11:16 AM	CMAKE File
OpenCVModules.cmake	9/4/2017 11:49 AM	CMAKE File
PACKAGE.vcxproj	9/4/2017 11:49 AM	VC++ Project
PACKAGE.vcxproj.filters	9/4/2017 11:49 AM	VC++ Project Filters F...
RUN_TESTS.vcxproj	9/4/2017 11:49 AM	VC++ Project
RUN_TESTS.vcxproj.filters	9/4/2017 11:49 AM	VC++ Project Filters F...
text_config.hpp	9/4/2017 11:44 AM	C/C++ Header
uninstall.vcxproj	9/4/2017 11:49 AM	VC++ Project
uninstall.vcxproj.filters	9/4/2017 11:49 AM	VC++ Project Filters F...
version_string.tmp	9/4/2017 11:48 AM	TMP File
ZERO_CHECK.vcxproj	9/4/2017 11:49 AM	VC++ Project

Figure 1-40. OpenCV Visual Studio solution file

Inside the Visual Studio program, select Release from the Solution Configurations menu (Figure 1-41); choose x64 from the Solution Platforms menu.

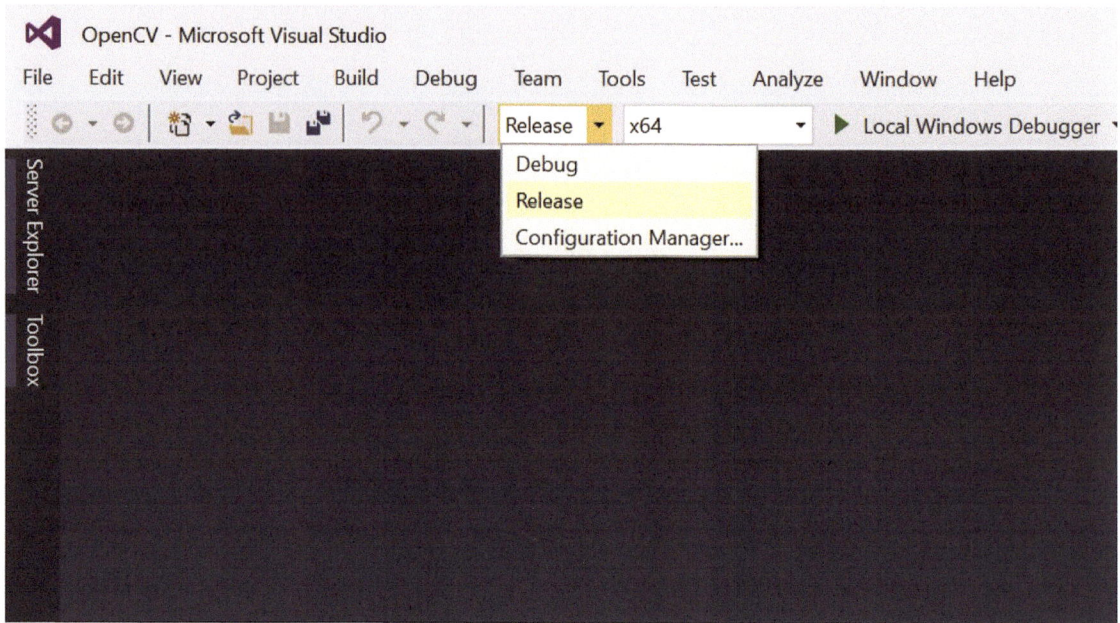

Figure 1-41. *Visual Studio project options*

From the Solution Explorer, expand CMakeTargets; then right-click the ALL_BUILD target and choose Build (Figure 1-42).

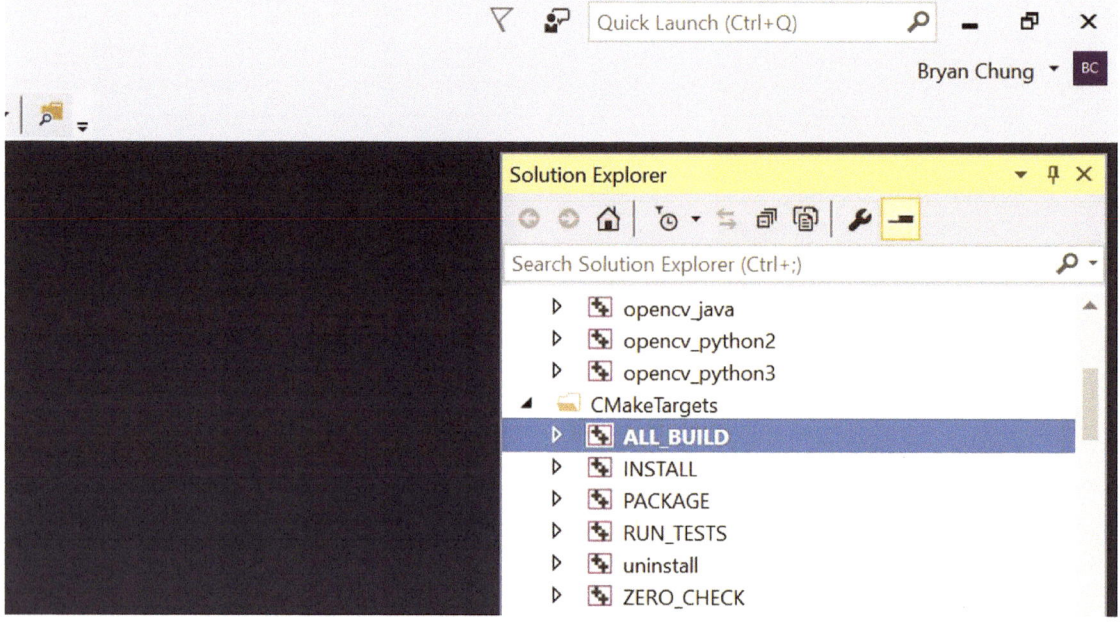

Figure 1-42. *Choosing the OpenCV build target*

After the successful build of the solution, quit Visual Studio and navigate into the `build` folder. Inside the `bin` folder, you will see the `opencv-310.jar` file, as shown in Figure 1-43.

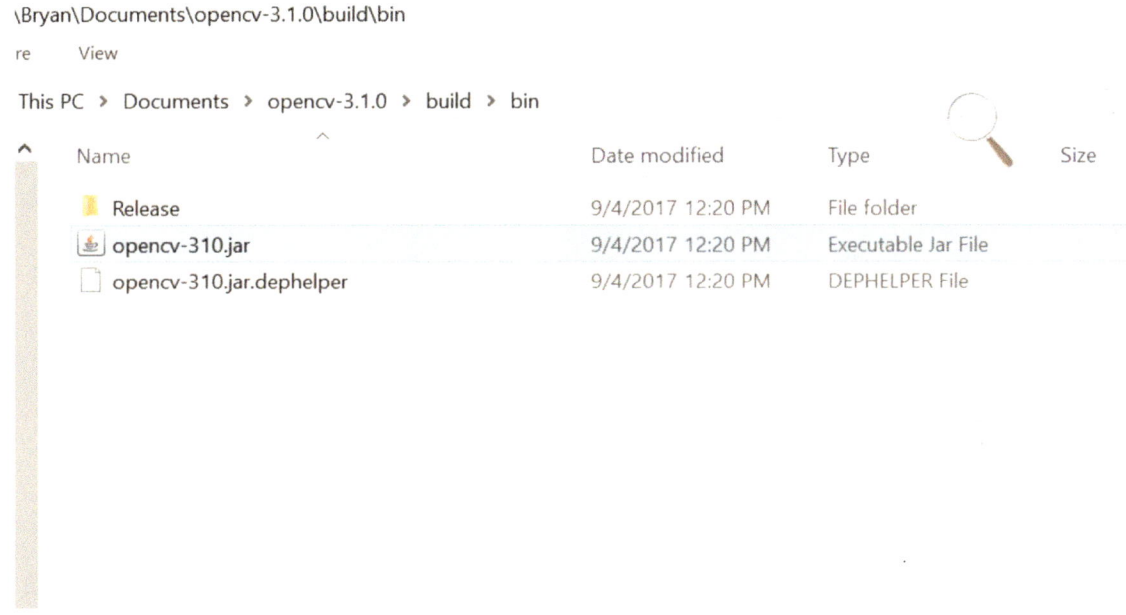

\Bryan\Documents\opencv-3.1.0\build\bin

re   View

This PC > Documents > opencv-3.1.0 > build > bin

Name	Date modified	Type	Size
Release	9/4/2017 12:20 PM	File folder	
opencv-310.jar	9/4/2017 12:20 PM	Executable Jar File	
opencv-310.jar.dephelper	9/4/2017 12:20 PM	DEPHELPER File	

Figure 1-43. *OpenCV Windows build file*

Double-click to open the `Release` folder inside the `bin` folder; the OpenCV Windows native library `opencv_java310.dll` will reside there, as shown in Figure 1-44.

Bryan\Documents\opencv-3.1.0\build\bin\Release

e   View

This PC > Documents > opencv-3.1.0 > build > bin > Release

Name	Date modified	Type	Size
opencv_annotation.exe	9/4/2017 12:19 PM	Application	8,
opencv_annotation.pdb	9/4/2017 12:19 PM	Program Debug Data...	26,9
opencv_createsamples.exe	9/4/2017 12:20 PM	Application	29,
opencv_createsamples.pdb	9/4/2017 12:20 PM	Program Debug Data...	35,4
opencv_java310.dll	9/4/2017 12:20 PM	Application extension	29,0
opencv_traincascade.exe	9/4/2017 12:20 PM	Application	8,2
opencv_traincascade.pdb	9/4/2017 12:20 PM	Program Debug Data...	27,6

Figure 1-44. *OpenCV Windows native library file*

Linux

The Linux distribution tested in the book is Ubuntu 16.04. For Linux systems, you can use the apt-get command to install the dependent software packages. The OpenCV 3.1.0 documentation has a page describing the detailed installation process. You can find the reference at http://docs.opencv.org/3.1.0/ d7/d9f/tutorial_linux_install.html. Before installing OpenCV, you need to set up the proper Java environment. In the book, you will use Oracle JDK 8 in the Linux installation. To obtain the proper version, enter the following in a Terminal session:

```
sudo add-apt-repository ppa:webupd8team/java
sudo apt-get update
sudo apt-get install oracle-java8-installer
```

After the Java installation, you need to set up the proper environment variable, JAVA_HOME, for the OpenCV build process. Use the text editor to edit the environment file.

```
sudo gedit /etc/environment
```

At the end of the file, insert the following line:

```
JAVA_HOME="/usr/lib/jvm/java-8-oracle"
```

Save and exit the environment file and reload it with the following:

```
source /etc/environment
```

Verify whether the environment variable was set correctly by using the echo command. It should return the proper location for the Java installation.

```
 echo $JAVA_HOME
```

After the successful installation of the JDK, you can proceed to install the dependent software packages for OpenCV with apt-get.

```
sudo apt-get install ant build-essential cmake git libgtk-2.0-dev pkg-config libavcodec-dev,
libavformat-dev libswscale-dev python-dev execstack
```

To simplify the build process, you can install the graphical user interface for cmake such that you can use ccmake to build the OpenCV.

```
sudo apt-get install cmake-curses-gui
```

First, you navigate to the build folder inside the OpenCV distribution folder, opencv-3.1.0. Start the configuration process by using the ccmake command.

```
ccmake ..
```

At the menu screen, type c to start the automatic configuration process. Fill in the options as shown in the following screenshots, starting with Figure 1-45.

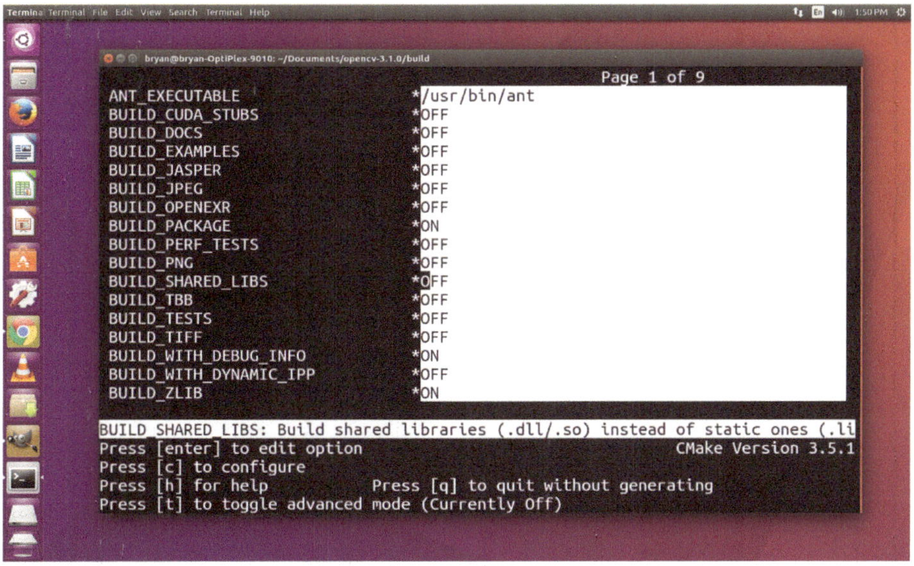

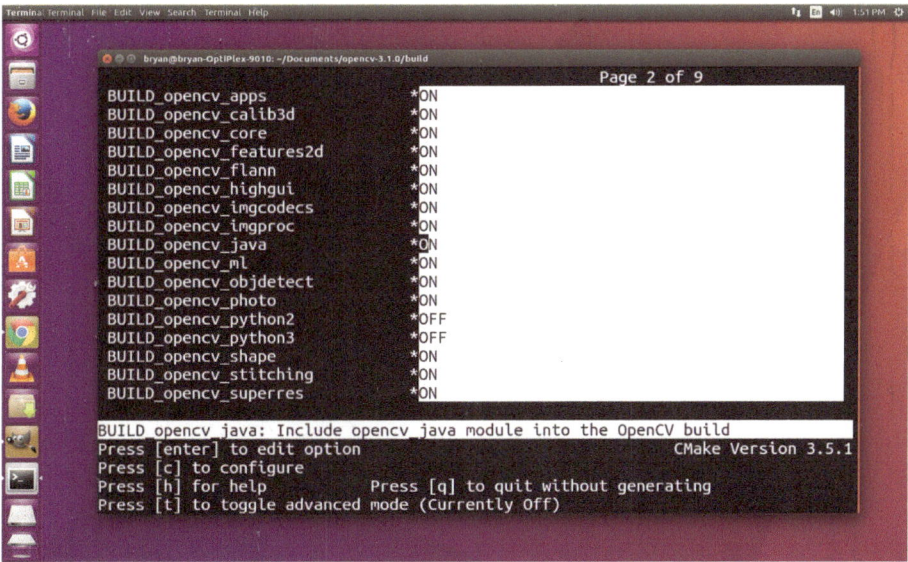

Figure 1-45. *BUILD_SHARED_LIBS option*

Please make sure to turn on the BUILD_opencv_java option, as shown in Figure 1-46.

Figure 1-46. *BUILD_opencv_java option*

Then enter the path information for the OpenCV extra modules in the OPENCV_EXTRA_MODULES_PATH option (Figure 1-47).

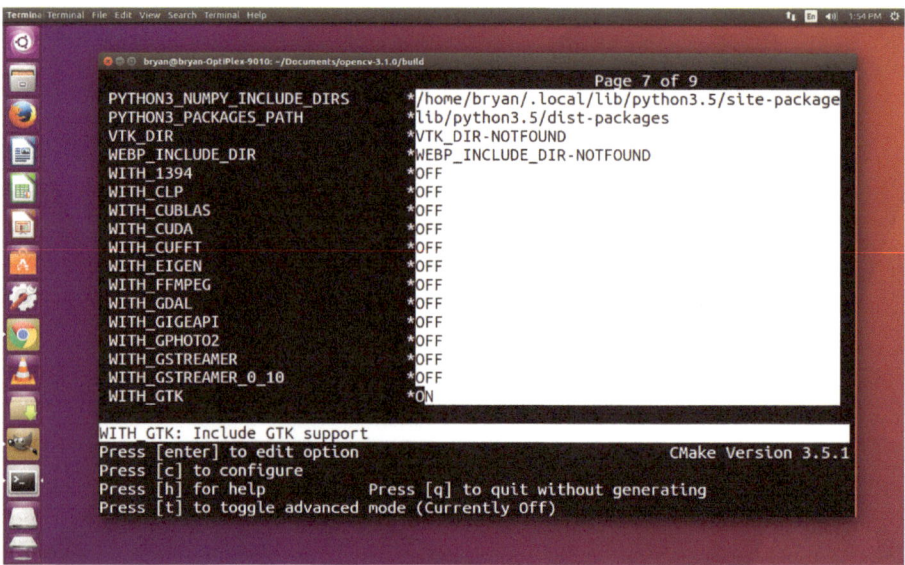

Figure 1-47. *OPENCV_EXTRA_MODULES_PATH option*

Include GTK support for the configuration by turning on the WITH_GTK option (Figure 1-48).

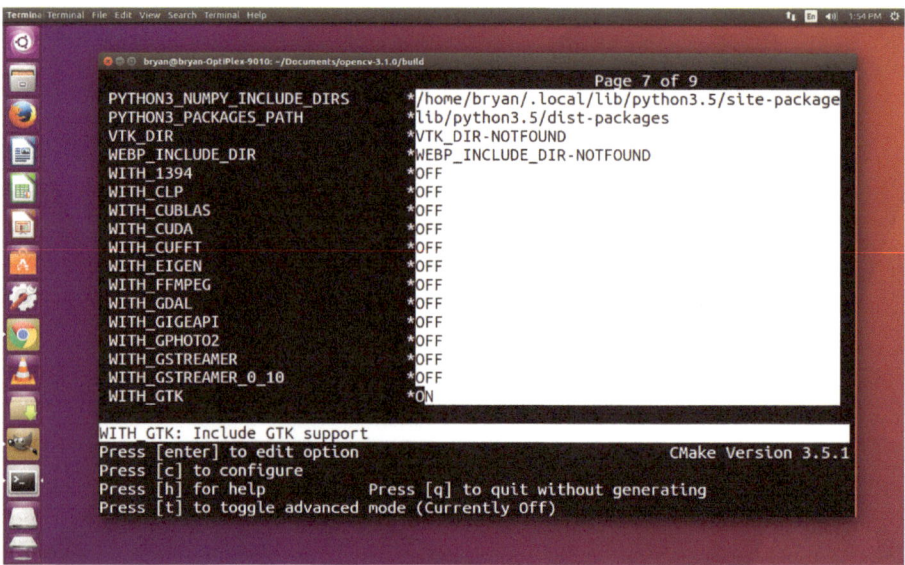

Figure 1-48. *WITH_GTK option*

Continue with the rest of the configuration options, as shown in Figure 1-49 and Figure 1-50.

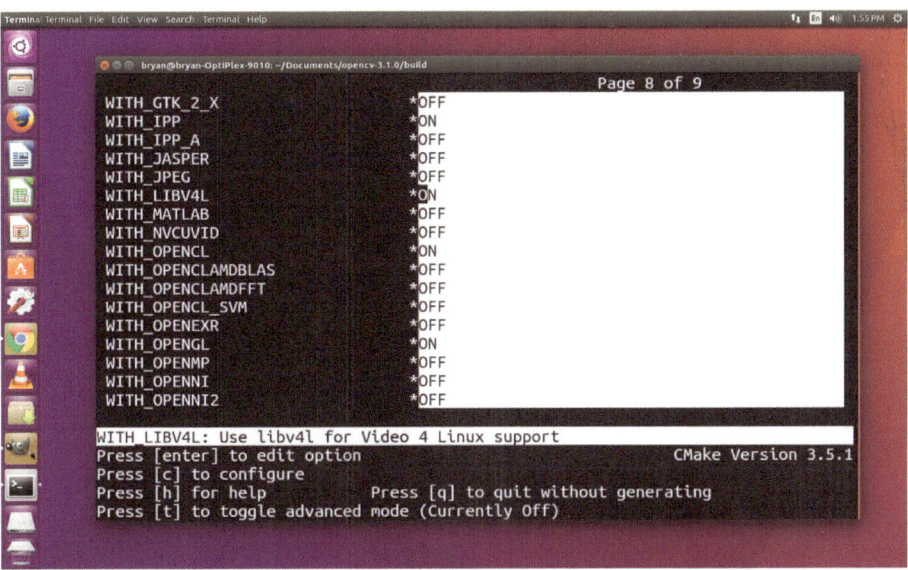

Figure 1-49. *WITH_LIBV4L option*

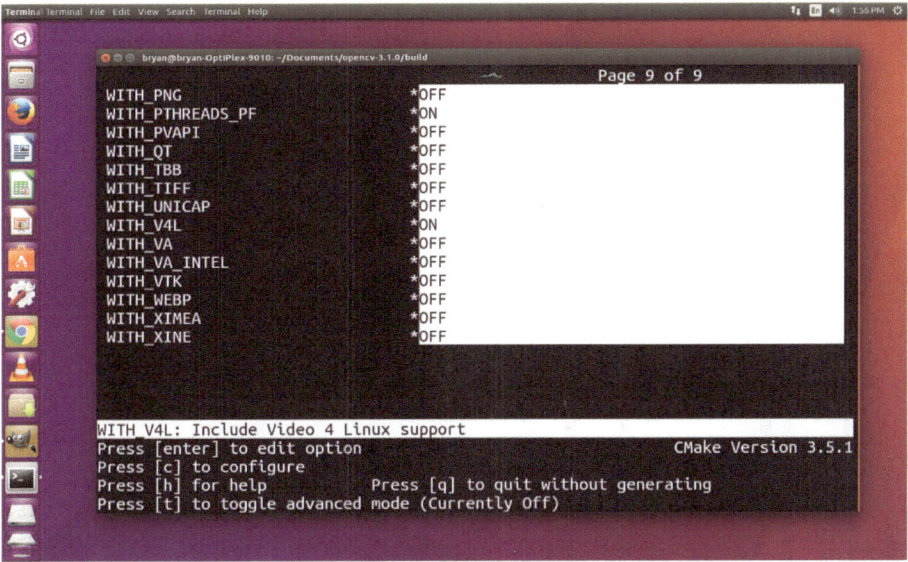

Figure 1-50. *WITH_V4L option*

After entering the last build option, type c to run the configuration with the extra modules. Choose OFF for the BUILD_FAT_JAVA_LIB option (Figure 1-51). Enter the ON options for BUILD_opencv_optflow and BUILD_opencv_ximgproc.

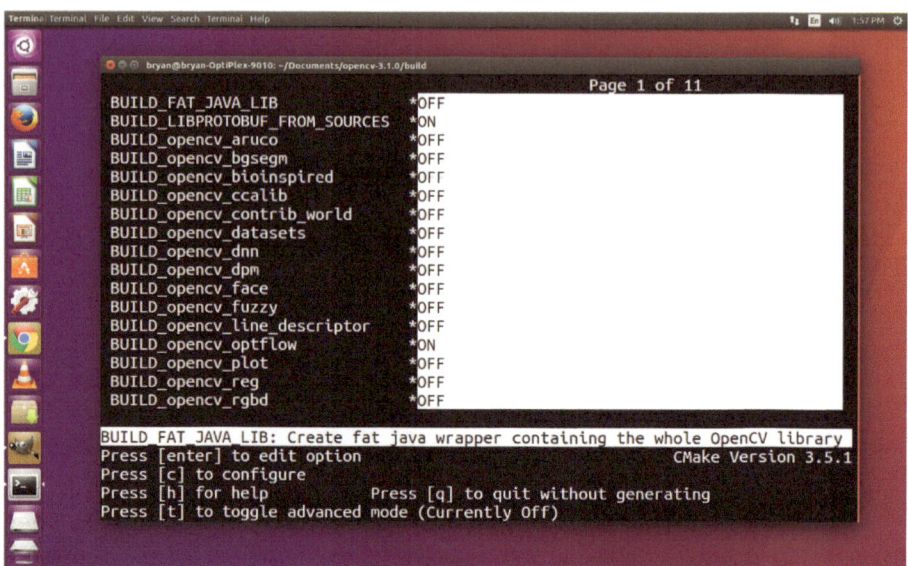

Figure 1-51. *BUILD_FAT_JAVA_LIB and BUILD_opencv_optflow options*

Keep the rest of the extra modules set to OFF (Figure 1-52).

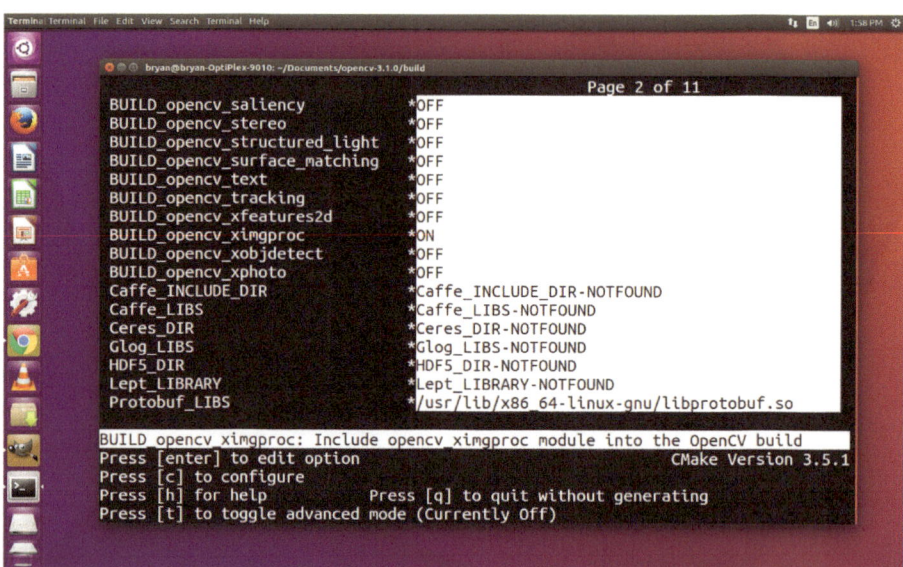

Figure 1-52. *BUILD_opencv_ximgproc option*

Type c again to run the final configuration. Type g to generate all the build files and quit (Figure 1-53).

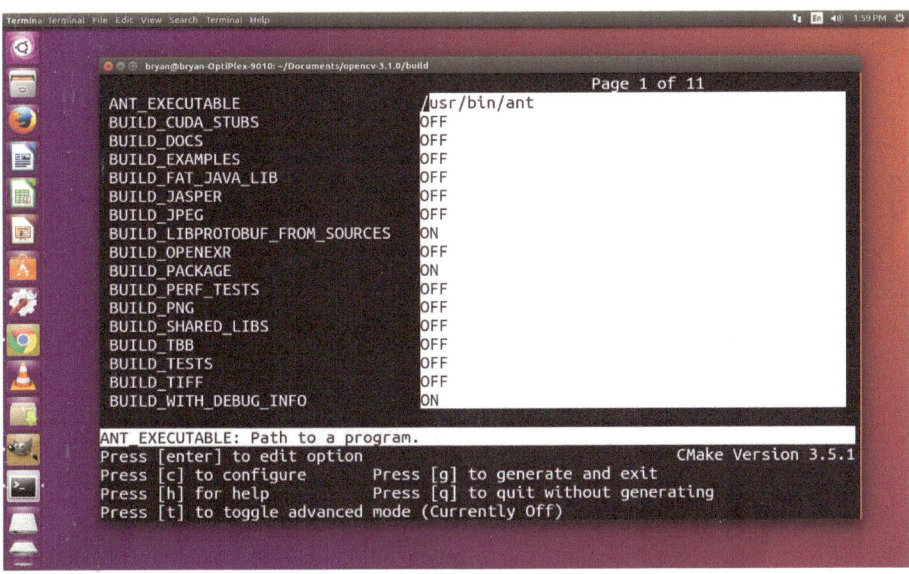

Figure 1-53. *Final configuration*

Start the build process by entering the following command:

```
make -j4
```

After the successful build of OpenCV, navigate into the bin folder within the current build folder (Figure 1-54). Spot the opencv-3.1.0.jar file.

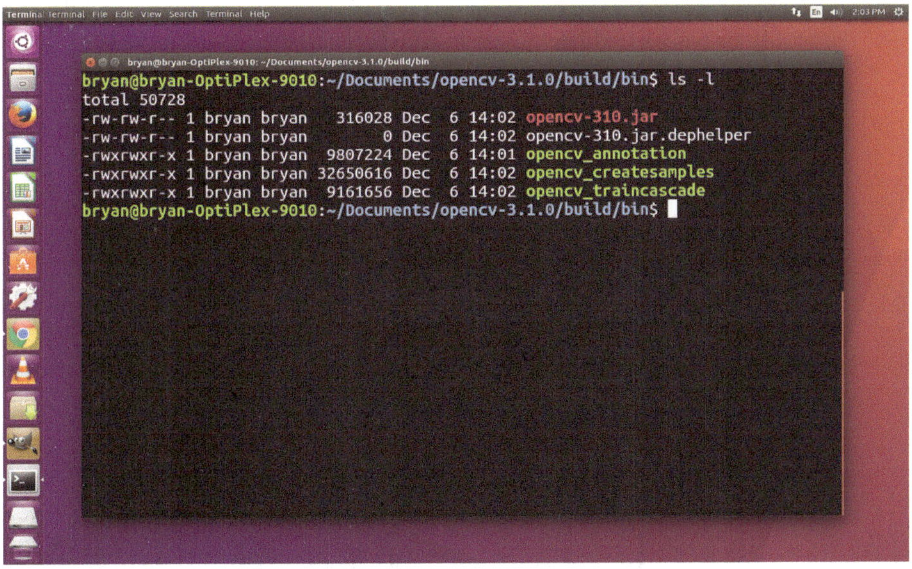

Figure 1-54. *Location of opencv-310.jar*

Then change the directory to the lib folder within the build folder. Find the libopencv_java310.so file. In the Terminal session, run execstack against the OpenCV library file to clear the executable stack flag (Figure 1-55).

```
execstack -c ./libopencv_java310.so
```

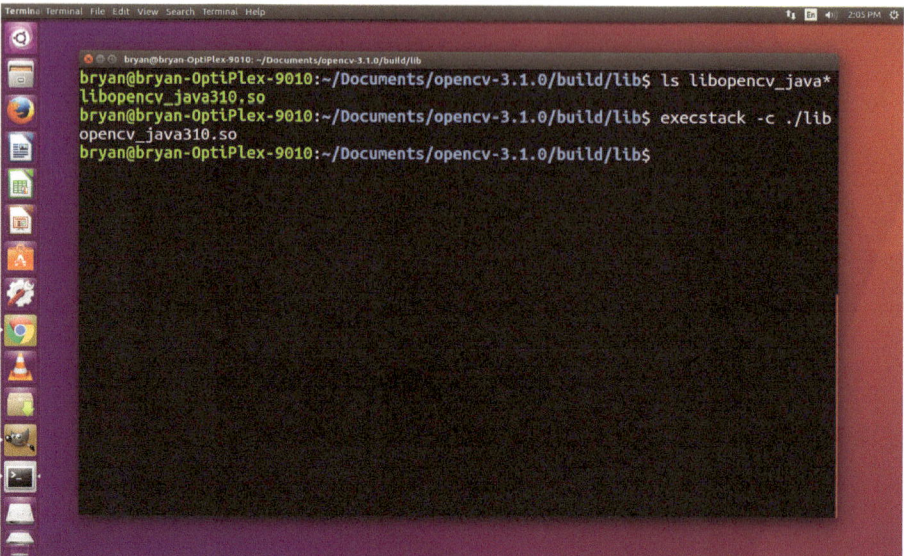

Figure 1-55. *Location of libopencv_java310.so*

Test Run

After you install Processing and build the Java version of OpenCV, you can start to write two programs to verify the installation and try the functionalities of the OpenCV library. The first program is a "Hello World" exercise to display the version information of the OpenCV library. The second program will define an OpenCV matrix data structure.

Hello World

Create a new Processing sketch named Chapter01_02. In the menu bar of the IDE, select Sketch ➤ Show Sketch Folder, as shown in Figure 1-56.

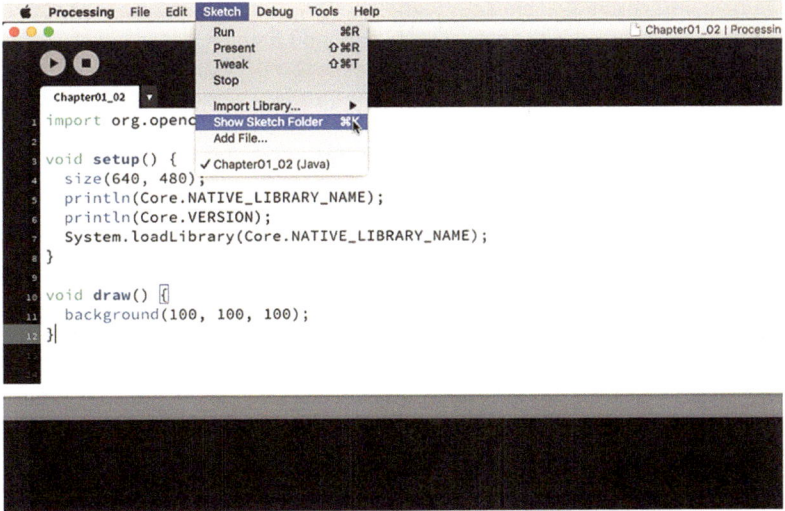

Figure 1-56. *Show Sketch Folder menu item in Processing IDE*

In the pop-up window, create a new folder named code. Copy all the OpenCV Java library files into it. It should contain the following files. You can just keep one of the opencv-310.jar files from the three platforms generated. Alternatively, you can copy only the related native library for the operating system you are using, such as libopencv_java310.dylib for macOS, libopencv_java310.so for Linux, or opencv_java310.dll for Windows.

- opencv-310.jar

- libopencv_java310.dylib

- libopencv_java310.so

- opencv_java310.dll

In the IDE main window, type the following code and click the Play button to execute:

```
import org.opencv.core.Core;

void setup() {
  size(640, 480);
  println(Core.NATIVE_LIBRARY_NAME);
  println(Core.VERSION);
  System.loadLibrary(Core.NATIVE_LIBRARY_NAME);
}

void draw() {
  background(100, 100, 100);
}
```

This will return the OpenCV native library name of opencv_java310 and the version number of 3.1.0 at the bottom of the IDE window. This location is the console window, and it's where messages will be displayed, as shown in Figure 1-57. The first import statement imports the OpenCV core module for subsequent reference. Within the setup function, the size function defines the size of the Java window for the program. The two println statements display the content of the two constants, Core.NATIVE_LIBRARY_NAME and Core.VERSION. The next statement, System.loadLibrary, loads the native library from the code folder. The draw routine has only one function to paint the window background in gray.

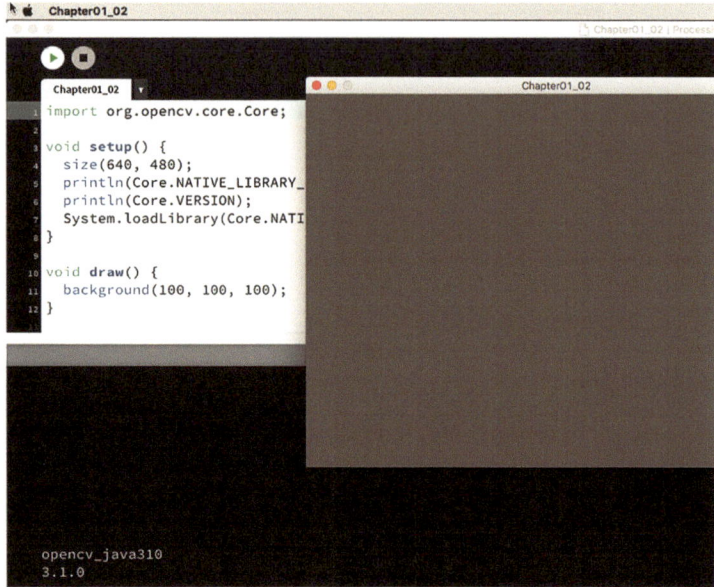

Figure 1-57. *Displaying OpenCV information in Processing*

Matrix Example

From the previous "Hello world" exercise, select the File menu; choose Save As to save the program with a new name, Chapter01_03. In this case, the content in the code folder will be duplicated in the new program. Use the following code for this exercise:

```
import org.opencv.core.Core;
import org.opencv.core.Mat;
import org.opencv.core.CvType;

void setup() {
  size(640, 480);
  System.loadLibrary(Core.NATIVE_LIBRARY_NAME);
  Mat m = Mat.eye(3, 3, CvType.CV_8UC1);
  println("Content of the matrix m is:");
  println(m.dump());
}
```

```
void draw() {
  background(100, 100, 100);
}
```

The three import statements include the definition of the OpenCV Core components, the Matrix data class, and the data type for the matrix elements. The new statement defines a matrix m and is an identity matrix with three rows and three columns.

```
Mat m = Mat.eye(3, 3, CvType.CV_8UC1);
```

Each data element in the matrix is an 8-bit unsigned character (one byte). The second println statement will dump the contents of the matrix m. (The next chapter will have a more detailed explanation about the matrix data structure and its representation and usage).

```
println(m.dump());
```

Figure 1-58 shows what the println statements display in the Processing window.

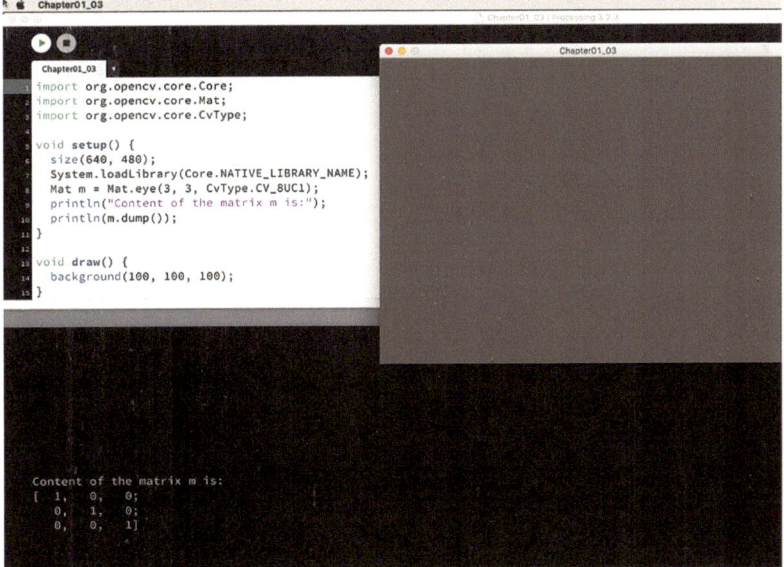

Figure 1-58. *Displaying matrix information*

Conclusion

This chapter guided you through the setup processes to install both Processing and OpenCV on the three most common platforms, macOS, Microsoft Windows, and Ubuntu Linux. At this point, you should be able to prepare the environment to proceed with working on image-processing and computer vision tasks. The next chapter will describe the representation of digital images in both Processing (Java) and OpenCV.

CHAPTER 2

Image Sources and Representations

The chapter explains the process of creating digital images in Processing and the internal representations of raster images in both Processing and OpenCV. It demonstrates how you can import external images into your programs and how to use different types of image manipulation functions. As an extended form of digital image, the use of digital video and live video streams are covered in the later sections of the chapter. The following are the basic concepts this chapter covers:

- Digital image fundamentals
- Images in Processing
- Moving images in Processing
- Matrices and images in OpenCV
- Image conversion between Processing and OpenCV

Digital Image Fundamentals

I usually use the metaphor of a grid to represent a digital image. The dimensions of an image equate to the size of the grid, with the *width* representing the number of columns and the *height* representing the number of rows. Therefore, the number of cells within the grid is equal to *width × height*. Each cell in the grid is a colored pixel. For a grayscale image, a *pixel* is a number representing the intensity of the gray tone. If you use one byte of data to represent each pixel, the grayscale will be within the range of 0 to 255. Figure 2-1 represents a grayscale image with eight columns and six rows.

100	200	10	5	77	22	34	75
255	200	100	90	10	33	66	55
123	45	46	47	1	99	0	23
3	5	8	13	21	101	71	4
167	84	256	222	123	21	17	5
23	22	180	250	89	16	81	66

Figure 2-1. *Grayscale image representation*

© Bryan WC Chung 2017
B. WC. Chung, *Pro Processing for Images and Computer Vision with OpenCV*,
DOI 10.1007/978-1-4842-2775-6_2

For a color image, a *pixel* is a group of numbers representing the intensity of individual color *channels*. Common color representations are RGB (red, green, blue) and HSB (hue, saturation, brightness). To bridge color formats between Processing and OpenCV, this book mainly adopts the ARGB representation. Each color pixel has four separate color channels, namely, alpha (transparency), red, green, and blue. For example, a fully opaque red will be (255, 255, 0, 0), or in hex notation #FFFF0000.

To summarize, you use *width* and *height* to describe the dimension of a digital image, *channel* to describe the number of color elements in each pixel, and *depth* to describe how many bits of data to represent each color.

Images in Processing

The main class in Processing that you use to handle digital images is PImage (https://processing.org/reference/PImage.html). It is modeled around the BufferedImage class (https://docs.oracle.com/javase/8/docs/api/java/awt/image/BufferedImage.html) in Java. Rather than asking you to study the Javadoc for the PImage class, I will walk you through the common image-processing tasks to do the following:

- Import an external image

- Create an image in Processing

- Display an image

- Export an image

Import an External Image

For this sequence of exercises, first create a Processing *sketch* (program) called Chapter02_01. The simplest way to add an external image is to drag the image directly onto the Processing IDE window. The process will create a data folder within your Processing sketch folder. Alternately, you can manually create a data folder inside your Processing sketch folder and copy the image into the data folder. Processing will automatically search this folder for external images, movies, and other data files such as Extensible Markup Language (XML) files. Inspect your data folder for the external image. The image used in this exercise is HongKong.png, as shown in Figure 2-2. The following code will load the image and display it in the Processing window. In this example, the size of the Processing window, 640×480, is the same as the size of the image. Cropping and padding may appear when they are of different sizes.

```
PImage img;

void setup() {

  size(640, 480);
  img = loadImage("HongKong.png");
  noLoop();
}

void draw() {
  image(img, 0, 0);
}
```

Figure 2-2. *Loading an external image*

The first statement defines an instance, img, of the PImage class and is the container for the external image. The statement inside the setup() function, as shown here, performs the actual loading of the image file HongKong.png into the img variable:

```
img = loadImage("HongKong.png");
```

The only statement inside the draw() function, as shown here, displays the image in the Processing graphic window at offset (0, 0):

```
image(img, 0, 0);
```

Note that there is a noLoop() statement inside the setup() function. It will perform the draw() function once instead of looping it in an animation mode.

In the next exercise, you will load an external image from the Internet (Figure 2-3). Create another Processing sketch called Chapter02_02. Enter the following code. Modify the String variable fName to point to the URL of any external image you want to import.

```
PImage img;
String fName;

void setup() {
  size(640, 480);
  background(255, 200, 200);
  fName = "http://www.magicandlove.com/blog/wp-content/uploads/2011/10/BryanChung-225x300.png";
  img = requestImage(fName);
}
```

41

```
void draw() {
  if (img.width > 0 && img.height > 0) {
    image(img, 360, 100);
  }
}
```

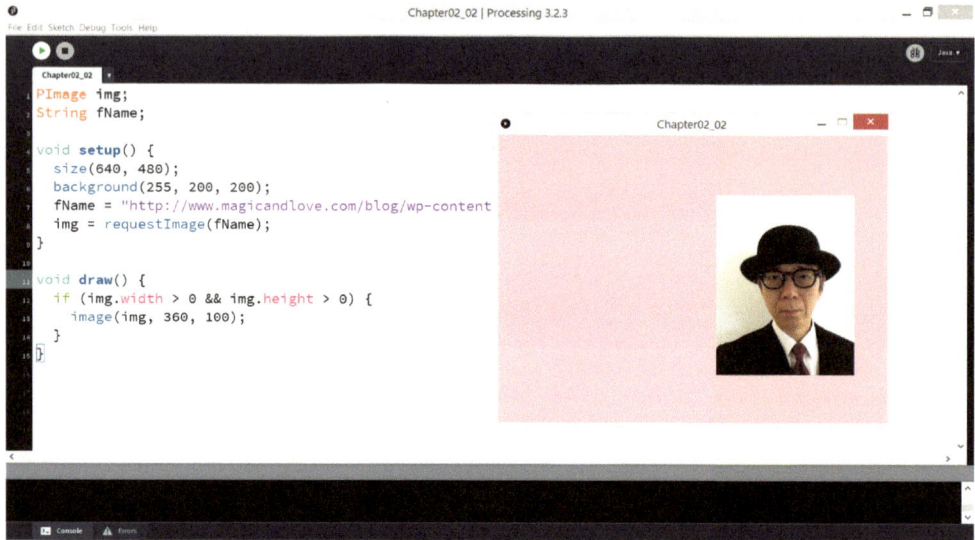

Figure 2-3. *Loading an image from the Internet*

In this exercise, you use the function requestImage() to load an external image, usually residing on some server on the Internet. The function performs asynchronous loading with another thread. It does not, however, come with a callback upon successful loading. You can make use of the two properties, width and height, of the PImage class to check whether the loading is complete. During the loading process, the values of the width and height properties of the image are 0. Upon successful completion of the loading, the values become the dimensions of the image loaded. The following code shows how to modify the previous code to print the values of width and height in the draw() function so you can check their values:

```
void draw() {
  println(img.width + ", " + img.height);
  if (img.width > 0 && img.height > 0) {
    image(img, 360, 100);
  }
}
```

If you purposely change the URL to a wrong address, you may find that the values for img.width and img.height both become -1.

Create an Image in Processing

In addition to loading an external image (Figure 2-4), you can create a digital image from scratch within Processing. The function to do so is createImage(), which will return an instance of the PImage class. The next program, Chapter02_03, will create an empty image and change all its pixels to yellow:

```
PImage img;

void setup() {
  size(640, 480);
  background(100, 100, 100);
  img = createImage(width, height, ARGB);
  color yellow = color(255, 255, 0);
  for (int y=0; y<img.height; y++) {
    for (int x=0; x<img.width; x++) {
      img.set(x, y, yellow);
    }
  }
}

void draw() {
  image(img, 0, 0);
}
```

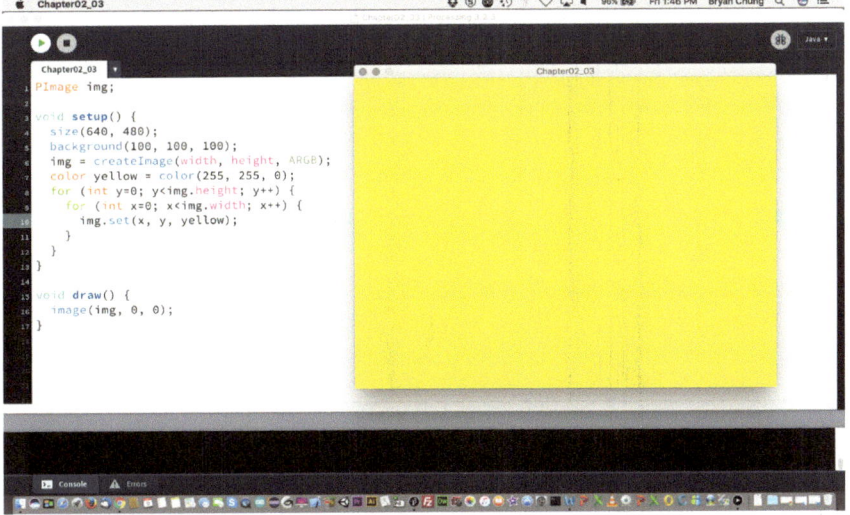

Figure 2-4. *Creating a yellow image within Processing*

The following statement creates a digital image of size width × height:

```
img = createImage(width, height, ARGB);
```

The variable width refers to the Processing window width as specified in the size() function. Its value is 640. Similarly, the variable height is 480, as defined in the size() function. The parameter ARGB defines a four-channel image (i.e., alpha, red, green, and blue). You can also define a three-channel image with RGB and a single alpha channel image with ALPHA. Nevertheless, the internal representation of the PImage class will remain as ARGB. The next statement defines a color variable named yellow:

```
color yellow = color(255, 255, 0);
```

Its value is yellow with maximum intensity (255) for the red and green channels. The nested for loops with indices y and x simply go through all the pixels of the image, img, and change the pixel color to yellow. Note the use of the set() function to modify the individual pixel color. This is a handy way to alter the pixel color at a specific point in the image with the use of the horizontal and vertical indices. The set() function is, however, not the most efficient way to do pixel manipulation. I will introduce other ways to achieve the effect later in this chapter.

```
img.set(x, y, yellow);
```

Graphics and Images

In the next exercise, Chapter02_04, you will look into the internal structure of the Processing canvas. The class PGraphics is the main graphics and rendering context. It is also a subclass of PImage. In this case, you can use the same image() function to display this graphics context. The following code will first draw a rectangle at the top-left corner of the canvas and then display the canvas by an offset. You will see two rectangles after the execution.

```
PGraphics pg;

void setup() {
  size(640, 480);
  background(100, 100, 100);
  pg = getGraphics();
  noLoop();
}

void draw() {
  rect(0, 0, 200, 120);
  image(pg, 200, 120);
}
```

Figure 2-5 shows the result of the execution. The first rectangle on the top left is the result of the rect() statement within the draw() function. The image() statement offsets the whole canvas by 200 pixels horizontally and 120 pixels vertically and displays the whole canvas. The technique is useful when you need to capture the current drawing canvas as an image.

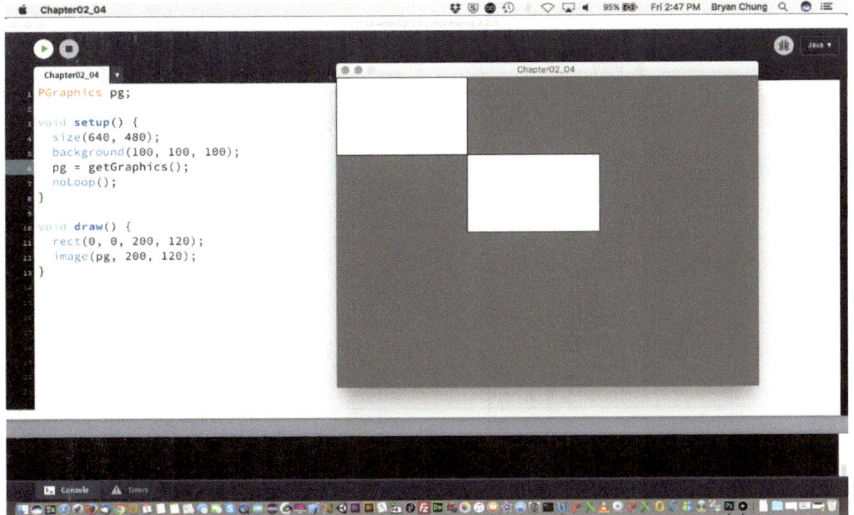

Figure 2-5. *Use of PGraphics as PImage*

In this exercise, Chapter02_05, you'll study the general use of the PGraphics class. You can consider a PGraphics instance a separate canvas such that you can draw on it off-screen. Whenever it is ready to display, you can use the image() function to display it in the Processing window.

```
PGraphics pg;
boolean toDraw;

void setup() {
  size(640, 480);
  background(0);
  pg = createGraphics(width, height);
  toDraw = false;
}

void draw() {
  if (toDraw)
    image(pg, 0, 0);
}

void mouseDragged() {
  pg.beginDraw();
  pg.noStroke();
  pg.fill(255, 100, 0);
  pg.ellipse(mouseX, mouseY, 20, 20);
  pg.endDraw();
}
```

```
void mousePressed() {
  pg.beginDraw();
  pg.background(0);
  pg.endDraw();
  toDraw = false;
}

void mouseReleased() {
  toDraw = true;
}
```

Figure 2-6 shows the result of a sample run of the sketch.

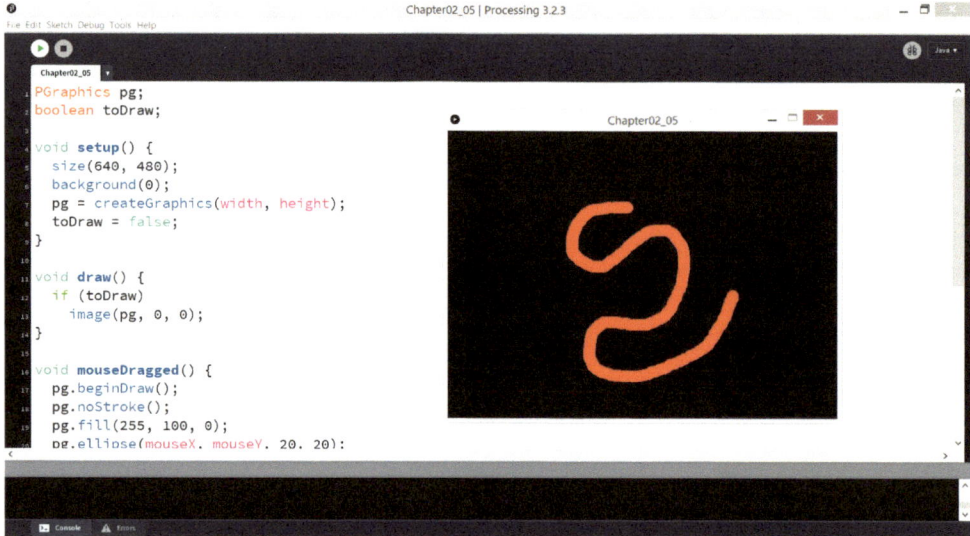

Figure 2-6. *Use of createGraphics() and the PGraphics*

Note the use of the following createGraphics() function to create an instance of the PGraphics class that is the same size as the Processing window. It will be used as an off-screen buffer to store the drawing that you made by dragging the mouse. The three callback functions, mousePressed(), mouseDragged(), and mouseReleased(), will be triggered whenever you press, drag, and release the mouse button. If you want to create any graphics in the PGraphics instance pg, you have to put the commands inside the pg.beginDraw() and pg.endDraw() block. Note also that you can specify grayscale color by putting in only one number, such as in the background(0) function, which clears the background with black. In the following line of code, the pair of variables mouseX and mouseY will return the current mouse position in the Processing graphic window, measured in pixels:

```
pg.ellipse(mouseX, mouseY, 20, 20);
```

In this statement, an ellipse/circle is drawn on the off-screen buffer pg in the current mouse position. Processing also provides another pair of variables, pmouseX and pmouseY, that store the previous mouse position in the last frame of the animation. The two pairs of mouse position variables will be useful when you need to draw a line segment from the previous mouse position to the current one.

BufferedImage in Processing

In previous sections, you learned how to use the main image-processing class in Processing, PImage. For those who are familiar with Java image processing, the class BufferedImage (https://docs.oracle.com/ javase/8/docs/api/java/awt/image/BufferedImage.html) is important for programmers to be able to manipulate images in Java. In Processing, you can also perform a conversion between the PImage class and the BufferedImage class. Sometimes it will be useful for you to incorporate other Java image-processing libraries in Processing that return a BufferedImage class. The following code demonstrates the conversion between a PImage class and a BufferedImage class in Processing:

```
import java.awt.image.BufferedImage;

PImage img;
BufferedImage bim;

void setup() {
  size(640, 480);
  noLoop();
}

void draw() {
  background(0);
  // create the PImage instance img
  img = createImage(width, height, ARGB);
  // create the BufferedImage instance bim from img
  bim = (BufferedImage) img.getNative();
  println(bim.getWidth() + ", " + bim.getHeight());
  // create a new PImage instance nim from BufferedImage bim
  PImage nim = new PImage(bim);
  println(nim.width + ", " + nim.height);
}
```

First, you use import java.awt.image.BufferedImage to include the reference of BufferedImage to your Processing sketch. Within the draw() function, you use the createImage() function to create an empty PImage instance, img. By using the getNative() method, you can create a copy of the original image in BufferedImage format. Given a BufferedImage, bim, you can again create a PImage out of it by using the new PImage(bim) command. In the following example, Chapter02_06, you can see a practical use of this conversion for a creative result:

```
import java.awt.Robot;
import java.awt.image.BufferedImage;
import java.awt.Rectangle;

Robot robot;

void setup() {
  size(640, 480);
  try {
    robot = new Robot();
  }
  catch (Exception e) {
    println(e.getMessage());
  }
}
```

```
void draw() {
  background(0);
  Rectangle rec = new Rectangle(mouseX, mouseY, width, height);
  BufferedImage img1 = robot.createScreenCapture(rec);
  PImage img2 = new PImage(img1);
  image(img2, 0, 0);
}
```

This Processing sketch mainly uses the Java Robot class (https://docs.oracle.com/javase/8/docs/api/java/awt/Robot.html) to do a screen capture. The output from the screen capture (Figure 2-7) is a BufferedImage that you can convert to a PImage for display within the draw() function. In the setup() function, you initialize the robot instance inside a try block to capture an AWTException. In the draw() function, you first use a Rectangle object to define the offset and size of the screen region to capture. The robot.createScreenCapture(rec) will perform the actual screen capture with the resulting image stored in img1, which is an instance of BufferedImage. The next statement converts the img1 instance to another PImage instance, img2, for display with an image() function. When you move the mouse within the Processing window, you can find a funny result similar to the feedback effect in video art. It is the image() function that modifies the screen content in every frame contributing to this feedback loop.

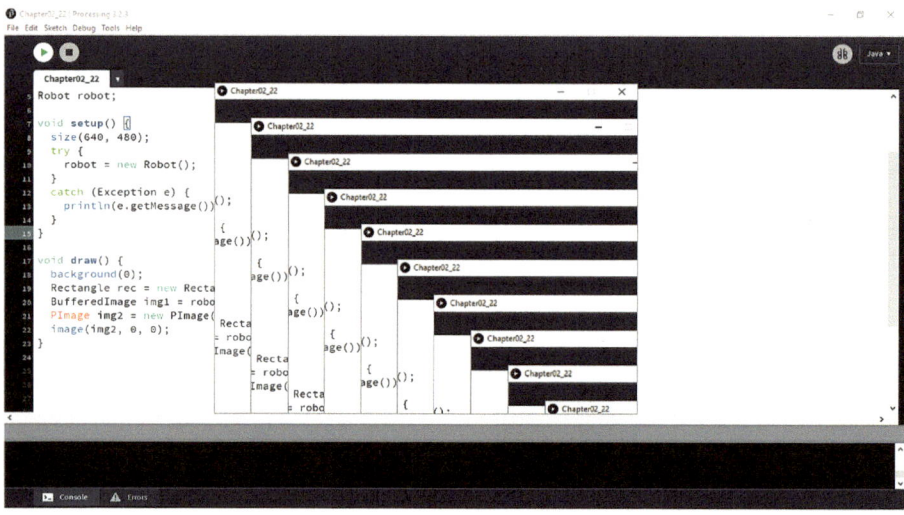

Figure 2-7. *Screen capture with PImage*

Moving Images in Processing

The external video library for Processing (https://processing.org/reference/libraries/video/index.html) that you installed in the previous chapter provides the necessary functions for video playback and capture. It is based on the Java binding in the GStreamer multimedia framework. The library contains two separate classes: Movie for video playback and Capture for live video capture. Both are subclasses of PImage. You can use similar methods to manipulate the pixel data.

Digital Movies

The next exercise, Chapter02_07, will perform a loop playback of the sample video, transit.mov, distributed in the video library. Like adding an image to the Processing sketch, you can simply drag the digital video file onto the Processing IDE window. Or you can create a data folder inside the sketch folder and copy the video file there. The following code performs an asynchronous playback of the digital video. Whenever a new frame is ready, the callback movieEvent() will be triggered to read the frame.

```
import processing.video.*;

Movie mov;

void setup() {
  size(640, 360);
  background(0);
  mov = new Movie(this, "transit.mov");
  mov.loop();
}

void draw() {
  image(mov, 0, 0);
}

void movieEvent(Movie m) {
  m.read();
}
```

Processing will automatically generate the first import statement when you select Sketch ➤ Import Library ➤ Video from the main menu. The next step is to define the Movie class instance, mov. The following statement will then create the new instance with the name of the video:

```
mov = new Movie(this, "transit.mov");
```

The keyword this refers to the current Processing sketch (i.e., Chapter02_07), which is necessary for the callback function movieEvent() to refer to it. Figure 2-8 shows the running sketch.

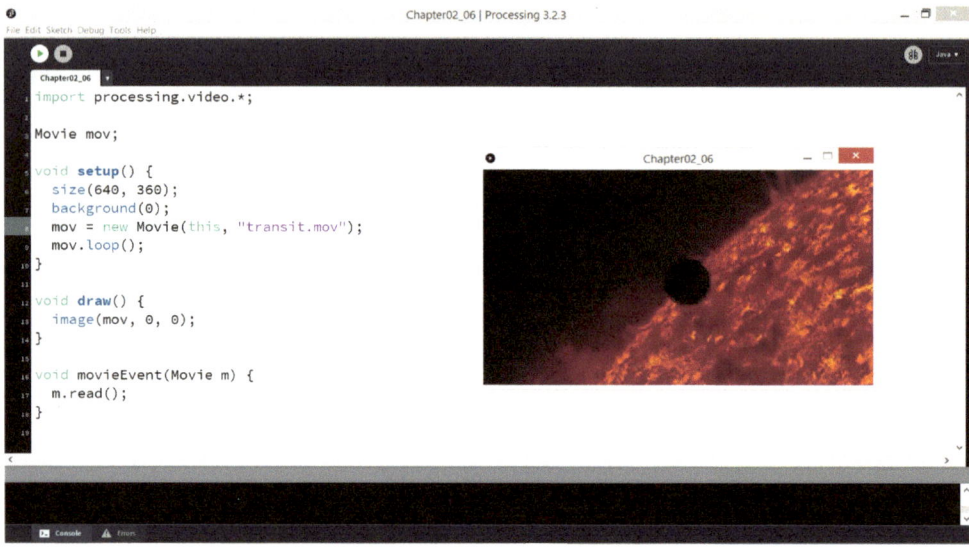

Figure 2-8. *Digital video playback example*

The next example, Chapter02_08, provides an alternative way to read the digital video. In this version, the sketch in each animation frame checks the availability of the new frame and reads it synchronously.

```
import processing.video.*;

Movie mov;

void setup() {
  size(640, 360);
  background(0);
  mov = new Movie(this, "transit.mov");
  mov.loop();
  frameRate(30);
}

void draw() {
  if (mov.available()) {
    mov.read();
  }
  image(mov, 0, 0);
}
```

Note in the setup() function there is a new frameRate() statement that specifies the frame rate per second for the draw() function. For slower computers, the actual frame rate may be slower than what is specified here.

As Movie is a subclass of PImage, you can use the get() method of PImage to retrieve the pixel color data from any frame of the video. The next Processing sketch, Chapter02_09, will demonstrate this:

```
import processing.video.*;

Movie mov;

void setup() {
  size(640, 360);
  background(0);
  mov = new Movie(this, "transit.mov");
  mov.loop();
  frameRate(30);
}

void draw() {
  if (mov.available()) {
    mov.read();
  }
  image(mov, 0, 0);
}

void mouseClicked() {
  color c = mov.get(mouseX, mouseY);
  println(red(c) + ", " + green(c) + ", " + blue(c));
}
```

In this exercise, you display the color information of the pixel that you click. This is done within the mouseClicked() callback function. You provide the horizontal and vertical positions of the pixel inside the mov frame. It returns the color data in the variable c. By using the red(), green(), and blue() functions, you can retrieve the three primary color components from it. The range of the numbers will be within 0 to 255.

Live Video Captures

In addition to digital video playback, Processing provides the class Capture to enable the live capture of video streams from regular webcams or capture devices. Like when using the Movie class, you need to import the video library, as shown in the following exercise, Chapter02_10:

```
import processing.video.*;

Capture cap;

void setup() {
  size(640, 480);
  background(0);
  cap = new Capture(this, width, height);
  cap.start();
}
```

```
void draw() {
  image(cap, 0, 0);
}

void captureEvent(Capture c) {
  c.read();
}
```

You use the Capture class with the instance cap. The new statement creates a new instance of the class and assigns it to cap. It also needs a start() method to start the capture device. Similar to the Movie class, the Capture class comes with the callback function called captureEvent() where the capture device can asynchronously notify the main Processing sketch to read in any new video frame available. Since Capture is a subclass of PImage, you can use the same image() function to display the capture frame in the Processing window.

In the next exercise, Chapter02_11, you use a synchronous read of the capture frame within the draw() function. At the same time, you introduce the mask() function to mask out a portion of the image by interactively drawing on a mask image.

```
import processing.video.*;

Capture cap;
PGraphics pg;

void setup() {
  size(640, 480);
  background(0);
  cap = new Capture(this, width, height);
  cap.start();
  pg = createGraphics(width, height);
  pg.beginDraw();
  pg.noStroke();
  pg.fill(255);
  pg.background(0);
  pg.endDraw();
}

void draw() {
  if (cap.available()) {
    cap.read();
  }
  tint(255, 0, 0, 40);
  cap.mask(pg);
  image(cap, 0, 0);
}

void mouseDragged() {
  pg.beginDraw();
  pg.ellipse(mouseX, mouseY, 20, 20);
  pg.endDraw();
}
```

In this exercise, you use a PGraphics instance called pg to serve as an off-screen buffer. In the mouseDragged() callback function, the user can create a white circular mark on the black background. In the draw() function, you introduce two new functions. The first one is tint(), where you tint the resulting image with red (255, 0, 0) and a bit of transparency, as indicated in the fourth parameter, 40. The second one is the mask() function, where you apply the mask, pg, to the original image (Figure 2-9), cap. The result is an interactive experience where you can drag the mouse to reveal the underlying live video stream.

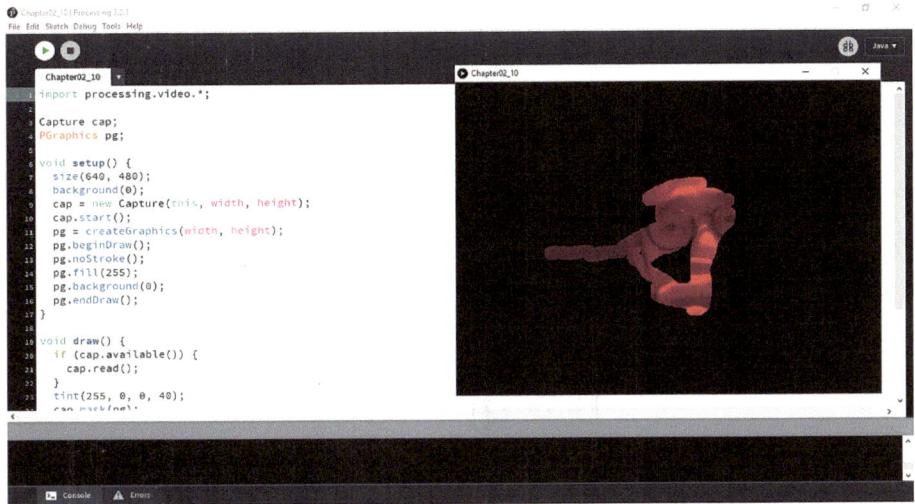

Figure 2-9. *Live video capture with a mask*

Matrices and Images in OpenCV

Now that I've finished introducing how to use external images, video, and live streaming for Processing, I will switch back to OpenCV to help you understand how it represents digital images. Before you start, remember to create a code folder in your next Processing sketch, Chapter02_12. Inside the code folder, put the OpenCV library files that you created in the previous chapter. The following are the OpenCV files in the folder:

- opencv-310.jar
- libopencv_java310.dylib (for macOS)
- libopencv_java310.so (for Linux, such as Ubuntu)
- opencv_java310.dll (for Windows)

In this exercise, you will define a number of empty matrices, Mat, with different options so you can understand the internal structure of the Mat class. The different classes I will cover are Mat, Size, CvType, and Scalar.

```
import org.opencv.core.*;

void setup() {
  size(640, 480);
  System.loadLibrary(Core.NATIVE_LIBRARY_NAME);
  noLoop();
}
```

```
void draw() {
  background(0);
  Mat m1 = new Mat();
  println(m1.dump());
  Mat m2 = new Mat(3, 4, CvType.CV_8UC1, Scalar.all(0));
  println(m2.dump());
  Mat m3 = new Mat(3, 4, CvType.CV_8UC3, Scalar.all(255));
  println(m3.dump());
  Mat m4 = new Mat(new Size(4, 3), CvType.CV_8UC3, new Scalar(0, 255, 0));
  println(m4.dump());
}
```

In this exercise, you have defined four matrices. The first matrix, m1, is an empty matrix without dimension information. The method m1.dump() will return a printable form of the matrix content. The second matrix, m2, has three rows and four columns, so the total number of elements is twelve. Each element is a number of 8 bits unsigned (CvType.CV_8UC1). The values of the elements are 0 (Scalar.all(0)) when the matrix is first created. The method m2.dump() will display 12 elements of 0 in three rows by four columns. The third matrix, m3, has the same dimensions as m2. Nevertheless, each element in m3 consists of three separate numbers or channels (CvType.CV_8UC3). All the elements will have a value of 255 (Scalar.all(255)). You use a different method to define the dimensions of the fourth matrix, m4. The new Size(4, 3) defines a new object instance of Size with a width of 4 and a height of 3, which is equivalent to a matrix with three rows and four columns. Each matrix element is the same with three channels. In m4, you initialize the matrix element with a Scalar instance with the value (0, 255, 0).

Before moving on with the next exercise, let's look at how the CvType class works. The data type specification after CvType is as follows:

CV_[bits][type]C[channels]

Here is an explanation:

- [bits] indicates the number of bits to represent each data element. It can be 8, 16, or 32.

- [type] indicates the type of data representation. It can be unsigned, U; signed, S; or float, F.

- [channels] indicates the number of channels for each data element in the matrix. It can be 1, 2, 3, or 4.

In the next exercise, Chapter02_13, you will explore a number of methods in the Mat class to understand the data type and representation of the matrix elements:

```
import org.opencv.core.*;

void setup() {
  size(640, 480);
  System.loadLibrary(Core.NATIVE_LIBRARY_NAME);
  noLoop();
}

void draw() {
  background(0);
  Mat m1 = new Mat(new Size(4, 3), CvType.CV_8UC3, new Scalar(0, 100, 0));
  println(m1.dump());
  println(m1.rows() + ", " + m1.cols());
  println(m1.width() + ", " + m1.height());
```

```
    println("Size: " + m1.size());
    println("Dimension: " + m1.dims());
    println("Number of elements: " + m1.total());
    println("Element size: " + m1.elemSize());
    println("Depth: " + m1.depth());
    println("Number of channels: " + m1.channels());
}
```

You should obtain the following output from your Processing console window:

```
[   0, 100,   0,   0, 100,   0,   0, 100,   0,   0, 100,   0;
    0, 100,   0,   0, 100,   0,   0, 100,   0,   0, 100,   0;
    0, 100,   0,   0, 100,   0,   0, 100,   0,   0, 100,   0]
3, 4
4, 3
Size: 4x3
Dimension: 2
Number of elements: 12
Element size: 3
Depth: 0
Number of channels: 3
```

Most of the information is straightforward. The element size is the number of bytes that each matrix element contains. The depth is the data type indicator of each channel. A value of 0 indicates the data type is 8-bit unsigned integers that you mainly use between Processing and OpenCV. Besides obtaining information from an existing matrix, the next exercise, Chapter02_14, will show how you can retrieve information from individual elements of a matrix, using the get() method:

```
import org.opencv.core.*;

void setup() {
  size(640, 480);
  System.loadLibrary(Core.NATIVE_LIBRARY_NAME);
  noLoop();
}

void draw() {
  background(0);
  Mat m1 = new Mat(new Size(4, 3), CvType.CV_8UC4, new Scalar(100, 200, 80, 255));
  double [] result = m1.get(0, 0);
  printArray(result);
  byte [] data = new byte[m1.channels()];
  m1.get(2, 2, data);
  for (byte b : data) {
    int i = (b < 0) ? b + 256 : b;
    println(i);
  }
}
```

Note in the previous code that the following statement uses the get() method to retrieve the data element located at row 0 and column 0 in m1. The returned data will be stored in a double array named result.

```
double [] result = m1.get(0, 0);
```

You may discover that even though each data element in the matrix is defined as a byte (8 bits), the result from the get() method with this syntax will always return a double array. The length of the double array result is 4, which is the number of channels defined in CV_8UC4. If you define the data element as CV_8UC1 (i.e., with only a single channel), the result returned will also be a double array with a length equal to 1. The second half of the exercise demonstrates that you can also explicitly define a byte array called data of length 4, use different syntax with the get() method to retrieve the data element from position row 2 column 2, and directly store it into the byte array data. Within the for loop, you also need to cater for the fact that Java does not have an unsigned byte data type. For a negative number, you have to add 256 to convert it to the original number that is greater than 127.

After the get() method, the next exercise, Chapter02_15, explores the put() method to change the content of a data element in the matrix. It demonstrates two ways of using the put() method. The first one updates the data element with a byte array. The second one updates the data element with a list of double numbers.

```
import org.opencv.core.*;

void setup() {
  size(640, 480);
  System.loadLibrary(Core.NATIVE_LIBRARY_NAME);
  noLoop();
}

void draw() {
  background(0);
  Mat m1 = new Mat(new Size(4, 3), CvType.CV_8UC4, new Scalar(100, 200, 80, 255));
  byte [] data1 = new byte[m1.channels()];
  byte [] data2 = new byte[m1.channels()];
  m1.get(1, 1, data1);
  data2[0] = data1[3];
  data2[1] = data1[2];
  data2[2] = data1[1];
  data2[3] = data1[0];
  m1.put(1, 1, data2);
  printArray(m1.get(1, 1));
  m1.put(2, 2, 123, 234, 200, 100);
  printArray(m1.get(2, 2));
}
```

The first part of this exercise is to retrieve the data element at row 1 column 1 into the data1 array. You then reorder the data1 array into the data2 array, which is the same length. The first put() method stores the data2 array into the same data element. You then use the printArray() function to display the individual channel information of that data element. In the second part of the exercise, you simply list the four numbers for the four-channel values in the put() method. They will be stored at row 2 column 2, as shown in the second printArray() statement. The result from the console window of the sketch is as follows:

```
[0] 255.0
[1] 80.0
[2] 200.0
[3] 100.0
[0] 123.0
[1] 234.0
[2] 200.0
[3] 100.0
```

Before ending this session, you are going to study another feature of the put() and get() functions, which is to do bulk information update and retrieval. The feature is essential when writing code to convert image data between Processing and OpenCV. In the upcoming exercise, Chapter02_16, you use a byte array and a sequence of numbers that is of the size of the matrix for bulk update and retrieval.

```
import org.opencv.core.*;

void setup() {
  size(640, 480);
  System.loadLibrary(Core.NATIVE_LIBRARY_NAME);
  noLoop();
}

void draw() {
  background(0);
  Mat m1 = new Mat(new Size(3, 2), CvType.CV_8UC1);
  for (int r=0; r<m1.rows(); r++) {
    for (int c=0; c<m1.cols(); c++) {
      m1.put(r, c, floor(random(100)));
    }
  }
  println(m1.dump());
  byte [] data = new byte[m1.rows()*m1.cols()*m1.channels()];
  m1.get(0, 0, data);
  printArray(data);

  Mat m2 = new Mat(new Size(3, 2), CvType.CV_8UC2, Scalar.all(0));
  m2.put(0, 0, 1, 2, 3, 4, 5, 6, 7, 8);
  println(m2.dump());
}
```

The first part of the exercise defines a small matrix with two rows and three columns. Each data element is a single-channel number stored in one byte. The for loop initializes the matrix m1 with random integer values smaller than 100. You then define an empty byte array called data that has a size determined by the matrix m1 size (i.e., $2 \times 3 \times 1 = 6$). After the get() method, all the matrix content is dumped into the data array. In the second part of the exercise, you define another matrix, m2, with two rows and three columns. Each data element is a two-channel number pair, as shown in CV_8UC2. The put() method will store the number sequence into the first four data elements of the array. The sequence will be in row order. The cells affected are (0, 0), (0, 1), (0, 2), (1, 0). The first number inside the brackets is the row number, while the second number is the column. The following statement will store (1, 2), (3, 4), (5, 6), (7, 8) into the locations at (0, 0), (0, 1), (0, 2), (1, 0):

```
m2.put(0, 0, 1, 2, 3, 4, 5, 6, 7, 8);
```

The remaining data elements will not be affected. Figure 2-10 shows the original and new matrices after the operation.

Original matrix

Row	Column		
	0	1	2
0	(0, 0)	(0, 0)	(0, 0)
1	(0, 0)	(0, 0)	(0, 0)

New matrix

Row	Column		
	0	1	2
0	(1,2)	(3,4)	(5,6)
1	(7,8)	(0, 0)	(0, 0)

Figure 2-10. *Operation of the matrix put() function*

You may note that even though you specify one matrix element in the get() and put() functions, the functions can affect the rest of the matrix content if the byte array you use covers more than the size of one element. You will use this technique to convert data between Processing's PImage and OpenCV's Mat in the next section.

Image Conversion Between Processing and OpenCV

This section is important for any applications that you want to use Processing with OpenCV. To use OpenCV, you have to convert the raw images that you create in the Processing environment, such as still photos, digital videos, or live webcam feeds, to the Mat format that OpenCV can operate on. After you have performed the OpenCV operations on the images, the last step is to convert them to the PImage format that Processing can display in its window.

At the beginning of this chapter, you learned that an image in Processing is a two-dimensional array of color pixels. The horizontal dimension is the width, and the vertical dimension is the height. Each pixel is of the data type color. The internal representation of a color pixel is an integer of 32 bits. The hex notation of a color instance is 0xAARRGGBB, corresponding to the alpha, red, green, and blue color channels. The range of value for each color channel is from 0 to 255. To define the color yellow, for instance, you can write the following:

```
color yellow = color(255, 255, 0);
```

If you just specify three color channels, the default alpha value will be set to 255 automatically. You can also write colors in hex notation like this:

```
color yellow = 0xFFFFFF00;
```

The following code segment will demonstrate the use of the color variable and the different ways to retrieve the color channel values from it:

```
color col = color(200, 100, 40);
println("Color value as integer");
println(col);
println("RGB from bitwise operations");
println(col & 0x000000FF);
```

```
println((col & 0x0000FF00) >> 8);
println((col & 0x00FF0000) >> 16);
println("RGB from functions");
println(red(col));
println(green(col));
println(blue(col));
```

Processing internally does not store the image as a two-dimensional array. Instead, it is stored as a one-dimensional integer array named pixels[]. The length of the array is the total number of pixels of the image as defined by its width × height. For the pixel at row y and column x in the image, the index to the pixels[] array is as follows:

index = y * width + x;

For example, when you have an image with just two rows and three columns as shown here, the two-dimensional array is as follows:

0 (0, 0)	1 (0, 1)	2 (0, 2)
3 (1, 0)	4 (1, 1)	5 (1, 2)

The two numbers inside the parentheses are the column and row indices. The single number outside the parentheses is the index in the one-dimensional array, pixels[], storing the image in Processing.

0 (0, 0)	1 (0, 1)	2 (0, 2)	3 (1, 0)	4 (1, 1)	5 (1, 2)

Within the pixels[] array, each cell is the color information of the pixel, stored as an integer with the format 0xAARRGGBB. Each integer consists of 4 bytes. Each byte within the integer stores a separate color channel for the pixel in ARGB order.

AARRGGBB	AARRGGBB	AARRGGBB	AARRGGBB	AARRGGBB	AARRGGBB

In OpenCV, the color pixel formats are more flexible, as shown in the previous section. To make OpenCV compatible with Processing, you will stick to the CV_8UC4 format so that you can have the same amount of storage to exchange between Processing and OpenCV. Nevertheless, a number of OpenCV functions rely on the use of a grayscale image (i.e., CV_8UC1) and a three-channel color image, such as (CV_8UC3) in BGR order. In this case, let's build in the flexibility to enable conversion into three channels and a single-channel color image.

Taking the same example with two rows and three columns you used for Processing, the OpenCV representation is as follows:

BB	GG	RR	AA	BB	GG	RR	AA	BB	GG	RR	AA	BB	GG	RR	AA	BB	GG	RR	AA	BB	GG	RR	AA

The total number of cells is width × height × channels, which is 24 in this example. The two-dimensional image matrix will be stored as a linear array of 24 bytes, or 48 hex characters. Four consecutive bytes make up a pixel with a channel order of BGRA. The byte array will be the internal representation of the image matrix for OpenCV.

Now you have two arrays. The first one is an integer array of size (width × height) from Processing; the second one is a byte array of size (width × height × channels) from OpenCV. The problem is how you can perform conversion between the two of them. The Java ByteBuffer and IntBuffer classes are the solution to the problem.

From Processing to OpenCV

You need to have a source image in the Processing environment. You will use the Capture class to retrieve a video frame for this exercise, Chapter02_17. In each run of the draw() function, you try to convert the frame into an OpenCV Mat. To verify whether the conversion is valid, the Processing sketch will allow users to click anywhere within the video frame to display its pixel color in the upper-right corner of the window.

```
import processing.video.*;
import org.opencv.core.*;
import java.nio.ByteBuffer;

Capture cap;
String colStr;
Mat fm;

void setup() {
  size(640, 480);
  System.loadLibrary(Core.NATIVE_LIBRARY_NAME);
  cap = new Capture(this, width, height);
  cap.start();
  frameRate(30);
  colStr = "";
  fm = new Mat();
}

void draw() {
  if (!cap.available())
    return;
  background(0);
  cap.read();
  fm = imgToMat(cap);
  image(cap, 0, 0);
  text(nf(round(frameRate), 2), 10, 20);
  text(colStr, 550, 20);
}

Mat imgToMat(PImage m) {
  Mat f = new Mat(new Size(m.width, m.height), CvType.CV_8UC4,
    Scalar.all(0));
  ByteBuffer b = ByteBuffer.allocate(f.rows()*f.cols()*f.channels());
  b.asIntBuffer().put(m.pixels);
  b.rewind();
  f.put(0, 0, b.array());
  return f;
}

void mouseClicked() {
  int x = constrain(mouseX, 0, width-1);
  int y = constrain(mouseY, 0, height-1);
  double [] px = fm.get(y, x);
  colStr = nf(round((float)px[1]), 3) + ", " +
    nf(round((float)px[2]), 3) + ", " +
    nf(round((float)px[3]), 3);
}
```

There are three global variables. The first one, cap, is the video capture object. The second one, fm, is the temporary OpenCV Mat storing the current frame of the webcam image. The third one is a String variable, colStr, keeping the RGB color value of a pixel where the user clicked. Within the draw() function, the program passes the current webcam image, cap, to the function imgToMat(). The function returns an OpenCV Mat to be stored in the variable fm. Whenever the user clicks the screen, the callback function mouseClicked() will obtain the pixel color data from the fm object by using the get(y, x) function. It will then return a double array called px[] that keeps the color pixel information in ARGB order. Note that you have not performed the channel reordering process to change from ARGB order in Processing to BGRA order in OpenCV.

The core of the program is the imgToMat() function. It accepts an input parameter of type PImage. The first statement defines a temporary OpenCV Mat f with the same size as the input, m. The second statement creates a ByteBuffer variable b with the size 640 × 480 × 4 = 1228800. It is the key buffer to exchange data between the Processing PImage and the OpenCV Mat. The next statement treats ByteBuffer as IntBuffer and puts the integer array m.pixels to itself as the content. After the put action, you rewind the buffer b so that the pointer will go back to its beginning for subsequent access. The last step is to put the content of the byte array buffer b to the Mat f with the following statement:

```
f.put(0, 0, b.array());
```

Figure 2-11 shows a sample screenshot of the test run of this Processing sketch to convert from a Processing video capture image to OpenCV. In the next section, you will go in the opposite direction to convert an OpenCV matrix to a Processing image.

Figure 2-11. *Conversion from Processing to OpenCV*

From OpenCV to Processing

In the next exercise, Chapter02_18, you will simply define a four-channel OpenCV matrix of solid color and convert it directly to a Processing PImage for display.

```
import org.opencv.core.*;
import java.nio.ByteBuffer;

void setup() {
  size(640, 480);
  System.loadLibrary(Core.NATIVE_LIBRARY_NAME);
  noLoop();
}

void draw() {
  background(0);
  Mat fm = new Mat(new Size(width, height), CvType.CV_8UC4, new Scalar(255, 255, 200, 0));
  PImage img = matToImg(fm);
  image(img, 0, 0);
}

PImage matToImg(Mat m) {
  PImage im = createImage(m.cols(), m.rows(), ARGB);
  ByteBuffer b = ByteBuffer.allocate(m.rows()*m.cols()*m.channels());
  m.get(0, 0, b.array());
  b.rewind();
  b.asIntBuffer().get(im.pixels);
  im.updatePixels();
  return im;
}
```

The core function for this program is matToImg(). It takes an OpenCV Mat as the only parameter and outputs a Processing PImage as the return value. The logic is just the opposite as in the previous section. It again makes use of a ByteBuffer class as a temporary storage location. The first statement of the function creates a temporary PImage variable, im, of the same size as the input Mat parameter m. The second statement defines the temporary storage of 1,228,800 bytes. The third statement uses the get() method of Mat to load the content into the ByteBuffer b. The fourth statement rewinds the ByteBuffer after loading. The next statement treats the ByteBuffer as IntBuffer and transfers its content as an integer array to the pixels of the temporary PImage variable im. You then do a updatePixels() for the PImage to refresh its content and return it to the caller. The result of this sketch will be a window filled with orange color as defined in Scalar(255, 255, 200, 0) in ARGB order.

In the next exercise, Chapter02_19, you will do a video capture in OpenCV and convert the Mat picture frame into a Processing PImage for display. There are a few new features that I will cover in this exercise. The first one is the videoio (video input-output) module in OpenCV that performs the video capture task. The second one is the imgproc (image-processing) module that helps you to perform color conversion. You use the same matToImg() function as in the previous exercise.

```
import org.opencv.core.*;
import org.opencv.videoio.*;
import org.opencv.imgproc.*;
import java.nio.ByteBuffer;
```

```
VideoCapture cap;
Mat fm;

void setup() {
  size(640, 480);
  System.loadLibrary(Core.NATIVE_LIBRARY_NAME);
  cap = new VideoCapture();
  cap.set(Videoio.CAP_PROP_FRAME_WIDTH, width);
  cap.set(Videoio.CAP_PROP_FRAME_HEIGHT, height);
  cap.open(Videoio.CAP_ANY);
  fm = new Mat();
  frameRate(30);
}

void draw() {
  background(0);
  Mat tmp = new Mat();
  cap.read(tmp);
  Imgproc.cvtColor(tmp, fm, Imgproc.COLOR_BGR2RGBA);
  PImage img = matToImg(fm);
  image(img, 0, 0);
  text(nf(round(frameRate), 2), 10, 20);
  tmp.release();
}

PImage matToImg(Mat m) {
  PImage im = createImage(m.cols(), m.rows(), ARGB);
  ByteBuffer b = ByteBuffer.allocate(m.rows()*m.cols()*m.channels());
  m.get(0, 0, b.array());
  b.rewind();
  b.asIntBuffer().get(im.pixels);
  im.updatePixels();
  return im;
}
```

The first step is to import all the new modules from OpenCV (i.e., org.opencv.videoio.* and org.opencv.imgproc.*) that you are going to use in this exercise. The new statements inside the setup() function are for the VideoCapture object instance cap. It needs the definitions for its capture frame size and the default camera available in the computer, Videoio.CAP_ANY. Inside the draw() function, the cap.read(tmp) statement grabs and retrieves the new video frame to a temporary Mat tmp. Unfortunately, the number of color channels in tmp is only three and arranged in BGR order. If you're interested, you can try to display the number of channels by using its channels() method. The next statement uses the imgproc module to convert the color space from BGR to RGBA and keep the new image in the matrix variable fm:

```
Imgproc.cvtColor(tmp, fm, Imgproc.COLOR_BGR2RGBA);
```

If you check out the Javadoc for OpenCV 3.1.0 (http://docs.opencv.org/java/3.1.0/), you actually will not find a color space conversion from BGR to ARGB directly. In this exercise, you can settle and see how the webcam image will look. You will learn how to deal with this in the next exercise. Figure 2-12 shows this Processing sketch.

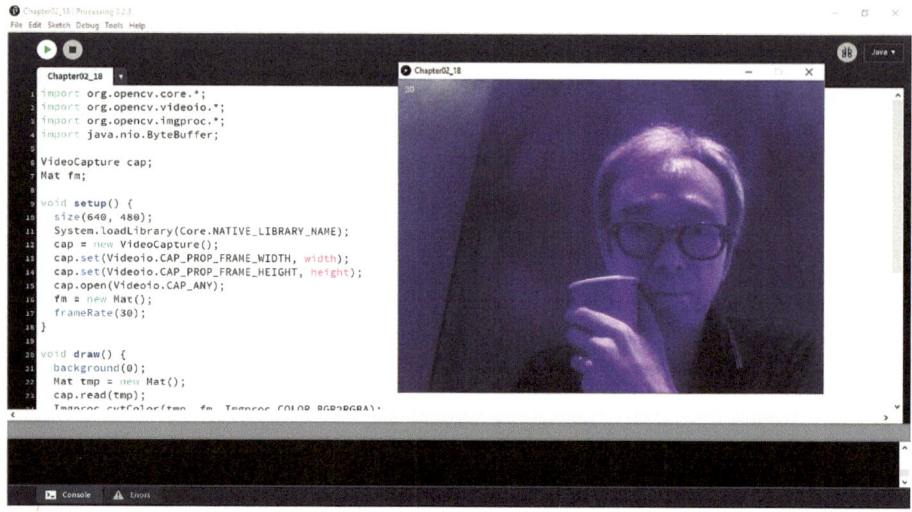

Figure 2-12. *Conversion from OpenCV to Processing*

As expected, the color is not natural because of the wrong order of the color channels. You'll fix it in the next exercise, Chapter02_20, by rearranging the order of the color channels:

```
import org.opencv.core.*;
import org.opencv.videoio.*;
import org.opencv.imgproc.*;
import java.nio.ByteBuffer;
import java.util.ArrayList;

VideoCapture cap;
Mat fm;

void setup() {
  size(640, 480);
  System.loadLibrary(Core.NATIVE_LIBRARY_NAME);
  cap = new VideoCapture();
  cap.set(Videoio.CAP_PROP_FRAME_WIDTH, width);
  cap.set(Videoio.CAP_PROP_FRAME_HEIGHT, height);
  cap.open(Videoio.CAP_ANY);
  fm = new Mat();
  frameRate(30);
}

void draw() {
  background(0);
  Mat tmp = new Mat();
  Mat src = new Mat();
  cap.read(tmp);
  Imgproc.cvtColor(tmp, src, Imgproc.COLOR_BGR2RGBA);
  fm = src.clone();
```

```
  ArrayList<Mat> srcList = new ArrayList<Mat>();
  ArrayList<Mat> dstList = new ArrayList<Mat>();
  Core.split(src, srcList);
  Core.split(fm, dstList);
  Core.mixChannels(srcList, dstList, new MatOfInt(0, 1, 1, 2, 2, 3, 3, 0));
  Core.merge(dstList, fm);
  PImage img = matToImg(fm);
  image(img, 0, 0);
  text(nf(round(frameRate), 2), 10, 20);
  src.release();
  tmp.release();
}

PImage matToImg(Mat m) {
  PImage im = createImage(m.cols(), m.rows(), ARGB);
  ByteBuffer b = ByteBuffer.allocate(m.rows()*m.cols()*m.channels());
  m.get(0, 0, b.array());
  b.rewind();
  b.asIntBuffer().get(im.pixels);
  im.updatePixels();
  return im;
}
```

The new functions you use in this exercise to rearrange the color channels are split(), mixChannels(), and merge(). You also use the ArrayList class in Java to handle the individual color channels for the image. Inside the draw() function, after the function Imgproc.cvtColor() converts the BGR color matrix to the RGBA color matrix, src, you plan to copy the Mat src to the destination Mat fm, with the color channels rearranged in the ARGB order. First, you duplicate the src matrix to fm. Second, you split the source Mat src into an ArrayList of four Mat, srcList. Each member of the list is a Mat with data type CV_8UC1, corresponding to a single-color channel. Third, you split the destination Mat fm into another ArrayList of Mat, named dstList. Fourth, the function Core.mixChannels() rearranges the order of the color channels, using the information specified in the MatOfInt parameter. MatOfInt is a subclass of Mat. It is similar to a vector in C++. The MatOfInt instance in this exercise is a matrix with one row and eight columns. The content of this matrix is four pairs of numbers, mapping the source channel position to the destination channel position. The original color channel order in src and srcList is RGBA. The destination color channel order in fm and dstList is ARGB.

- *Source*: R(0), G(1), B(2), A(3)

- *Destination*: A(0), R(1), G(2), B(3)

Source channel 0 maps to destination channel 1 for red. Source channel 1 maps to destination channel 2 for green. Source channel 2 maps to destination 3 for blue. Source channel 3 maps to destination 0 for alpha. This is exactly what the new MatOfInt(0, 1, 1, 2, 2, 3, 3, 0) command specifies. After the Core.mixChannels() function, the ArrayList called dstList contains the four single-channel matrices with the correct color order. The next function, Core.merge(), will combine the four matrices into a single matrix with four color channels in ARGB order. The program then applies the matToImg() function to fm and returns a PImage instance to img, which is shown in the window through the image() function. Figure 2-13 shows how to run the sketch in Processing.

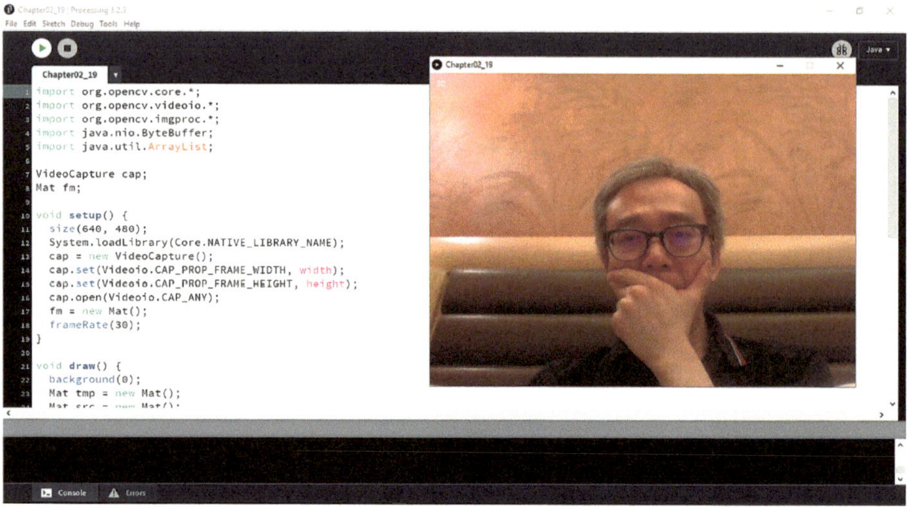

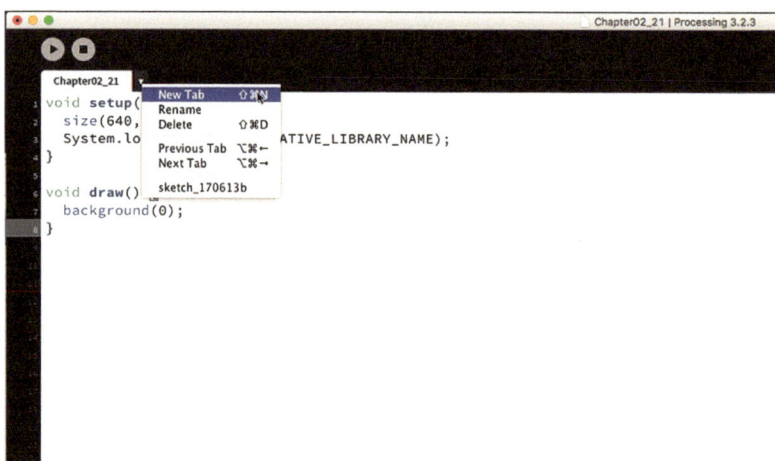

Figure 2-13. *Conversion from OpenCV to Processing with correct color channel order*

For the last exercise in this chapter, Chapter02_21, you will encapsulate the conversion between Processing and OpenCV in a Java class so that you do not need to explicitly invoke them in subsequent exercises in the book. Since the conversion functions ride on the class PImage in Processing, it is convenient to extend the PImage class to define a subclass of it. In the exercise, you name the new class CVImage. In the Processing IDE, you can add a new tab to create a new class, as shown in Figure 2-14. Name the new tab CVImage.

Figure 2-14. *Adding a new tab to create a class in Processing*

The content of the class CVImage is as follows:

```
import org.opencv.core.*;
import org.opencv.imgproc.*;
import java.nio.ByteBuffer;
import java.util.ArrayList;

public class CVImage extends PImage {
  final private MatOfInt BGRA2ARGB = new MatOfInt(0, 3, 1, 2, 2, 1, 3, 0);
  final private MatOfInt ARGB2BGRA = new MatOfInt(0, 3, 1, 2, 2, 1, 3, 0);
  // cvImg - OpenCV Mat in BGRA format
  // pixCnt - number of bytes in the image
  private Mat cvImg;
  private int pixCnt;

  public CVImage(int w, int h) {
    super(w, h, ARGB);
    System.loadLibrary(Core.NATIVE_LIBRARY_NAME);
    pixCnt = w*h*4;
    cvImg = new Mat(new Size(w, h), CvType.CV_8UC4, Scalar.all(0));
  }

  public void copyTo() {
    // Copy from the PImage pixels array to the Mat cvImg
    Mat tmp = new Mat(new Size(this.width, this.height), CvType.CV_8UC4, Scalar.all(0));
    ByteBuffer b = ByteBuffer.allocate(pixCnt);
    b.asIntBuffer().put(this.pixels);
    b.rewind();
    tmp.put(0, 0, b.array());
    cvImg = ARGBToBGRA(tmp);
    tmp.release();
  }

  public void copyTo(PImage i) {
    // Copy from an external PImage to here
    if (i.width != this.width || i.height != this.height) {
      println("Size not identical");
      return;
    }
    PApplet.arrayCopy(i.pixels, this.pixels);
    this.updatePixels();
    copyTo();
  }

  public void copyTo(Mat m) {
    // Copy from an external Mat to both the Mat cvImg and PImage pixels array
    if (m.rows() != this.height || m.cols() != this.width) {
      println("Size not identical");
      return;
    }
```

```java
    Mat out = new Mat(cvImg.size(), cvImg.type(), Scalar.all(0));
    switch (m.channels()) {
    case 1:
      // Greyscale image
      Imgproc.cvtColor(m, cvImg, Imgproc.COLOR_GRAY2BGRA);
      break;
    case 3:
      // 3 channels colour image BGR
      Imgproc.cvtColor(m, cvImg, Imgproc.COLOR_BGR2BGRA);
      break;
    case 4:
      // 4 channels colour image BGRA
      m.copyTo(cvImg);
      break;
    default:
      println("Invalid number of channels " + m.channels());
      return;
    }
    out = BGRAToARGB(cvImg);
    ByteBuffer b = ByteBuffer.allocate(pixCnt);
    out.get(0, 0, b.array());
    b.rewind();
    b.asIntBuffer().get(this.pixels);
    this.updatePixels();
    out.release();
  }

  private Mat BGRAToARGB(Mat m) {
    Mat tmp = new Mat(m.size(), CvType.CV_8UC4, Scalar.all(0));
    ArrayList<Mat> in = new ArrayList<Mat>();
    ArrayList<Mat> out = new ArrayList<Mat>();
    Core.split(m, in);
    Core.split(tmp, out);
    Core.mixChannels(in, out, BGRA2ARGB);
    Core.merge(out, tmp);
    return tmp;
  }

  private Mat ARGBToBGRA(Mat m) {
    Mat tmp = new Mat(m.size(), CvType.CV_8UC4, Scalar.all(0));
    ArrayList<Mat> in = new ArrayList<Mat>();
    ArrayList<Mat> out = new ArrayList<Mat>();
    Core.split(m, in);
    Core.split(tmp, out);
    Core.mixChannels(in, out, ARGB2BGRA);
    Core.merge(out, tmp);
    return tmp;
  }
```

```
public Mat getBGRA() {
  // Get a copy of the Mat cvImg
  Mat mat = cvImg.clone();
  return mat;
}

public Mat getBGR() {
  // Get a 3 channels Mat in BGR
  Mat mat = new Mat(cvImg.size(), CvType.CV_8UC3, Scalar.all(0));
  Imgproc.cvtColor(cvImg, mat, Imgproc.COLOR_BGRA2BGR);
  return mat;
}

public Mat getGrey() {
  // Get a greyscale copy of the image
  Mat out = new Mat(cvImg.size(), CvType.CV_8UC1, Scalar.all(0));
  Imgproc.cvtColor(cvImg, out, Imgproc.COLOR_BGRA2GRAY);
  return out;
}
}
```

The most important part of the class definition is the Mat variable cvImg. It maintains a copy of the OpenCV matrix with type CV_8UC4 and a color channel order in BGRA. There are three versions of the copyTo() method. The first one without a parameter copies the current local pixels array to the OpenCV matrix cvImg. The second one with a PImage parameter copies the input parameter pixels array to the local PImage pixels array and updates cvImg as well. The third one with a Mat parameter is the most complex one. Depending on the number of channels of the input parameter, the method first converts the input Mat into the standard four-color channel in BGRA format to store in cvImg, with the use of the Imgproc.cvtColor() function. At the same time, with the use of a ByteBuffer b, it copies the image content to the internal pixels array with ARGB color channel order for use in Processing. The remaining three methods return the different types of OpenCV Mat to the caller. The getGrey() method returns a grayscale image with type CV_8UC1. The getBGR() method returns a color image with the OpenCV standard three-color channel in BGR order. The getBGRA() method returns a color image Mat stored as cvImg with four channels in BGRA order.

To demonstrate its usage, the main program will use the video capture class to start the webcam image stream and obtain a grayscale image from the CVImage object instance, img. The grayscale image is copied back to the instance for display. The final display in the Processing window will be a grayscale version of the original webcam image.

```
import processing.video.*;

Capture cap;
CVImage img;

void setup() {
  size(640, 480);
  System.loadLibrary(Core.NATIVE_LIBRARY_NAME);
  cap = new Capture(this, width, height);
  cap.start();
  img = new CVImage(cap.width, cap.height);
  frameRate(30);
}
```

```
void draw() {
  if (!cap.available())
    return;
  background(0);
  cap.read();
  img.copyTo(cap);
  Mat grey = img.getGrey();
  img.copyTo(grey);
  image(img, 0, 0);
  text(nf(round(frameRate), 2), 10, 20);
  grey.release();
}
```

Let's add one more function to the previous code before concluding the chapter. You will often want to save the content of an image for later use. To do that, you can use the save() method in the PImage class in Processing. The parameter for the save() method is the full path name of the image file you want to save. It can accept the TARGA, TIFF, JPEG, and PNG formats. The following code will save the image with the name screenshot.jpg to the data folder of the sketch whenever the user presses the left mouse button:

```
void mousePressed() {
  img.save(dataPath("screenshot.jpg"));
}
```

Conclusion

This chapter explained the different image representations in both Processing and OpenCV. By following the exercises, you have acquired the essential skills to create and manipulate images in the Processing environment. You learned how to convert images between Processing and OpenCV. The class defined in the last exercise will form the base of the book for you to learn OpenCV and Processing without going back into the tedious details related to format conversion. In the next chapter, you will start to manipulate individual pixels of images to generate creative pictures.

CHAPTER 3

Pixel-Based Manipulations

This chapter introduces the different ways to manipulate individual pixel color values and thus create interesting effects for images. You will learn how to work on individual pixels in both algorithmic and interactive ways. In this chapter, you will focus on changing only the color value of the pixels, not their positions and total numbers within an image. Before you work on the technical details of image processing, the chapter will also introduce the basic graphical properties commonly used in art and design. This chapter will cover the following topics:

- Visual properties
- Pixel color manipulation
- Randomness
- Drawing with existing images
- Blending multiple images

Visual Properties

In visual art and design, you study how to create visual materials and create compositions of them. For any visual material, you can often describe its properties with the following:

- Position
- Size
- Shape
- Orientation
- Color
- Value

In the classic book *Semiology of Graphics*, Jacque Bertin used the term *retinal variables* to describe the similar properties of visual elements. Let's go through these properties to see whether any one of them relates to the discussion of pixel color manipulation.

© Bryan WC Chung 2017
B. WC. Chung, *Pro Processing for Images and Computer Vision with OpenCV*,
DOI 10.1007/978-1-4842-2775-6_3

Position

Each pixel in an image has a position. As shown in Figure 3-1, the origin of measurement is in the top-left corner, instead of the bottom-left corner as you might have learned in school. The horizontal position is the x-axis, with the value increasing as it goes toward the right side. The vertical position is the y-axis, with the value increasing as it goes toward the bottom.

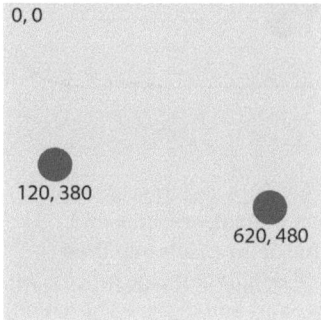

Figure 3-1. *Pixel position in an image*

You can change the pixel color information according to its position within an image to achieve a gradation effect. Figure 3-2 shows a typical example.

Figure 3-2. *Gradation effect*

Size

A pixel does not have any size information. To be precise, each pixel is of the size 1 by 1. You can imagine increasing the size of a pixel by changing the adjacent pixels around it to the same color. This is the mosaic effect you are probably familiar with, as shown in Figure 3-3.

Figure 3-3. *Mosaic effect*

Shape

It is difficult to describe the shape of a pixel. In fact, since its size is only one pixel, it is meaningless to describe the shape of a pixel. Conceptually, in a rectangular grid representation, you can consider a pixel as a tiny square or a tiny circle.

Orientation

If a pixel has no definite shape, you cannot describe its orientation (i.e., the amount of rotation on a two-dimensional plane). You can, however, describe the orientation/rotation of a digital image as a whole. In this case, you are transforming the position of the pixels in the image, which will be the topics of the next chapter.

Color

The color information of a pixel is the main concern in this chapter. You are going to see in different ways how you can modify the color. You can use color to communicate information in an image. If two images have two different solid colors, you can easily conclude that they are different. As shown in Figure 3-4, you cannot tell instantly which one is "higher" or "lower" if you choose the colors arbitrarily.

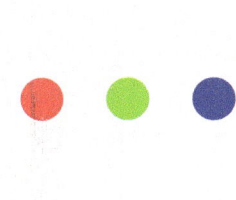

Figure 3-4. *Color difference*

Value

The value is sometimes referred to as the *intensity* or *brightness* of the color. This makes more sense if you just use a grayscale image, as shown in Figure 3-5. Unlike the arbitrary use of colors, it creates a comparison to suggest order information. For example, using dark and light gray may suggest a weight comparison to indicate that one is heavier or lighter. In Processing, besides using RGB as the default color representation, you can use HSB (hue, saturation, brightness). In this case, if you keep the hue and saturation constant and change only the brightness, you can create a comparison that suggests order.

Figure 3-5. *Grayscale image with value comparison*

Pixel Color Manipulation

In the previous chapter, you used the `get()` and `set()` methods of `PImage` in Processing to obtain and update pixel color information. The `PImage` object has an internal array to store the color information for each pixel. In this chapter, I will introduce a direct way to update the internal array, `pixels[]`, of the `PImage` object. In the first exercise, `Chapter03_01`, the sketch just creates a solid color image by changing all the pixels to one color using the `pixels[]` array.

```
PImage img;

void setup() {
  size(750, 750);
  background(0);
  img = createImage(width, height, ARGB);
  noLoop();
}

void draw() {
  img.loadPixels();
  color orange = color(255, 160, 0);
  for (int i=0; i<img.pixels.length; i++) {
    img.pixels[i] = orange;
  }
  img.updatePixels();
  image(img, 0, 0);
}
```

Note that the code uses a PImage object instance called img. It is created using the createImage() function in that setup. You also use the noLoop() function to run the draw() function once, without looping. In the draw() function, you use the loadPixels() method to load the image data into the pixels array for img, and you use a updatePixels() method to make the color change after updating the pixels array elements in the for loop. In the for loop, you perform repetition with index i from 0 until the length of the pixels array. Each pixel will have the same color as defined in the variable, orange. The pixels[] array is an integer array with a size equal to width × height of the PImage (i.e., the number of pixels in the image). Each pixel is a 32-bit integer storing the four color channels in ARGB format. Instead of writing an integer directly for a color, you can use the color() function to specify a color with four numbers as color(red, green, blue, alpha). By default, each of the red, green, blue, and alpha values is a number in the range of 0 to 255.

Color Change with Pixel Position

In the next exercise, Chapter03_02, you will take into account the pixel position to alter its color. The resulting image it creates will be the gradation effect you learned about in the "Visual Properties" section.

```
PImage img;

void setup() {
  size(750, 750);
  img = createImage(width, height, ARGB);
  noLoop();
}

void draw() {
  background(0);
  img.loadPixels();
  float xStep = 256.0/img.width;
  float yStep = 256.0/img.height;
  for (int y=0; y<img.height; y++) {
    int rows = y*img.width;
    for (int x=0; x<img.width; x++) {
      img.pixels[rows+x] = color(x*xStep, 0, y*yStep);
    }
  }
  img.updatePixels();
  image(img, 0, 0);
}
```

Figure 3-6 shows the result of running the Processing sketch.

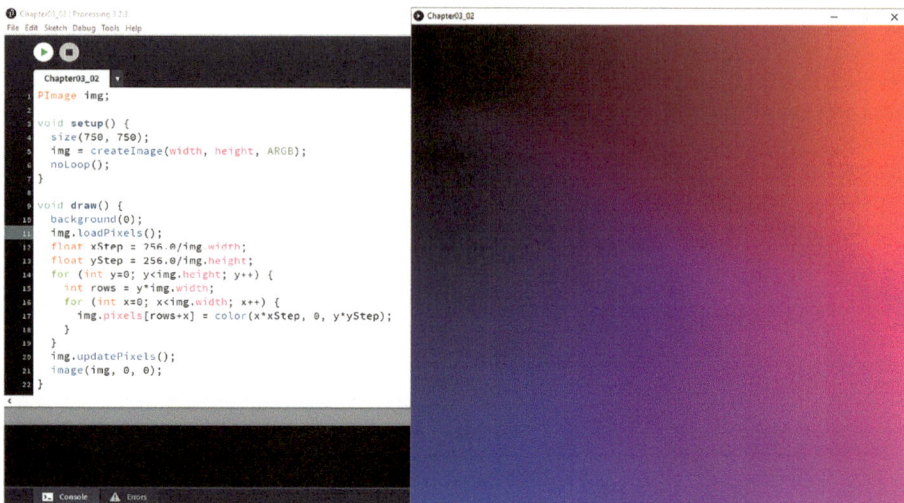

Figure 3-6. *Gradation image in two colors, red and blue*

In the previous exercise, you changed the color RGB components according to the linear change of the position of the pixel. You can, however, try another, nonlinear approach to see the differences. In the following exercise, Chapter03_03, you can see a demonstration of this approach:

```
PImage img;

void setup() {
  size(750, 750);
  img = createImage(width, height, ARGB);
  noLoop();
}

void draw() {
  background(0);
  img.loadPixels();
  float colStep = 256.0/colFunc(img.height);
  for (int y=0; y<img.height; y++) {
    int rows = y*img.width;
    color col = color(colFunc(y)*colStep);
    for (int x=0; x<img.width; x++) {
      img.pixels[rows+x] = col;
    }
  }
  img.updatePixels();
  image(img, 0, 0);
}

float colFunc(float v) {
  return v;
}
```

In the first version, you use a linear color gradation, which was actually a grayscale gradation in the *y*-axis. For the sake of flexibility, you use a separate function called colFunc() to calculate the relation between the color change and the y position of the pixel. In the first run, you just return the y position value as the output from the function. In the draw() function, you define the variable colStep by dividing by 256, which is the maximum value for grayscale with colFunc(img.height), the maximum value from colFunc(). In each step of the for loop of the *y*-axis, the color variable col is calculated by multiplying colFunc(y) with the colStep value. In this case, the minimum value for col is 0 when the y position is 0, and the maximum value for col is 255 when the y position is img.height - 1. Figure 3-7 shows the result of running the Processing sketch.

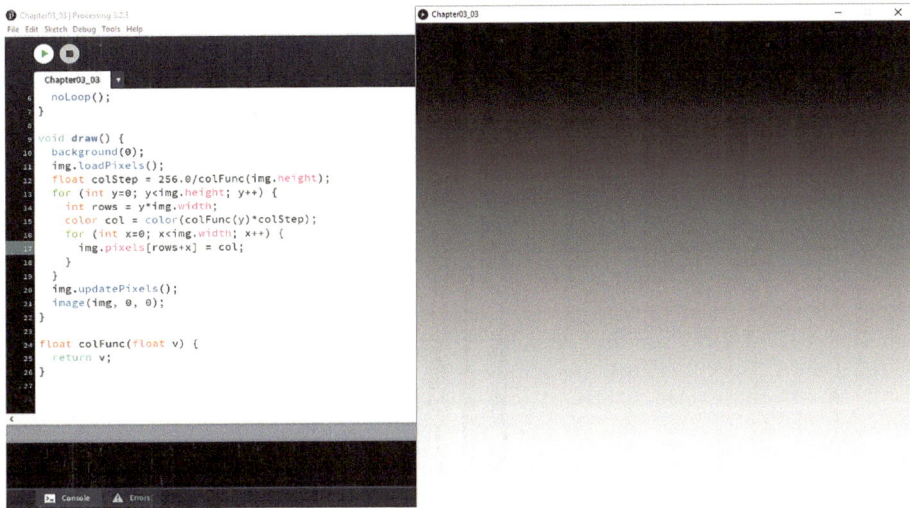

Figure 3-7. *Grayscale gradation with linear function*

In the second version, you can modify the colFunc() function by returning, for example, the square of v, as shown here:

```
float colFunc(float v) {
  return v*v;
}
```

Figure 3-8 shows the result of this version with the nonlinear change of grayscale according to the y position.

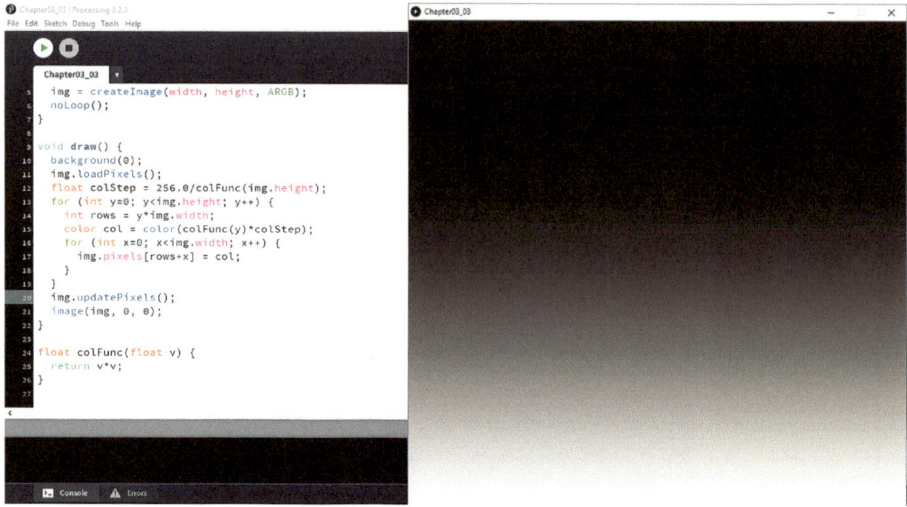

Figure 3-8. *Grayscale gradation with nonlinear change, y-square*

In the last version of this exercise, you replace the colFunc() function with a more general mathematical function called pow() with a non-integer value. You can try, for example, taking the parameter v to the power of 1.5. The new colFunc() definition is as follows:

```
float colFunc(float v) {
  return (float) Math.pow(v, 1.5);
}
```

Figure 3-9 is included here so you can compare it with the last two.

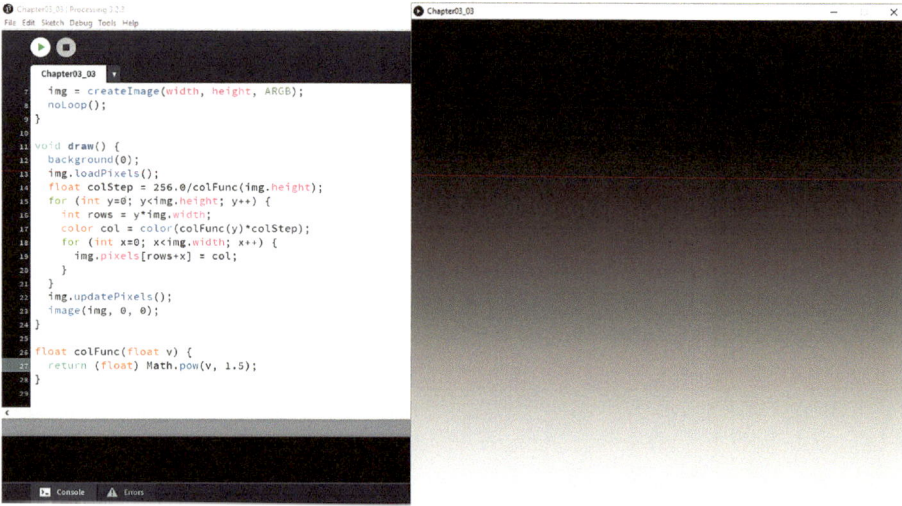

Figure 3-9. *Grayscale gradation with nonlinear change, y to the power of 1.5*

Color Change with Pixel Distance

In addition to changing the color value according to the pixel's position, you can change the color value according to the pixel's distance from another position on the screen. In the following exercises, you will experiment with different distance functions and positions and also see the results. First, try to compare the distance of a pixel from the center of the image with this exercise, Chapter03_04:

```
PImage img;

void setup() {
  size(750, 750);
  img = createImage(width, height, ARGB);
  noLoop();
}

void draw() {
  background(0);
  img.loadPixels();
  float colStep = 256.0/max(img.width/2, img.height/2);
  PVector ctr = new PVector(img.width/2, img.height/2);
  for (int y=0; y<img.height; y++) {
    int rows = y*img.width;
    for (int x=0; x<img.width; x++) {
      float d = distance(ctr, new PVector(x, y));
      color col = color(d*colStep, 0, 255-d*colStep);
      img.pixels[rows+x] = col;
    }
  }
  img.updatePixels();
  image(img, 0, 0);
}

float distance(PVector p1, PVector p2) {
  float d = abs(p1.x-p2.x) + abs(p1.y-p2.y);
  return d;
}
```

Note the use of a custom distance function in the program called distance(). It has two parameters of type PVector (https://processing.org/reference/PVector.html), which is a useful class in Processing to simplify the use of vector calculation. A PVector has three attributes: x, y, and z. These correspond to the position in three-dimensional space. For this exercise, you only use the x and y in 2D graphics. This version of the distance function uses the sum of the absolute values of the differences between the x and y positions of the two points. In the draw() function, you calculate the distance of every pixel from the center of the image and use it to compute the red and blue color components. Figure 3-10 shows the result of running the Processing sketch.

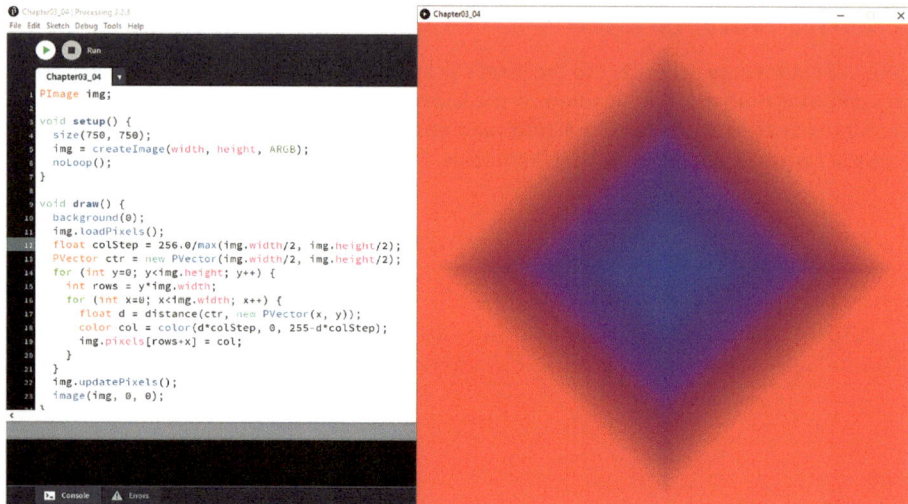

Figure 3-10. *Color change with distance from center*

You can modify the `distance()` function to use the more common Euclidean distance to test the result. The following is the new definition of the `distance()` function:

```
float distance(PVector p1, PVector p2) {
  float d = p1.dist(p2);
  return d;
}
```

It employs the built-in `dist()` method of `PVector` to calculate the distance between two points in two-dimensional space. The resulting image (shown in Figure 3-11) will resemble a circle instead of a diamond shape.

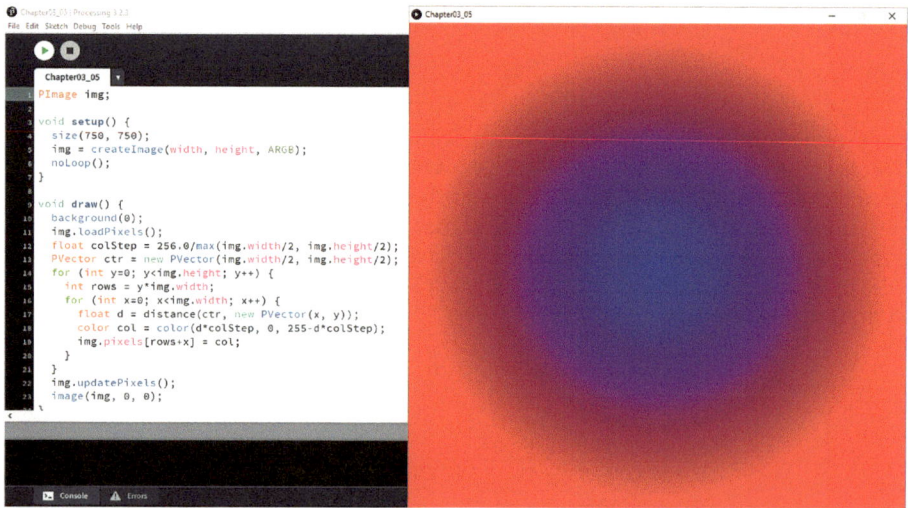

Figure 3-11. *Color change with distance from center*

In the next exercise, Chapter03_05, you enhance the computation within the draw() function so that you can make use of some nice features in Processing to simplify your code:

```
PImage img;

void setup() {
  size(750, 750);
  img = createImage(width, height, ARGB);
  noLoop();
}

void draw() {
  background(0);
  img.loadPixels();
  float distMax = max(img.width/2, img.height/2);
  PVector ctr = new PVector(img.width/2, img.height/2);
  for (int y=0; y<img.height; y++) {
    int rows = y*img.width;
    for (int x=0; x<img.width; x++) {
      float d = distance(ctr, new PVector(x, y));
      float c = map(d, 0, distMax, 0, 255);
      color col = color(c, 0, 255-c);
      img.pixels[rows+x] = col;
    }
  }
  img.updatePixels();
  image(img, 0, 0);
}

float distance(PVector p1, PVector p2) {
  float d = p1.dist(p2);
  return d;
}
```

The new feature used is the map() function. It takes in the variable d in the example and maps it from the source range of 0 to distMax to the destination range of 0 to 255. It simplifies the linear mapping calculation for a lot of applications.

A quick variation of the program is to introduce interactivity to the variable ctr. Imagine if it could follow the movement of the mouse; you could generate an interactive version of it by using the mouseX and mouseY variables.

```
PImage img;
float distMax;

void setup() {
  size(750, 750);
  img = createImage(width, height, ARGB);
  img.loadPixels();
  distMax = max(img.width, img.height);
}
```

```
void draw() {
  background(0);
  PVector ctr = new PVector(mouseX, mouseY);
  for (int y=0; y<img.height; y++) {
    int rows = y*img.width;
    for (int x=0; x<img.width; x++) {
      float d = distance(ctr, new PVector(x, y));
      float c = map(d, 0, distMax, 0, 255);
      color col = color(c, 0, 255-c);
      img.pixels[rows+x] = col;
    }
  }
  img.updatePixels();
  image(img, 0, 0);
}

float distance(PVector p1, PVector p2) {
  float d = p1.dist(p2);
  return d;
}
```

Color Change with Trigonometric Functions

Trigonometric functions refer to the sine, cosine, and tangent functions you learned about in school. The sine and cosine functions have a periodic nature in terms of their output values. Processing has the built-in sin() and cos() functions adopted from Java. They have one input value, measured in radians. The normal range of the input value is within the range of -PI to PI to complete a cycle. The output range of both functions is within the range of -1 to 1. In the next exercise, Chapter03_07, you map the input range (i.e., the distance between a pixel and the mouse position) to between -PI and PI and, at the same time, map the output range between -1 to 1 to the color range of 0 to 255.

```
PImage img;
float num;

void setup() {
  size(750, 750);
  img = createImage(width, height, ARGB);
  img.loadPixels();
  num = 8;
}

void draw() {
  background(0);
  PVector mouse = new PVector(mouseX, mouseY);
  for (int y=0; y<img.height; y++) {
    int rows = y*img.width;
    for (int x=0; x<img.width; x++) {
      PVector dist = distance(mouse, new PVector(x, y));
      float xRange = map(dist.x, -img.width, img.width, -PI*num, PI*num);
      float yRange = map(dist.y, -img.height, img.height, -PI*num, PI*num);
      float xCol = map(cos(xRange), -1, 1, 0, 255);
```

```
      float yCol = map(sin(yRange), -1, 1, 0, 255);
      color col = color(xCol, 0, yCol);
      img.pixels[rows+x] = col;
    }
  }
  img.updatePixels();
  image(img, 0, 0);
}

PVector distance(PVector p1, PVector p2) {
  return PVector.sub(p1, p2);
}
```

You modify the distance() function to return a PVector storing the subtraction result from the two input vectors. In the input range, you also introduce a new variable, num, to extend the original range (-PI, PI). The image will then consist of more repetitions. Figure 3-12 shows the result of the test run.

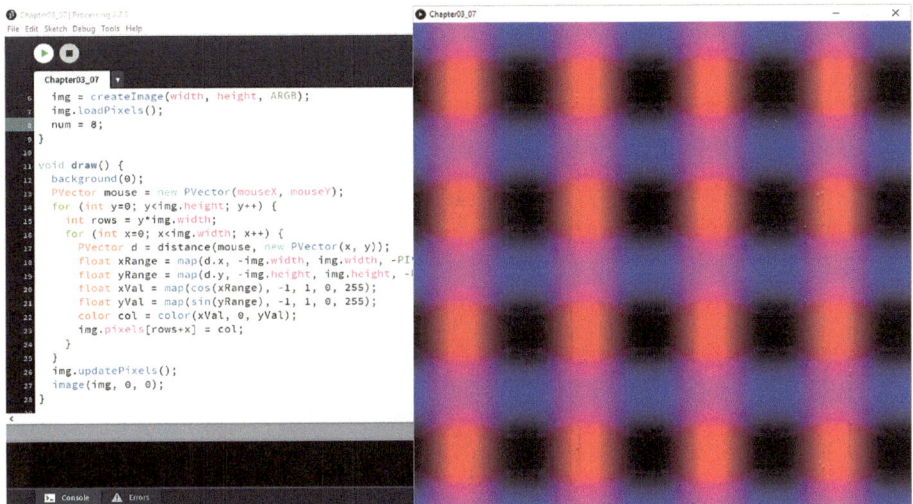

Figure 3-12. *Color change with trigonometric functions*

To enhance the complexity of the image, you can simply add the x and y for loop variables into the input range calculation, as shown in the next exercise, Chapter03_08. At the same time, you need to reduce the value for the variable num so that the xRange and yRange values will not become too large.

```
PImage img;
float num;

void setup() {
  size(750, 750);
  img = createImage(width, height, ARGB);
  img.loadPixels();
  num = 0.1;
}
```

```
void draw() {
  background(0);
  PVector mouse = new PVector(mouseX, mouseY);
  for (int y=0; y<img.height; y++) {
    int rows = y*img.width;
    for (int x=0; x<img.width; x++) {
      PVector dist = distance(mouse, new PVector(x, y));
      float xRange = map(dist.x, -img.width, img.width, -PI*num*y, PI*num*x);
      float yRange = map(dist.y, -img.height, img.height, -PI*num*x, PI*num*y);
      float xCol = map(cos(xRange), -1, 1, 0, 255);
      float yCol = map(sin(yRange), -1, 1, 0, 255);
      color col = color(xCol, 0, yCol);
      img.pixels[rows+x] = col;
    }
  }
  img.updatePixels();
  image(img, 0, 0);
}

PVector distance(PVector p1, PVector p2) {
  return PVector.sub(p1, p2);
}
```

This will generate a more psychedelic effect similar to the optical art graphics commonly found in the 1960s and 1970s, as shown in Figure 3-13. Since you include both the x and y values in the calculation of the xRange and yRange values, the result will be less predictable.

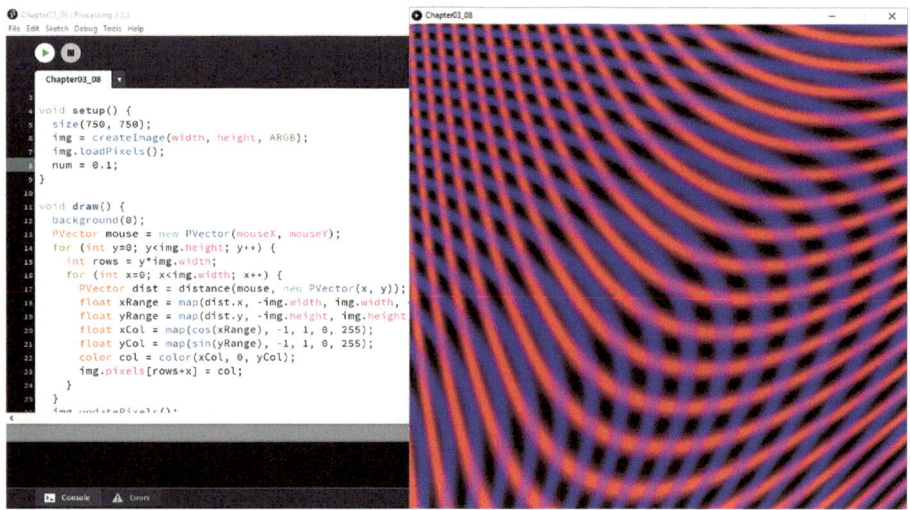

Figure 3-13. *Another example with trigonometric function*

In the next exercise, Chapter03_09, you simplify the distance() function and use only a single value, dist, in the draw() function to generate the input range to the sine and cosine functions. The modification is not substantial, but the visual result differs a lot from the previous one.

```
PImage img;
float num;

void setup() {
  size(750, 750);
  img = createImage(width, height, ARGB);
  img.loadPixels();
  num = 2;
}

void draw() {
  background(0);
  PVector mouse = new PVector(mouseX, mouseY);
  for (int y=0; y<img.height; y++) {
    int rows = y*img.width;
    for (int x=0; x<img.width; x++) {
      float dist = distance(mouse, new PVector(x, y));
      float range = map(dist, -img.width, img.width, -PI*num*y, PI*num*x);
      float xCol = map(sin(range), -1, 1, 0, 255);
      float yCol = map(cos(range), -1, 1, 0, 255);
      color col = color(0, 255-xCol, yCol);
      img.pixels[rows+x] = col;
    }
  }
  img.updatePixels();
  image(img, 0, 0);
}

float distance(PVector p1, PVector p2) {
  return p1.dist(p2);
}
```

Both the xCol and yCol color variables share the same input range value but use different trigonometric functions. The visual result may resemble a circle because you know that a circle can be represented as follows:

- x = radius * cos(angle)

- y = radius * sin(angle)

In this exercise, the image is much more complex because the input range, indicated as angle here, does not just range from -PI to PI. Figure 3-14 shows the image after running the program.

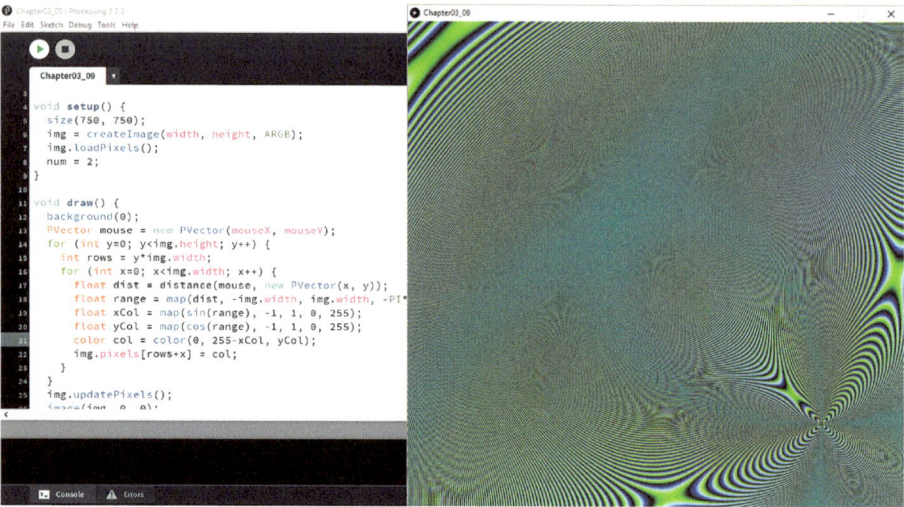

Figure 3-14. *Color change with more trigonometric function*

You can have a lot of fun playing with trigonometric functions in image processing. Feel free to explore more variations. In the next section, I will start to explain how the idea of randomness can help you generate interesting images.

Randomness

Processing provides a random number generator based on the `java.util.Random` class. You can create various types of random color images using the `random()` function. For the next exercise, `Chapter03_10`, you use random numbers to fill in an image with grayscale color:

```
PImage img;

void setup() {
  size(750, 750);
  img = createImage(width, height, ARGB);
  img.loadPixels();
  noLoop();
}

void draw() {
  background(0);
  for (int i=0; i<img.pixels.length; i++) {
    img.pixels[i] = color(floor(random(0, 256)));
  }
  img.updatePixels();
  image(img, 0, 0);
}
```

The for loop within the draw() function traverses all the pixels in the PImage and sets the color to a random value between 0 to 255, using the function random(0, 256). The resulting image is completely chaotic, without any identifiable patterns, as shown in Figure 3-15.

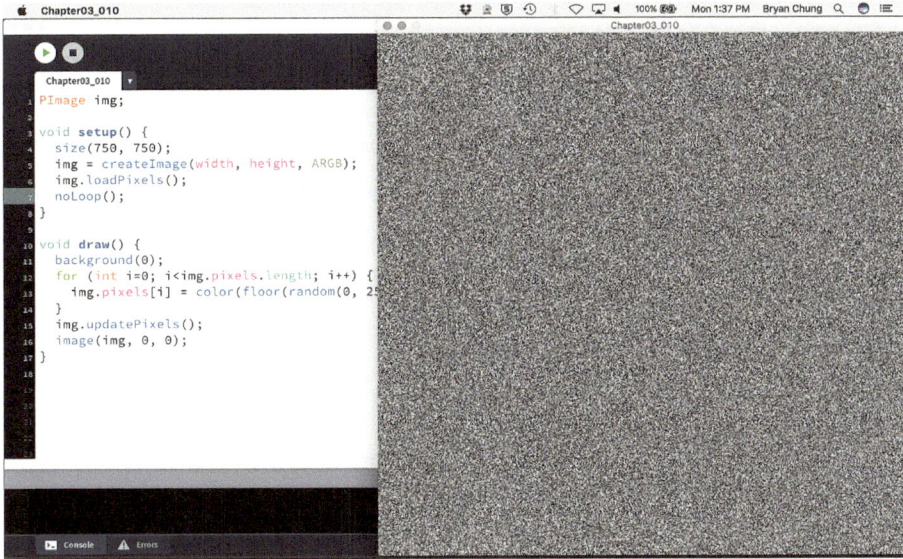

Figure 3-15. *Random grayscale image*

If you want to create a more visually pleasant image with randomness, you can reduce the degree of randomness by imposing rules in the color information. The next exercise, Chapter03_11, will initialize the first pixel in the image with a random gray tone. The next pixel will either increase or decrease the gray tone value by a random portion. Compare the two results to see whether there are any patterns in the second version.

```
PImage img;
float value1;
float range;

void setup() {
  size(750, 750);
  img = createImage(width, height, ARGB);
  img.loadPixels();
  value1 = floor(random(0, 256));
  range = 50;
  noLoop();
}

void draw() {
  background(0);
  for (int i=0; i<img.pixels.length; i++) {
    float v = random(-range, range);
    value1 += v;
```

```
    value1 = constrain(value1, 0, 255);
    img.pixels[i] = color(value1);
  }
  img.updatePixels();
  image(img, 0, 0);
}
```

The code basically uses the `random(-range, range)` statement to introduce a controlled version of randomness in the `draw()` function. The image will consist of random gray tone pixels, but the randomness is controlled within a smaller range and at the same time depends on the previous pixel, as shown in Figure 3-16.

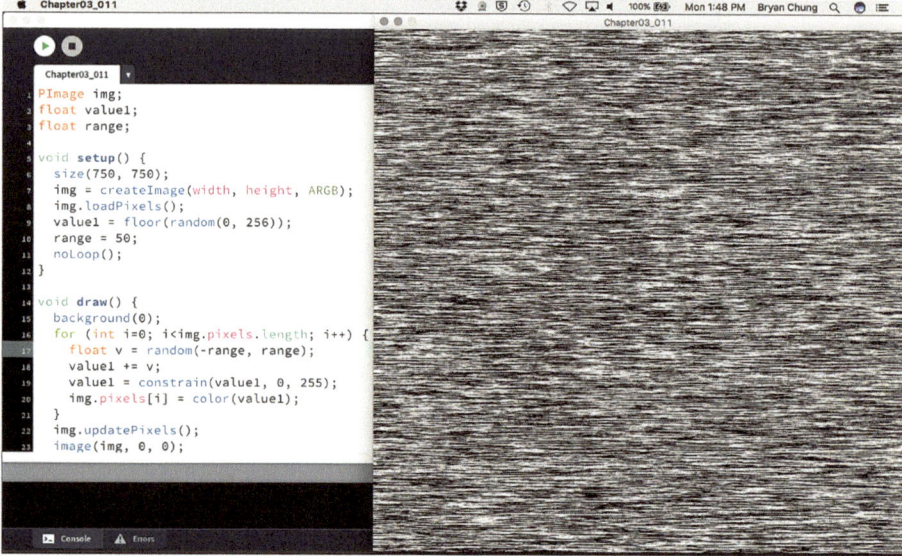

Figure 3-16. *Random grayscale image with patterns*

As the pixel color information is dependent on the last one with a certain degree of randomness, you can easily identify the horizontal texture of the image because the arrangement of pixels in the array is sorted in row order first.

The next exercise, `Chapter03_12`, uses the `noise()` function in Processing to explore randomness. This is the Perlin noise function developed by Ken Perlin. The output from the function displays a more natural and smooth sequence of numbers. Processing provides up to three dimensions of the Perlin noise function. In this exercise, you use the two-dimensional version of the noise values to fill up an image with gray tone.

```
PImage img;
float xScale, yScale;

void setup() {
  size(750, 750);
  background(0);
  img = createImage(width, height, ARGB);
  img.loadPixels();
```

```
    xScale = 0.01;
    yScale = 0.01;
    noLoop();
}

void draw() {
    for (int y=0; y<img.height; y++) {
        int rows = y*img.width;
        for (int x=0; x<img.width; x++) {
            img.pixels[rows+x] = color(floor(noise(x*xScale, y*yScale)*256));
        }
    }
    img.updatePixels();
    image(img, 0, 0);
}
```

Note that for the x and y positions of the pixel, you use the xScale and yScale variables to reduce the range to achieve a smoother noise effect in the image, as shown in Figure 3-17.

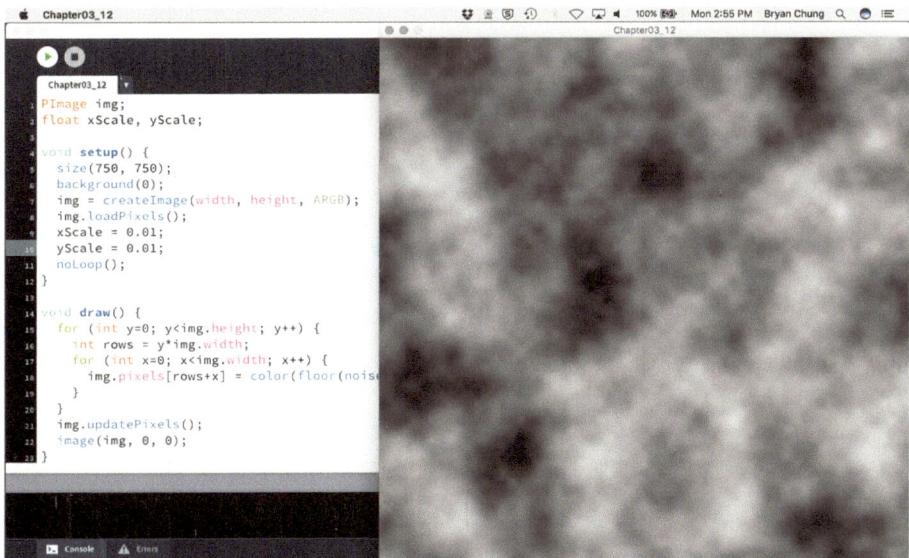

Figure 3-17. *Grayscale color with Perlin noise*

So far, you have created an image using algorithmic ways to fill in the color for each pixel. And you learned how to create an image with random colors in the pixels. In the next section, you will import an existing image and use the steps from previous sections to manipulate the pixel colors.

Drawing with Existing Images

The next exercise, Chapter03_13, with an existing image is to convert a color image into gray tone. Of course, you can use the built-in functions from both Processing and OpenCV to do the conversion. You can use this exercise as a starting point to learn how simple image processing can be coded.

```
PImage img1, img2;

void setup() {
  size(1500, 750);

  background(0);
  img1 = loadImage("landscape.png");
  img1.loadPixels();
  img2 = createImage(img1.width, img1.height, ARGB);
  img2.loadPixels();
  noLoop();
}

void draw() {
  for (int i=0; i<img1.pixels.length; i++) {
    color col = img1.pixels[i];
    img2.pixels[i] = color((red(col) + green(col) + blue(col))/3);
  }
  img2.updatePixels();
  image(img1, 0, 0);
  image(img2, img1.width, 0);
}
```

In the program, you define the Processing window to be double the width of the photo to lay out the original and modified images side by side. You use two PImage variables. The first one, img1, loads the external image. The second one, img2, makes a copy of the first one with the color pixels converted into a single gray tone color, using a simple average of the red, green, and blue colors. Figure 3-18 shows the conversion.

Figure 3-18. *Color to grayscale conversion with simple averaging*

There is another approach to calculate the luminance of a grayscale image from the original RGB one. The visual perception does not detect RGB with equal intensity. In this version of the exercise, Chapter03_14, you use the following formula to come up with the luminance value:

```
img2.pixels[i] = color(0.2*red(col) + 0.7*green(col) + 0.1*blue(col));
```

Figure 3-19 shows the resulting image for comparison.

Figure 3-19. *Color to grayscale conversion with relative luminance*

For the next exercise, Chapter03_15, you write an inverse filter to invert all the red, green, and blue color channels of the original color image. To achieve the effect, you use 255 and subtract all three color channel values. The formula is as follows:

```
img2.pixels[i] = color(255-red(col), 255-green(col), 255-blue(col));
```

Figure 3-20 shows the resulting image.

Figure 3-20. *Color change with inverse effect*

You can also swap the three color channels to mix them in a different order to obtain other effects that can be found in Photoshop. Here is one example, Chapter03_16, that swaps the order of the three channels and inverts the original red channel:

```
img2.pixels[i] = color(blue(col), 255-red(col), green(col));
```

Figure 3-21 shows the output using the same image.

Figure 3-21. *Color change by swapping different color channels*

Processing has a filter() function (https://processing.org/reference/filter_.html) that provides a number of image-processing presets such as the following:

- THRESHOLD

- GRAY

- OPAQUE

- INVERT

- POSTERIZE

- BLUR

- ERODE

- DILATE

In addition to these presets, you can implement your own. The following exercises will illustrate how you can draw on the canvas based on an existing image. The first preset you are going to test is the mosaic effect found in Photoshop. The mosaic effect is essentially a reduction in the image resolution while keeping the size of the image. Let's take a look at the code of this exercise, Chapter03_17:

```
PImage img;
int step;

void setup() {
  size(1500, 750);
  background(0);
  img = loadImage("landscape.png");
  img.loadPixels();
  step = 10;
  noStroke();
  noLoop();
}

void draw() {
  for (int y=0; y<img.height; y+=step) {
    int rows = y*img.width;
    for (int x=0; x<img.width; x+=step) {
      color col = img.pixels[rows+x];
      fill(col);
      rect(x+img.width, y, step, step);
    }
  }
  image(img, 0, 0);
}
```

Note that in the nested for loops, you do not go through every single pixel. Instead, you increment the indices with a value in the variable called step. You then sample the color for these pixels and use it as the fill() color for the squares. Figure 3-22 shows both the original photograph and the mosaic image together.

Figure 3-22. *Mosaic effect example*

If you replace the rect() command with the ellipse() command, you can achieve the circular mosaic effect, as shown in Figure 3-23.

Figure 3-23. *Mosaic effect with circles*

The previous two exercises use the fill() color for the rectangles and circles. If you use stroke() color to draw lines instead, you can have a different rendering of the same photograph, similar to Figure 3-24.

Figure 3-24. *Mosaic effect with short line segments*

In the draw() function, you use a random mechanism, floor(random(2)), to select which direction of the line segment will be drawn. Its result will be either 0 or 1. You use it to determine the direction of your diagonal line segments.

```
PImage img;
int step;

void setup() {
  size(1500, 750);
  background(0);
  img = loadImage("landscape.png");
  img.loadPixels();
  step = 10;
  smooth();
  noFill();
  noLoop();
}

void draw() {
  for (int y=0; y<img.height; y+=step) {
    int rows = y*img.width;
    for (int x=0; x<img.width; x+=step) {
      color col = img.pixels[rows+x];
      stroke(col);
      int num = floor(random(2));
      if (num == 0) {
        line(x+img.width, y, x+img.width+step, y+step);
      } else {
```

```
        line(x+img.width+step, y, x+img.width, y+step);
      }
    }
  }
  image(img, 0, 0);
}
```

The next exercise, Chapter03_20, explores a common barcode effect in image processing. Famous designers such as Irma Boom have also sampled old classic paintings and represented them in vertical color bars, similar to what you plan to do in this exercise. First, you take a color photograph and add a horizontal line across the middle of it (Figure 3-25).

Figure 3-25. *Sample photograph with a horizontal line*

Along that horizontal line, you sample each pixel on the line and retrieve its color value. By using the color value, you draw a vertical line for each of the pixels along the horizontal line. Here is the code:

```
PImage img;

void setup() {
  size(1200, 900);
  background(0);
  img = loadImage("christmas.png");
  img.loadPixels();
  noFill();
  noLoop();
}
```

```
void draw() {
  int y = img.height/2;
  for (int x=0; x<img.width; x++) {
    color c = img.pixels[y*img.width+x];
    stroke(c);
    line(x, 0, x, img.height-1);
  }
}
```

The program is straightforward. The visual result is a barcode representation of the original photograph, as shown in Figure 3-26.

Figure 3-26. *Barcode effect example*

You can experiment with an interactive version of this program by changing the variable y to mouseY and removing the noLoop() function. In this case, the result is a beautiful animation generated by just one photograph.

So far, you have explored various ways to create new imagery based on an existing image, either by replacing the pixel color or by drawing on the canvas referring to the pixel color. In the next section, you will learn how to combine two images.

Blending Multiple Images

Processing has a blend() function (https://processing.org/reference/blend_.html) that provides a number of options to combine two images. The working mechanism is similar to the layer options in Photoshop. This section will not explain each option in detail. The exercises in this section will illustrate the underlying logic of combining two images. The following exercise, Chapter03_21, demonstrates the use of the blend() function in Processing with the option ADD:

```
PImage img1, img2;

void setup() {
  size(1200, 900);
  background(0);
  img1 = loadImage("hongkong.png");
  img2 = loadImage("sydney.png");
  noLoop();
}

void draw() {
  img1.blend(img2, 0, 0, img2.width, img2.height,
    0, 0, img1.width, img1.height, ADD);
  image(img1, 0, 0);
}
```

You have two PImage instances, img1 and img2, each loaded with an external image from the data folder. In the draw() function, the img2 instance will be blended into the img1 instance through the method img1.blend(). The rest of the parameters are the source offset (x, y) and dimension (width, height), destination offset (x, y) and dimension (width, height), and the blend option, ADD. Note that, after the blend() function, the content of img1 will change. The two images used in the exercise have the same size (1200×900 pixels). The blend() function here, however, will alter the resolution of img2 if the two images do not have the same size. Figure 3-27 shows the resulting image.

Figure 3-27. *Blending two images with the ADD option*

You can also perform this blending effect in Processing with your own code. For the ADD option, you can just add the two pixel-color components from the two images. Since the valid range for RGB is 0 to 255, you can constrain the values in this range. Here is the source for the exercise, Chapter03_22. In this version, you assume the two images have the same size (1200×900 pixels).

```
PImage img1, img2, img3;

void setup() {
  size(1200, 900);
  background(0);
  img1 = loadImage("hongkong.png");
  img2 = loadImage("sydney.png");
  img3 = createImage(img1.width, img1.height, ARGB);
  noLoop();
}

void draw() {
  for (int i=0; i<img1.pixels.length; i++) {
    color c1 = img1.pixels[i];
    color c2 = img2.pixels[i];
    float r = constrain(red(c1) + red(c2), 0, 255);
    float g = constrain(green(c1) + green(c2), 0, 255);
    float b = constrain(blue(c1) + blue(c2), 0, 255);
    img3.pixels[i] = color(r, g, b);
  }
  img3.updatePixels();
  image(img3, 0, 0);
}
```

The logic is simple. The draw() function has a for loop to go through all the pixels in img1 and img2. The three color components are added together and constrained within the range of 0 to 255. The third PImage instance, img3, stores all the new pixel color values and displays the image on-screen.

As a demonstration, the last exercise in the section, Chapter03_23, will also present a version done in OpenCV. To use OpenCV in the Processing environment, remember to copy the code folder into your sketch folder and re-create the CVImage class in a new tab, as shown in the previous chapter. You'll create three instances of the CVImage class to maintain hongkong.png, sydney.png, and the resulting image. The sample code for the main program is shown here. Again, you assume the two source images have the same size (1200×900 pixels).

```
CVImage img1, img2, img3;

void setup() {
  size(1200, 900);
  System.loadLibrary(Core.NATIVE_LIBRARY_NAME);
  background(0);
  PImage tmp = loadImage("hongkong.png");
  img1 = new CVImage(tmp.width, tmp.height);
  img2 = new CVImage(tmp.width, tmp.height);
  img3 = new CVImage(tmp.width, tmp.height);
  img1.copyTo(tmp);
  tmp = loadImage("sydney.png");
```

```
  img2.copyTo(tmp);
  noLoop();
}

void draw() {
  Mat m1 = img1.getBGR();
  Mat m2 = img2.getBGR();
  Mat m3 = new Mat(m1.size(), m1.type());
  Core.add(m1, m2, m3);
  img3.copyTo(m3);
  image(img3, 0, 0);
  m1.release();
  m2.release();
  m3.release();
}
```

The main command of the program is the Core.add() function. It adds the first two source matrices to the third one as the destination. It also relies on the CVImage class that you developed in the previous chapter. The image objects use the copyTo() and getBGR() methods to convert between the Processing and OpenCV formats.

Conclusion

This chapter went through the basic tasks of image processing by changing the individual pixel color. You now understand how to implement simple image filters such as the grayscale and invert filters. You also learned how to create graphical images from scratch and modify existing images for creative outputs. In the next chapter, you are going to change the pixels' position so you can achieve more dynamic image-processing effects.

CHAPTER 4

Geometry and Transformation

In this chapter, you'll continue to work on the transformation of digital images. In the previous chapter, you modified mainly the pixel color information for an image, using the built-in and custom functions in Processing. In this chapter, you will focus on deforming the pixel grid of the image without changing the image content. Essentially, this changes the position of each pixel within an image and thus modifies the geometry of the original image. As the Processing language lacks such functions, you will use OpenCV to work on the exercises. At the same time, you will explore the three-dimensional features in Processing to achieve a geometric transform of digital images. The following are the topics covered in this chapter:

- Image transformation
- Image orientation
- Image resizing
- Affine transform
- Perspective transform
- Linear vs. polar coordinates
- Three-dimensional space
- General pixel mapping

Image Transformation

The first type of image transformation is the translation. In this type, as shown in Figure 4-1, the whole digital image, as defined by its rectangular grid, is moved in a horizontal or vertical direction. The size and orientation of the image remain the same before and after the transformation.

© Bryan WC Chung 2017
B. WC. Chung, *Pro Processing for Images and Computer Vision with OpenCV*,
DOI 10.1007/978-1-4842-2775-6_4

Figure 4-1. *Image translation*

The second and third types of transformation shown in this chapter alter the orientation of the image. They are rotation and flipping. In rotation, the image rotates on the 2D plane, along the imaginary *z*-axis, without any size changes or deformation, as shown in Figure 4-2. In Processing, the anchor point for rotation is the top-left corner at (0, 0).

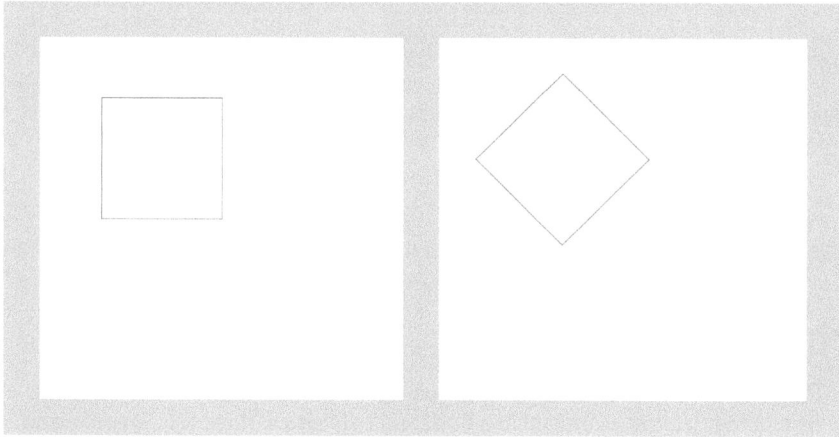

Figure 4-2. *Image rotation*

Flipping is the reflection along the *x*-axis and/or *y*-axis. In the exercise that you are going to work on, you can flip an image in a single axis or both. Figure 4-3 shows a vertical flip of a square image.

Figure 4-3. *Image flipping*

These three types of transformations preserve the size and shape of the original image. The next type of transformation, shown in Figure 4-4 will, however, alter the size of the image. It is a resize transform.

Figure 4-4. *Image resize*

The previous four types of transformation covered preserve the shape of the image. The next type, affine transform, will distort the original shape, but it still preserves parallel lines. The rectangular pixel grid will transform into a parallelogram, as shown in Figure 4-5.

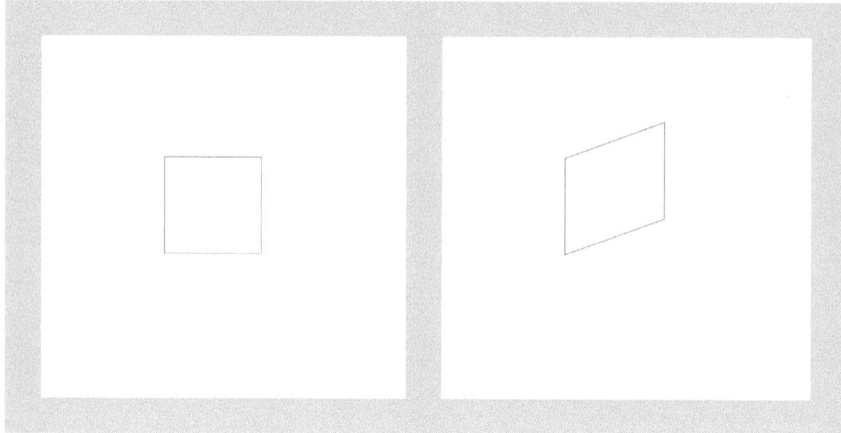

Figure 4-5. *Affine transform*

The last type of geometric transform I will cover is a perspective transform. It converts the rectangular image grid into any four-point convex polygon. The transform also corresponds to the perspective projection where the 3D object is projected onto a 2D plane with a nearby camera. Figure 4-6 shows an example of a perspective transform.

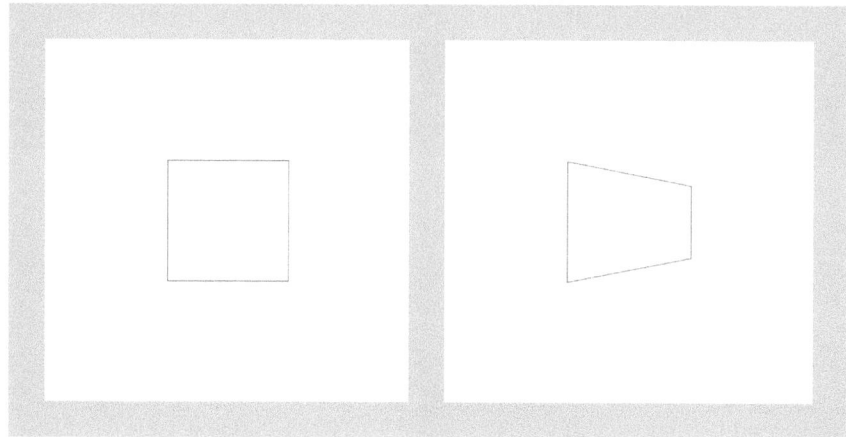

Figure 4-6. *Perspective transform*

Image Orientation

By *image orientation*, I am referring to tasks such as flipping and rotating an image in a two-dimensional plane. Flipping, or reflecting, an image is easy to achieve in OpenCV by using the flip() function. In two-dimensional graphics, you can have flipping along the horizontal axis, the vertical axis, or both axes. The syntax and parameters for the flip() function are as follows:

```
public static void flip(Mat src, Mat dst, int flipCode);
```

The command will flip the src matrix to the dst matrix, according to what is specified in the flipCode value. A zero value for flipCode will flip along the *x*-axis, a positive value will flip along the *y*-axis, and a negative value will flip along both axes. The following exercise, Chapter04_01, demonstrates the use of flipping in Processing with OpenCV. Remember, as covered in Chapter 1, to include the code folder in the Processing sketch and the CVImage class definition. The code folder contains all the necessary OpenCV Java and native files. The Processing window size caters to displaying two images side by side. The original image (600×600 pixels) will be on the left, and the flipped image will be on the right.

```
import org.opencv.core.*;

PImage img;
CVImage cv;

void setup() {

  size(1200, 600);

  System.loadLibrary(Core.NATIVE_LIBRARY_NAME);
  img = loadImage("hongkong.png");
  cv = new CVImage(img.width, img.height);
  noLoop();
}

void draw() {
  background(0);
  cv.copyTo(img);
  Mat mat = cv.getBGR();
  Core.flip(mat, mat, -1);
  cv.copyTo(mat);
  image(img, 0, 0);
  image(cv, img.width, 0);
  mat.release();
}
```

The resulting image from the program contains two parts, as shown in Figure 4-7. The left side is the original image, and the right side is the flipped one along both axes.

Figure 4-7. *Transform with flip in both axes*

The next exercise, Chapter04_02, will help you study the commands for image rotation. There are two steps you need to follow to rotate an image. The first step is to compute the rotation transform matrix. The second step is to apply the rotation transform matrix to the source image. The syntax for the first command to obtain the rotation matrix is as follows:

```
public static Mat Imgproc.getRotationMatrix2D(Point center, double angle, double scale)
```

The first parameter, center, is the coordinate of the center point of the rotation in the source image. The second parameter, angle, is the rotation angle measured in degrees. Note that Processing rotation is measured in radians, while OpenCV rotation is in degrees. The third parameter, scale, is the scaling factor applied in the transformation. The function will output a two-by-three matrix as follows:

```
a     b     (1-a)*center.x-b*center.y
-b    a     b*center.x+(1-a)*center.y
```

Here, a = scale*cos(angle) and b = scale*sin(angle).

Once you have the rotation transform matrix, you can apply the matrix to the source image with the warpAffine() function. The syntax is as follows:

```
public static void Imgproc.warpAffine(Mat src, Mat dst, Mat m, Size dsize)
```

The first parameter, src, is the source image. The second parameter, dst, is the destination image with the same type as src and the same size as what was specified in the fourth parameter, dsize. The third parameter, m, is the rotation transform matrix you obtained from the previous step. The fourth parameter, dsize, is the size of the destination image. Again, make sure the code folder, with the OpenCV libraries and the CVImage class, are in the Processing sketch folder. The original image is 600×600 pixels. The rotated image will be displayed on the right side of the original one. The complete source code for the exercise, Chapter04_02, is as follows:

```
import org.opencv.core.*;
import org.opencv.imgproc.*;

CVImage cvout;
Mat in;
PImage img;
Point ctr;
float angle;

void setup() {
  size(1200, 600);
  System.loadLibrary(Core.NATIVE_LIBRARY_NAME);
  img = loadImage("hongkong.png");
  CVImage cvin = new CVImage(img.width, img.height);
  cvout = new CVImage(cvin.width, cvin.height);
  cvin.copyTo(img);
  in = cvin.getBGR();
  ctr = new Point(img.width/2, img.height/2);
  angle = 0;
  frameRate(30);
}
```

```
void draw() {
  background(0);
  Mat rot = Imgproc.getRotationMatrix2D(ctr, angle, 1.0);
  Mat out = new Mat(in.size(), in.type());
  Imgproc.warpAffine(in, out, rot, out.size());
  cvout.copyTo(out);
  image(img, 0, 0);
  image(cvout, img.width, 0);
  angle += 0.5;
  angle %= 360;
  out.release();
  rot.release();

}
```

In the code you use CVImage cvout to maintain the rotated image. Mat in keeps the input image in OpenCV matrix format. The OpenCV class Point ctr is the center of the image as the pivot point for rotation. float angle is the current rotation angle. It will be incremented by half a degree for every turn in the draw() function. Figure 4-8 shows a sample of the Processing window running the sketch.

Figure 4-8. *Rotation transform with digital image*

By using the Processing tint() function, you can have more fun with the rotation display. Before the image() function, you can alter the transparency of the fill color by specifying an alpha value less than 255, such as tint(255, 20). In the draw() function, if you remove background(0) and add two tint() functions, you can achieve a motion blur effect in the rotating image. The new draw() function is as follows:

```
void draw() {
  //  background(0);
  Mat rot = Imgproc.getRotationMatrix2D(ctr, angle, 1.0);
  Mat out = new Mat(in.size(), in.type());
  Imgproc.warpAffine(in, out, rot, out.size());
  cvout.copyTo(out);
  tint(255, 255);
  image(img, 0, 0);
  tint(255, 20);
```

```
  image(cvout, img.width, 0);
  angle += 0.5;
  angle %= 360;
  out.release();
  rot.release();
}
```

The tint(255, 20) function before image(cvout, img.width, 0) will set the fill color with transparency. In this case, only the rotating image will have the motion blur effect, not the original image on the left side. Figure 4-9 shows the result.

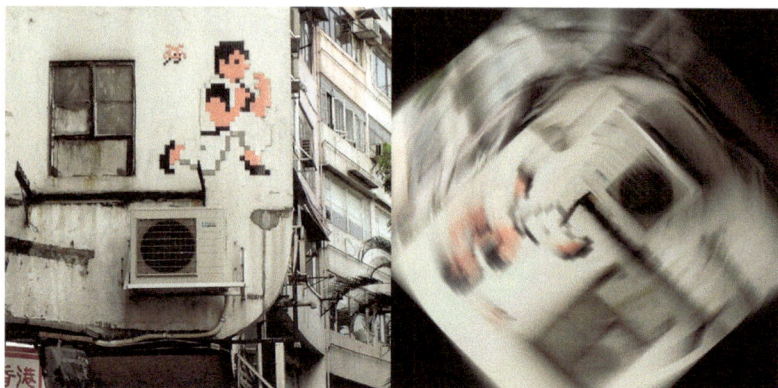

Figure 4-9. *Rotation transform with motion blur*

Image Resizing

In the previous section, the transformations flip and rotation do not change the size/area of the image. If you want to change the image size while maintaining its shape, you can use the resize transform. The function is resize() from the OpenCV Imgproc module, as shown here:

```
public static void Imgproc.resize(Mat src, Mat dst, Size dsize)
```

The first parameter, src, is the source image. The second parameter, dst, is the destination image. The third parameter, dsize, is the size of the destination image. It belongs to the OpenCV Size class. The following sketch, Chapter04_03, demonstrates the use of the resize() function for a graphic composition. The size of the original image in the program is 800×600 pixels.

```
import org.opencv.core.*;
import org.opencv.imgproc.*;

PImage img;
CVImage cv;

void setup() {
  size(1200, 600);
  System.loadLibrary(Core.NATIVE_LIBRARY_NAME);
```

```
  img = loadImage("hongkong.png");

  cv = new CVImage(img.width, img.height);
  cv.copyTo(img);
  noLoop();
}

void draw() {
  background(0);
  Mat in = cv.getBGR();
  Mat out = new Mat(new Size(img.width*0.5, img.height*0.5), in.type());
  Imgproc.resize(in, out, out.size());
  CVImage small = new CVImage(out.cols(), out.rows());
  small.copyTo(out);
  image(img, 0, 0);
  tint(255, 100, 100);
  image(small, img.width, 0);
  tint(100, 100, 255);
  image(small, img.width, small.height);
}
```

The program created a copy of the original image img, with half the width and height. The smaller image, small, is displayed twice with different color tints on the right side of the Processing window, as shown in Figure 4-10.

Figure 4-10. *Resize transform with color tint*

Without using OpenCV, you can also achieve the same result with the copy() method of the PImage class. The next exercise, Chapter04_04, will show how you can create the same composition with the copy() method. The size of the image for testing is 800×600 pixels.

```
PImage img;

void setup() {
  size(1200, 600);
  img = loadImage("hongkong.png");
  noLoop();
}
```

```
void draw() {
  background(0);
  PImage small = createImage(round(img.width*0.5),
    round(img.height*0.5), ARGB);
  small.copy(img, 0, 0, img.width, img.height,
    0, 0, small.width, small.height);
  small.updatePixels();
  image(img, 0, 0);
  tint(255, 100, 100);
  image(small, img.width, 0);
  tint(100, 100, 255);
  image(small, img.width, small.height);

}
```

The copy() method copies the pixels from the original image, img, to the destination, small. Other than the source image, the parameters also include the offset (x, y) and size (width, height) of the source image and the destination image.

Affine Transform

The next geometric transform is the affine transform that can preserve parallel lines in the transformation. To define the transformation matrix, you need to have three points in the source image and their corresponding positions in the destination image. In the next exercise, Chapter04_05, you will use the top-left, top-right, and bottom-right corners of the image to define the transformation. Assume you have the original image, img. The three points from the source image are as follows:

- 0, 0
- img.width-1, 0
- img.width-1, img.height-1

After the affine transform, you assume that the three points will be moved to the following positions, respectively:

- 50, 50
- img.width-100, 100
- img.width-50, img.height-100

In this program, you need to compute the transform matrix based on the mapping of the six corner points. With the matrix, you apply it to the whole image to create the output image. The image size used for testing is 600×600 pixels. Here is the code:

```
import org.opencv.core.*;
import org.opencv.imgproc.*;

PImage img;
CVImage cv;
```

```
void setup() {
  size(1200, 600);
  System.loadLibrary(Core.NATIVE_LIBRARY_NAME);
  img = loadImage("hongkong.png");
  cv = new CVImage(img.width, img.height);
  cv.copyTo(img);
  noLoop();
}

void draw() {
  background(0);

  MatOfPoint2f srcMat = new MatOfPoint2f(new Point(0, 0),
    new Point(img.width-1, 0),
    new Point(img.width-1, img.height-1));
  MatOfPoint2f dstMat = new MatOfPoint2f(new Point(50, 50),
    new Point(img.width-100, 100),
    new Point(img.width-50, img.height-100));

  Mat affine = Imgproc.getAffineTransform(srcMat, dstMat);
  Mat in = cv.getBGR();
  Mat out = new Mat(in.size(), in.type());
  Imgproc.warpAffine(in, out, affine, out.size());
  cv.copyTo(out);
  image(img, 0, 0);
  image(cv, img.width, 0);
  in.release();
  out.release();
  affine.release();
}
```

There are two steps in the draw() function. The first one is to compute the transform matrix based on the six corner points. This is done with the Imgproc.getAffineTransform() function.

```
public static Mat Imgproc.getAffineTransform(MatOfPoint2f src, MatOfPoint2f dst)
```

The first parameter consists of the three points in the source image. The second parameter consists of the three corresponding points in the destination image. Both parameters belong to the OpenCV class MatOfPoint2f. It is similar to vector in C++ and ArrayList in Java. You can consider it as an ordered collection of the base class, Point. The second step is to apply an affine matrix to the source image, in, and generate the destination matrix, out, using the warpAffine() function you learned in the previous section. Figure 4-11 shows the resulting image displayed in the Processing window.

Figure 4-11. *Affine transform*

The next exercise, Chapter04_06, is a more practical usage of the affine transform in image processing. The program will allow users to alter the anchor points to manipulate the degree of transformation. In the source code, you will introduce one more class, Corner, to represent each of the anchor points that you can drag around to change the transformation. The definition of the Corner class is as follows:

```
public class Corner {
  float radius;
  PVector pos;
  boolean picked;

  public Corner(float x, float y) {
    pos = new PVector(x, y);
    radius = 10.0;
    picked = false;
  }

  PVector getPos() {
    return pos;
  }

  void drag(float x, float y) {
    if (picked) {
      PVector p = new PVector(x, y);
      pos.set(p.x, p.y);
    }
  }

  void pick(float x, float y) {
    PVector p = new PVector(x, y);
    float d = p.dist(pos);
    if (d < radius) {
      picked = true;
      pos.set(p.x, p.y);
    }
  }
```

```
  void unpick() {
    picked = false;
  }

  void draw() {
    pushStyle();
    fill(255, 255, 0, 160);
    noStroke();
    ellipse(pos.x, pos.y, radius*2, radius*2);
    popStyle();
  }
}
```

The class will display a circle to indicate the corners of the digital image. In an affine transform, you use only three corners. For the exercise, you use the top-left, top-right, and bottom-right corners. Users can click and drag to move the corner points. You will reuse the class when you work with the perspective transform in the next section. The main program for Chapter04_06 is shown here:

```
import org.opencv.core.*;
import org.opencv.imgproc.*;

PImage img;
CVImage cvout;
PVector offset;
MatOfPoint2f srcMat, dstMat;
Mat in;
Corner [] corners;

void setup() {
  size(720, 720);
  System.loadLibrary(Core.NATIVE_LIBRARY_NAME);
  img = loadImage("hongkong.png");
  CVImage cvin = new CVImage(img.width, img.height);
  cvin.copyTo(img);
  in = cvin.getBGR();
  cvout = new CVImage(img.width, img.height);
  offset = new PVector((width-img.width)/2, (height-img.height)/2);
  srcMat = new MatOfPoint2f(new Point(0, 0),
    new Point(img.width-1, 0),
    new Point(img.width-1, img.height-1));
  dstMat = new MatOfPoint2f();
  corners = new Corner[srcMat.rows()];
  corners[0] = new Corner(0+offset.x, 0+offset.y);
  corners[1] = new Corner(img.width-1+offset.x, 0+offset.y);
  corners[2] = new Corner(img.width-1+offset.x, img.height-1+offset.y);
}

void draw() {
  background(0);
  drawFrame();
  Point [] points = new Point[corners.length];
  for (int i=0; i<corners.length; i++) {
    PVector p = corners[i].getPos();
```

113

```
      points[i] = new Point(p.x-offset.x, p.y-offset.y);
    }
    dstMat.fromArray(points);
    Mat affine = Imgproc.getAffineTransform(srcMat, dstMat);
    Mat out = new Mat(in.size(), in.type());
    Imgproc.warpAffine(in, out, affine, out.size());
    cvout.copyTo(out);
    image(cvout, offset.x, offset.y);
    for (Corner c : corners) {
      c.draw();
    }
    out.release();
    affine.release();
}

void drawFrame() {
  pushStyle();
  noFill();
  stroke(100);
  line(offset.x-1, offset.y-1,
    img.width+offset.x, offset.y-1);
  line(img.width+offset.x, offset.y-1,
    img.width+offset.x, img.height+offset.y);
  line(offset.x-1, img.height+offset.y,
    img.width+offset.x, img.height+offset.y);
  line(offset.x-1, offset.y-1,
    offset.x-1, img.height+offset.y);
  popStyle();
}

void mousePressed() {
  for (Corner c : corners) {
    c.pick(mouseX, mouseY);
  }
}

void mouseDragged() {
  for (Corner c : corners) {
    if (mouseX<offset.x ||
      mouseX>offset.x+img.width ||
      mouseY<offset.y ||
      mouseY>offset.y+img.height)
      continue;
    c.drag(mouseX, mouseY);
  }
}

void mouseReleased() {
  for (Corner c : corners) {
    c.unpick();
  }
}
```

114

The program adds the mouse event handlers to manage the mouse click actions with the anchor points as defined by the Corner class. Within the draw() function, you use another method to initialize the dstMat matrix. You have defined points as an array of Point. In every frame, you copy the anchor points information from corners to points and use the fromArray() method to initialize dstMat for subsequent processing. The rest of the program is similar to the last one. Figure 4-12 shows the visual display of the program.

Figure 4-12. *Interactive affine transform*

Perspective Transform

The usage of a perspective transform is similar to the affine transform in the previous section, except that you need to use four points to define the transform rather than three points. After the transformation, it cannot preserve parallel lines as that in the affine transform. The function to generate the perspective transform matrix is as follows:

```
public static Mat Imgproc.getPerspectiveTransform(MatOfPoint2f src, MatOfPoint2f dst)
```

The first parameter, src, is the collection (MatOfPont2f) of the four anchor points from the source image. In the exercise, Chapter04_07, you use the four corners of the input image, img. They are as follows:

- 0, 0: Top-left corner

- img.width-1, 0: Top-right corner

- img.width-1, img.height-1: Bottom-right corner

- 0, img.height-1: Bottom-left corner

The second parameter, dst, is the collection (MatOfPoint2f) of the four corner points of the output image after the transformation. You adopt the class Corner from the previous exercise. Users can click/drag the corner points to interactively change the transform matrix. The source code is similar to the previous one. You merely replace the affine transform with the perspective transform and use four points instead of three. The size of the original image you use here is 700×700 pixels.

```
PImage img;
CVImage cvout;
PVector offset;
MatOfPoint2f srcMat, dstMat;
Mat in;
Corner [] corners;
```

```
void setup() {
  size(720, 720);
  System.loadLibrary(Core.NATIVE_LIBRARY_NAME);
  img = loadImage("hongkong.png");
  CVImage cvin = new CVImage(img.width, img.height);
  cvin.copyTo(img);
  in = cvin.getBGR();
  cvout = new CVImage(img.width, img.height);
  offset = new PVector((width-img.width)/2, (height-img.height)/2);
  srcMat = new MatOfPoint2f(new Point(0, 0),
    new Point(img.width-1, 0),
    new Point(img.width-1, img.height-1),
    new Point(0, img.height-1));
  dstMat = new MatOfPoint2f();
  corners = new Corner[srcMat.rows()];
  corners[0] = new Corner(0+offset.x, 0+offset.y);
  corners[1] = new Corner(img.width-1+offset.x, 0+offset.y);
  corners[2] = new Corner(img.width-1+offset.x, img.height-1+offset.y);
  corners[3] = new Corner(0+offset.x, img.height-1+offset.y);
}

void draw() {
  background(0);
  drawFrame();
  Point [] points = new Point[corners.length];
  for (int i=0; i<corners.length; i++) {
    PVector p = corners[i].getPos();
    points[i] = new Point(p.x-offset.x, p.y-offset.y);
  }
  dstMat.fromArray(points);
  Mat transform = Imgproc.getPerspectiveTransform(srcMat, dstMat);
  Mat out = new Mat(in.size(), in.type());
  Imgproc.warpPerspective(in, out, transform, out.size());
  cvout.copyTo(out);
  image(cvout, offset.x, offset.y);
  for (Corner c : corners) {
    c.draw();
  }
  out.release();
  transform.release();
}

void drawFrame() {
  pushStyle();
  noFill();
  stroke(100);
  line(offset.x-1, offset.y-1,
    img.width+offset.x, offset.y-1);
  line(img.width+offsct.x, offset.y-1,
    img.width+offset.x, img.height+offset.y);
  line(offset.x-1, img.height+offset.y,
    img.width+offset.x, img.height+offset.y);
```

```
    line(offset.x-1, offset.y-1,
      offset.x-1, img.height+offset.y);
    popStyle();
}

void mousePressed() {
  for (Corner c : corners) {
    c.pick(mouseX, mouseY);
  }
}

void mouseDragged() {
  for (Corner c : corners) {
    if (mouseX<offset.x ||
      mouseX>offset.x+img.width ||
      mouseY<offset.y ||
      mouseY>offset.y+img.height)
      continue;
    c.drag(mouseX, mouseY);
  }
}

void mouseReleased() {
  for (Corner c : corners) {
    c.unpick();
  }
}
```

To perform the perspective transform, you use the new warpPerspective() function with the matrix transform, which was generated from the last getPerspectiveTransform() matrix, as shown in Figure 4-13.

Figure 4-13. *Perspective transform with interactivity*

Note that when users click/drag the corner points, you do not check whether the new shape is convex. When the new shape is not convex, a distorted image may result.

Linear vs. Polar Coordinates

The *x, y* coordinate system you are using is linear, or Cartesian coordinate. The two axes are straight lines perpendicular to each other. Besides the linear coordinate system, you can also represent a point (*x, y*) in a two-dimensional plane by using the measurements of *radius* and *angle*, as shown in Figure 4-14.

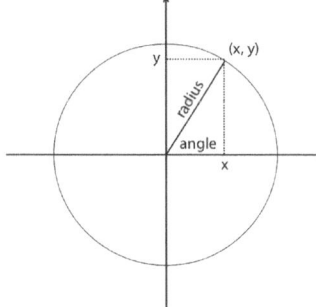

Figure 4-14. *Linear and polar coordinates*

OpenCV provides the transformation functions to convert an image in linear coordinate space to polar coordinate space, with the image-processing module Imgproc. The function is as follows:

```
public static void Imgproc.linearPolar(Mat src, Mat dst, Point center, double maxRadius,
int flags)
```

The first parameter, src, is the source image. The second parameter, dst, is the destination image with the same size and type as the source. The third parameter, center, is the transformation center. You usually set it to the center of the image. The fourth parameter, maxRadius, is the radius of the bounding circle to transform. The fifth parameter, flags, is a combination of interpolation methods. You use the bilinear interpolation, INTER_LINEAR, and fill all the destination pixels, WARP_FILL_OUTLIERS. In the demonstration exercise, Chapter04_08, you will use a live webcam as the input image and show both the source image and the transformed image side by side.

```
import processing.video.*;
import org.opencv.core.*;
import org.opencv.imgproc.*;

Capture cap;
CVImage img, out;
int capW, capH;

void setup() {
  size(1280, 480);
  System.loadLibrary(Core.NATIVE_LIBRARY_NAME);
  capW = width/2;
  capH = height;
  cap = new Capture(this, capW, capH);
  cap.start();
  img = new CVImage(cap.width, cap.height);
  out = new CVImage(cap.width, cap.height);
}
```

```
void draw() {
  if (!cap.available())
    return;
  background(0);
  cap.read();
  img.copyTo(cap);
  Mat linear = img.getBGR();
  Mat polar = new Mat();
  Point ctr = new Point(cap.width/2, cap.height/2);
  double radius = min(cap.width, cap.height)/2.0;
  Imgproc.linearPolar(linear, polar, ctr, radius,
    Imgproc.INTER_LINEAR+Imgproc.WARP_FILL_OUTLIERS);
  out.copyTo(polar);
  image(cap, 0, 0);
  image(out, cap.width, 0);
  linear.release();
  polar.release();
}
```

In the exercise, you set the radius to half the height of the video image. Figure 4-15 shows the Processing window image.

Figure 4-15. *Linear to polar transform*

OpenCV also provides another polar coordinate transform, `logPolar()`. It is similar to the `linearPolar()` function except that it uses the natural logarithm of the distance. The following exercise, Chapter04_09, shows how you can use the `logPolar()` function with the webcam image:

```
import processing.video.*;
import org.opencv.core.*;
import org.opencv.imgproc.*;

Capture cap;
CVImage img, out;
int capW, capH;

void setup() {
  size(1280, 480);
  System.loadLibrary(Core.NATIVE_LIBRARY_NAME);
```

```
  capW = width/2;
  capH = height;
  cap = new Capture(this, capW, capH);
  cap.start();
  img = new CVImage(cap.width, cap.height);
  out = new CVImage(cap.width, cap.height);
}

void draw() {
  if (!cap.available())
    return;
  background(0);
  cap.read();
  img.copyTo(cap);
  Mat linear = img.getBGR();
  Mat polar = new Mat();
  Point ctr = new Point(cap.width/2, cap.height/2);
  double radius = (double)min(cap.width, cap.height)/2.0;
  double m = (double)cap.width/log((float)radius);
  Imgproc.logPolar(linear, polar, ctr, m,
    Imgproc.INTER_LINEAR+Imgproc.WARP_FILL_OUTLIERS);
  out.copyTo(polar);
  image(cap, 0, 0);
  image(out, cap.width, 0);
  linear.release();
  polar.release();
}
```

The function claims to emulate the human "foveal" vision and appears to be more "natural." Figure 4-16 shows the resulting image.

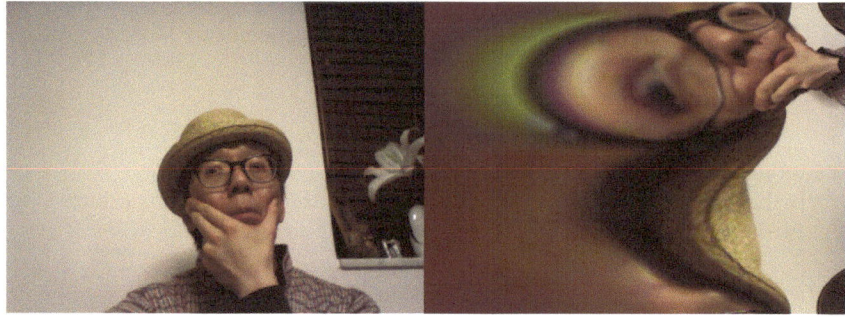

Figure 4-16. *Linear to log polar transform*

Three-Dimensional Space

Besides using the image-processing module in OpenCV, you can use the 3D graphical features in Processing to transform images. In most of this book's exercises, you are using the image() function to display the PImage object instance directly on the screen. In Processing, there are other ways to display the image.

The following exercise, Chapter04_10, demonstrates how to use the PShape class (https://processing.org/reference/PShape.html) with a PImage class as the mapped texture. The exercise is a composition of two images. The first one is the background image from a PImage instance. The second one is the foreground image from the Capture instance. The rotation in 3D space simulates a perspective transform.

```
import processing.video.*;

Capture cap;
PImage img;
PShape canvas;
int capW, capH;
float angle;

void setup() {
  size(800, 600, P3D);
  hint(DISABLE_DEPTH_TEST);
  capW = 640;
  capH = 480;
  cap = new Capture(this, capW, capH);
  cap.start();
  img = loadImage("hongkong.png");
  canvas = createShape(RECT, 0, 0, cap.width, cap.height);
  canvas.setStroke(false);
  canvas.setTexture(cap);
  shapeMode(CENTER);
  angle = 0;
}

void draw() {
  if (!cap.available())
    return;
  cap.read();
  background(0);
  image(img, 0, 0);
  translate(width/2, height/2, -100);
  rotateX(radians(angle));
  shape(canvas, 0, 0);
  angle += 0.5;
  angle %= 360;
}
```

The first change in the program is the size() function. It has an additional parameter, P3D, to indicate that you are now in 3D display mode. Advanced users can use the OpenGL hint function to control the rendering parameters (https://processing.org/tutorials/rendering/). The hint() function you used here has a parameter to disable a depth test in the rendering, such that the surface in the front will not occlude that in the back. In the setup() function, you define the PShape instance canvas with the following function:

```
createShape(RECT, 0, 0, cap.width, cap.height);
```

This creates a shape as a rectangle, RECT, with the top-left corner at (0, 0) and the width and height equal to the webcam capture's width and height. The next statement disables the stroke color. You also use canvas.setTexture(cap) to associate PImage cap from the webcam as the texture for the shape, canvas.

In the draw() function, you first clear the background to black and then display directly the background image, img, onto the Processing window. The translate() function displaces the drawing to the center of the screen and also with negative value in the z direction. The rotateX() function rotates the drawing by the amount specified in angle along the X axis. Note that the rotation takes radians as the unit of measurement. If you are using degrees, you need to use the radians() function to do the conversion. The final step is to use the shape() function to display the PShape instance canvas in the center (0, 0). Note also that in the setup() function, you set shapeMode to CENTER, rather than the top-left corner. The sample display will be similar to what is shown in Figure 4-17.

Figure 4-17. *Perspective transform in Processing by rotation*

In the previous exercise, you define the shape using a built-in rectangular shape. In fact, you can define your own vertices. The following exercise, Chapter04_11, will define the same shape using a sequence of vertex() commands. After that, you can retrieve the individual vertex and alter its position to achieve a more dynamic animation.

```
import processing.video.*;

Capture cap;
PImage img;
PShape canvas;
int capW, capH;
float angle;
int vCnt;

void setup() {
  size(800, 600, P3D);
  hint(DISABLE_DEPTH_TEST);
  capW = 640;
  capH = 480;
  cap = new Capture(this, capW, capH);
  cap.start();
  img = loadImage("hongkong.png");
  canvas = createShape();
  canvas.beginShape();
  canvas.textureMode(NORMAL);
  canvas.texture(cap);
  canvas.noStroke();
  canvas.vertex(0, 0, 0, 0, 0);
  canvas.vertex(cap.width, 0, 0, 1, 0);
```

```
  canvas.vertex(cap.width, cap.height, 0, 1, 1);
  canvas.vertex(0, cap.height, 0, 0, 1);
  canvas.endShape(CLOSE);
  shapeMode(CENTER);
  angle = 0;
  vCnt = canvas.getVertexCount();
}

void draw() {
  if (!cap.available())
    return;
  cap.read();
  background(0);
  image(img, 0, 0);
  for (int i=0; i<vCnt; i++) {
    PVector pos = canvas.getVertex(i);
    if (i < 2) {
      pos.z = 100*cos(radians(angle*3));
    } else {
      pos.z = 100*sin(radians(angle*5));
    }
    canvas.setVertex(i, pos);
  }
  translate(width/2, height/2, -100);
  rotateY(radians(angle));
  shape(canvas, 0, 0);
  angle += 0.5;
  angle %= 360;
}
```

Figure 4-18 shows the result.

Figure 4-18. *Perspective transform with custom shape*

The previous exercises use only four corners of the rectangle to specify the rectangle. The image is not distorted too much. If you use a wireframe grid as the skeleton for the texture mapping, you can modify each point to further distort the image. Figure 4-19 shows the grid and the image mapped on top of it.

123

Figure 4-19. *Image text-mapped on a grid*

To define the grid in Processing, you use the QUAD_STRIP shape. First, you define a GROUP shape for the whole grid. Second, you create each row of the grid as a QUAD_STRIP shape. To create a cell in the QUAD_STRIP, you have to define the points in this order: top-left, bottom-left, top-right, and bottom-right. Third, you add each row to the GROUP shape as a child. Figure 4-20 explains the detailed configuration of this shape.

Figure 4-20. *A GROUP shape with QUAD_STRIP as children*

The next exercise, Chapter04_12, shows how you can use a GROUP PShape called canvas to define the grid for the detailed texture mapping:

```
import processing.video.*;

Capture cap;
PShape canvas;
int capW, capH;
float step;

void setup() {
  size(800, 600, P3D);
  hint(DISABLE_DEPTH_TEST);
  capW = 640;
  capH = 480;
  step = 40;
  cap = new Capture(this, capW, capH);
  cap.start();
  initShape();
  shapeMode(CENTER);
}
```

```
void initShape() {
  // initialize the GROUP PShape grid
  canvas = createShape(GROUP);
  int nRows = floor(cap.height/step) + 1;
  int nCols = floor(cap.width/step) + 1;
  for (int y=0; y<nRows-1; y++) {
    // initialize each row of the grid
    PShape tmp = createShape();
    tmp.beginShape(QUAD_STRIP);
    tmp.texture(cap);
    for (int x=0; x<nCols; x++) {
      // initialize the top-left, bottom-left points
      int x1 = (int)constrain(x*step, 0, cap.width-1);
      int y1 = (int)constrain(y*step, 0, cap.height-1);
      int y2 = (int)constrain((y+1)*step, 0, cap.height-1);
      tmp.vertex(x1, y1, 0, x1, y1);
      tmp.vertex(x1, y2, 0, x1, y2);
    }
    tmp.endShape();
    canvas.addChild(tmp);
  }
}

void draw() {
  if (!cap.available())
    return;
  cap.read();
  background(100);
  translate(width/2, height/2, -80);
  rotateX(radians(20));
  shape(canvas, 0, 0);
}
```

The difficult part is done in the initShape() function. You first define PShape for the whole grid as

```
canvas = createShape(GROUP)
```

Then you loop through every cell in the grid. Note that you need to take care of the right and bottom margins by adding 1 to the total number of rows, nRows, and the total number of columns, nCols. For each row, you define the temporary variable tmp as a QUAD_STRIP shape. After you create all the vertices in the QUAD_STRIP, you add it to the canvas shape by using canvas.addChild(tmp). Now you can map the video capture image onto the grid as a texture. Nevertheless, you are not going to stop here. Your intention is to alter the z position of the vertices on the screen, such that you can have a distorted image of the video capture.

The next exercise, Chapter04_13, will maintain a two-dimensional array of vertices in the grid. Also, you will set a random initial z position for each of the vertices.

```
import processing.video.*;

Capture cap;
PShape canvas;
int capW, capH;
float step;
PVector [][] points;
float angle;
```

125

```
void setup() {
  size(800, 600, P3D);
  hint(DISABLE_DEPTH_TEST);
  capW = 640;
  capH = 480;
  step = 20;
  cap = new Capture(this, capW, capH);
  cap.start();
  initGrid();
  initShape();
  shapeMode(CENTER);
  angle = 0;
}

void initGrid() {
  // initialize the matrix of points for texture mapping
  points = new PVector[floor(cap.height/step)+1][floor(cap.width/step)+1];
  for (int y=0; y<points.length; y++) {
    for (int x=0; x<points[y].length; x++) {
      float xVal = constrain(x*step, 0, cap.width-1);
      float yVal = constrain(y*step, 0, cap.height-1);
      // random z value
      points[y][x] = new PVector(xVal, yVal, noise(x*0.2, y*0.2)*60-30);
    }
  }
}

void initShape() {
  // initialize the GROUP PShape grid
  canvas = createShape(GROUP);
  for (int y=0; y<points.length-1; y++) {
    // initialize each row of the grid
    PShape tmp = createShape();
    tmp.beginShape(QUAD_STRIP);
    tmp.noStroke();
    tmp.texture(cap);
    for (int x=0; x<points[y].length; x++) {
      PVector p1 = points[y][x];
      PVector p2 = points[y+1][x];
      tmp.vertex(p1.x, p1.y, p1.z, p1.x, p1.y);
      tmp.vertex(p2.x, p2.y, p2.z, p2.x, p2.y);
    }
    tmp.endShape();
    canvas.addChild(tmp);
  }
}

void draw() {
  if (!cap.available())
    return;
  cap.read();
  lights();
```

```
  background(100);
  translate(width/2, height/2, -100);
  rotateX(radians(angle*1.3));
  rotateY(radians(angle));
  shape(canvas, 0, 0);
  angle += 0.5;
  angle %= 360;
}
```

The 2D array of PVector, called points, maintains all the vertices of the grid. The function initGrid() initializes the position information. For the z position, you use the Perlin noise function to initialize it. The initShape() function will copy the information in the points array to create the GROUP PShape, canvas, with proper texture mapping. Note that you also use the lights() function to enable the default lighting condition in the draw() function. The resulting image (shown in Figure 4-21) will resemble a 3D terrain with the webcam image mapped on top of it.

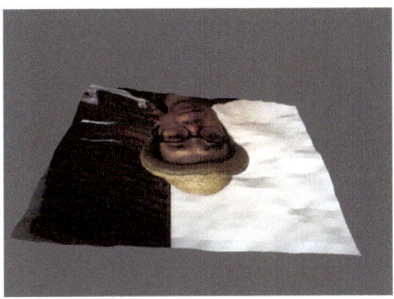

Figure 4-21. *Texture map with irregular surface*

In the previous exercise, notice that the vertices in the grid do not move. They are created once in the setup() function, without any further changes. In the next exercise, Chapter04_14, you will try to animate the vertices according to the webcam image so that you can achieve an interactive viewing experience. Instead of putting a random number for the z position of each vertex, you intend to change its value by using color information from the webcam. In Processing, the default color mode is RGB. You can, however, switch it to HSB (hue, saturation, brightness) if you want to make explicit use of the brightness information. In this exercise, you will aim to swap the vertex's z position with the brightness information of that pixel. The function you can use is brightness().

```
import processing.video.*;

Capture cap;
int capW, capH;
float step;
PVector [][] points;
float angle;
PShape canvas;

void setup() {
  size(800, 600, P3D);
  hint(DISABLE_DEPTH_TEST);
  capW = 640;
```

```
    capH = 480;
    step = 10;
    cap = new Capture(this, capW, capH);
    cap.start();
    initGrid();
    initShape();
    shapeMode(CENTER);
    angle = 0;
}

void initGrid() {
    // initialize the matrix of points for texture mapping
    points = new PVector[floor(cap.height/step)+1][floor(cap.width/step)+1];
    for (int y=0; y<points.length; y++) {
        for (int x=0; x<points[y].length; x++) {
            float xVal = constrain(x*step, 0, cap.width-1);
            float yVal = constrain(y*step, 0, cap.height-1);
            points[y][x] = new PVector(xVal, yVal, 0);
        }
    }
}

void initShape() {
    canvas = createShape(GROUP);
    for (int y=0; y<points.length-1; y++) {
        // initialize each row of the grid
        PShape tmp = createShape();
        tmp.beginShape(QUAD_STRIP);
        tmp.noFill();
        for (int x=0; x<points[y].length; x++) {
            PVector p1 = points[y][x];
            PVector p2 = points[y+1][x];
            tmp.vertex(p1.x, p1.y, p1.z);
            tmp.vertex(p2.x, p2.y, p2.z);
        }
        tmp.endShape();
        canvas.addChild(tmp);
    }
}

color getColor(int x, int y) {
    // obtain color information from cap
    int x1 = constrain(floor(x*step), 0, cap.width-1);
    int y1 = constrain(floor(y*step), 0, cap.height-1);
    return cap.get(x1, y1);
}
```

```
void updatePoints() {
  // update the depth of vertices using color
  // brightness from cap
  float factor = 0.3;
  for (int y=0; y<points.length; y++) {
    for (int x=0; x<points[y].length; x++) {
      color c = getColor(x, y);
      points[y][x].z = brightness(c)*factor;
    }
  }
}

void updateShape() {
  // update the color and depth of vertices
  for (int i=0; i<canvas.getChildCount(); i++) {
    for (int j=0; j<canvas.getChild(i).getVertexCount(); j++) {
      PVector p = canvas.getChild(i).getVertex(j);
      int x = constrain(floor(p.x/step), 0, points[0].length-1);
      int y = constrain(floor(p.y/step), 0, points.length-1);
      p.z = points[y][x].z;
      color c = getColor(x, y);
      canvas.getChild(i).setStroke(j, c);
      canvas.getChild(i).setVertex(j, p);
    }
  }
}

void draw() {
  if (!cap.available())
    return;
  cap.read();
  updatePoints();
  updateShape();
  background(0);
  translate(width/2, height/2, -100);
  rotateX(radians(angle));
  shape(canvas, 0, 0);
  angle += 0.5;
  angle %= 360;
}
```

The initGrid() function initializes the points array. The initShape() function uses the information from the points array to initialize PShape canvas. In the function, you do not set the texture directly in each of the QUAD_STRIP children. You enable the stroke color but disable the fill color for the child shapes. In the draw() function, you write the updatePoints() function to update the vertices' *z* position according to the color brightness. The updateShape() function goes through all the children of PShape canvas and updates the vertices' *z* position and the stroke color. Figure 4-22 shows a sample of the display window.

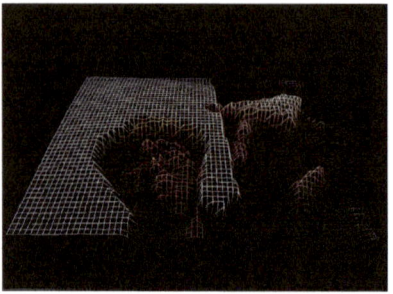

Figure 4-22. *3D effect using brightness as depth*

Note that in the image those areas with darker color will appear to be deeper, while the lighter areas will be higher in the grid plane. If you change the `tmp.noFill()` statement in the `initShape()` function to `tmp.noStroke()` and change the `canvas.getChild(i).setStroke(j, c)` statement in the `updateShape()` function to `canvas.getChild(i).setFill(j, c)`, you can switch the wireframe display to a solid filled version, as shown in Figure 4-23.

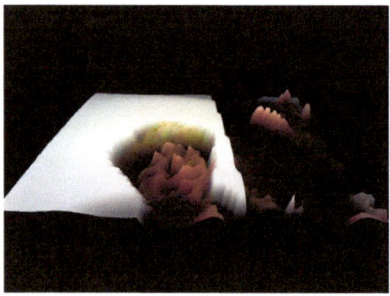

Figure 4-23. *3D effect with brightness as depth*

General Pixel Mapping

In addition to the built-in functions in Processing and OpenCV for image transformation, you can write the generic image transform algorithm by mapping pixel by pixel from the source image to the destination image. In the last exercise, `Chapter04_15`, of this chapter, you will try to work on copying individual pixels from the first image, `img1`, to the second image, `img2`. The transformation will be based on the harmonic motion generated from the sine and cosine functions. The size of the image used here is 600×600 pixels.

```
PImage img1, img2;
float angle;

void setup() {
  size(1200, 600);
  img1 = loadImage("hongkong.png");
  img2 = createImage(img1.width, img1.hcight, ARGB);
  angle = 0;
}
```

```
void draw() {
  // Variables rx, ry are for the radii of the sine/cosine functions
  // Variables ax, ay are for the angles of the sine/cosine functions
  background(0);
  for (int y=0; y<img2.height; y++) {
    float ay = y*angle/img2.height;
    float ry = y*angle/360.0;
    for (int x=0; x<img2.width; x++) {
      float ax = x*angle/img2.width;
      float rx = x*angle/360.0;
      int x1 = x + (int)(rx*cos(radians(ay)));
      int y1 = y + (int)(ry*sin(radians(ax)));
      x1 = constrain(x1, 0, img1.width-1);
      y1 = constrain(y1, 0, img1.height-1);
      img2.pixels[y*img2.width+x] = img1.pixels[y1*img1.width+x1];
    }
  }
  angle += 1;
  angle %= 360;
  img2.updatePixels();
  image(img1, 0, 0);
  image(img2, img1.width, 0);
}
```

The first image, img1, is the source image. The second image, img2, is of the same size as img1. Within the nested for loops in the draw() function, you go from the opposite direction through each pixel in the destination image, img2. For each pixel, you find from the source image which pixel you should copy from it to the destination. For the source pixel, you adopt the sine and cosine functions with variables affecting the radii and angles. The overall result is an animation of a warping effect working on the source image, shown in Figure 4-24. Figure 4-24 and Figure 4-25 shows two sample displays at different points of time.

Figure 4-24. *General mapping of pixels sample 1*

131

It is the second moment you capture from the animation (Figure 4-25).

Figure 4-25. *General mapping of pixels sample 2*

The reason why you work from the destination back to the source image is not to leave any of the destination pixels empty. This is common practice when developing a pixel-mapping transformation.

Conclusion

This chapter described the steps to modify an image by changing its pixels' position and thus altering its geometry. Both Processing and OpenCV have geometric transform functionalities. You can choose which one to use according to the application requirements in order to simplify the coding tasks. Alternately, you can write your own image transform functions by specifying all the pixels in the destination image and where they come from in the source image. So far, you have modify images for creative results only. You have not tried to understand the images yet. In the next chapter, you will start to make sense of the content in the image.

CHAPTER 5

Identification of Structure

After working on image processing in the previous two chapters, you will start to explore computer vision with Processing and OpenCV. In previous chapters, a webcam image was the source material for creative outputs. You have not attempted to make sense of the content of the image. In this chapter, you can use the concepts of computer vision to identify structures in the image. Through the structures, you will make more sense of the content of the image. The topics this chapter will cover are as follows:

- Image preparation
- Edge detection
- Line detection
- Circle detection
- Contours processing
- Shape detection

Image Preparation

Before you send a source image for detection, it is often necessary to optimize the image. By optimization, I am referring to the process of reducing unnecessary information in the raw image. For example, when you want to identify straight lines in an image, you often do not need to have a color image. A grayscale one will do. Sometimes a black-and-white image may just be enough to serve the purpose of shape detection. The following are the steps to follow to prepare the image for detection:

1. Conversion to grayscale
2. Conversion to a black-and-white image
3. Morphological operations (erode, dilate)
4. Blur operations (smoothing)

Conversion to Grayscale

You learned how to convert a color RGB image into grayscale by changing each pixel in Chapter 2. In the following exercises, you will explore different ways in Processing and OpenCV to achieve the same effect. The first exercise, Chapter05_01, will use the filter() function in Processing. The size of the sample image used in this exercise is 600×600 pixels.

© Bryan WC Chung 2017
B. WC. Chung, *Pro Processing for Images and Computer Vision with OpenCV*,
DOI 10.1007/978-1-4842-2775-6_5

```
PImage source, grey;

void setup() {
  size(1200, 600);
  source = loadImage("sample04.jpg");
  grey = createImage(source.width, source.height, ARGB);
  noLoop();
}

void draw() {
  background(0);
  arrayCopy(source.pixels, grey.pixels);
  grey.updatePixels();
  grey.filter(GRAY);
  image(source, 0, 0);
  image(grey, source.width, 0);
}
```

The program also demonstrates the use of the `arrayCopy()` function to efficiently copy from one array to another of the same size. The actual function to convert the image is `grey.filter(GRAY)`. The program will display the original image and the grayscale one side by side for comparison, as shown in Figure 5-1.

Figure 5-1. *Grayscale conversion in Processing*

The next version, `Chapter05_02`, will use the OpenCV function to perform the grayscale conversion. Note that in the `CVImage` class defined in the Chapter 2 example, `Chapter02_21`, you have already written the `getGrey()` method to return a grayscale image matrix. Please remember to copy the code folder and the `CVImage` definition to the sketch folder before using OpenCV in Processing. The size of the sample image is 600×600 pixels.

```
PImage source;
CVImage srccv, greycv;

void setup() {
  size(1200, 600);
  System.loadLibrary(Core.NATIVE_LIBRARY_NAME);
```

```
  source = loadImage("sample04.jpg");

  srccv = new CVImage(source.width, source.height);
  srccv.copyTo(source);
  greycv = new CVImage(source.width, source.height);
  noLoop();
}

void draw() {
  background(0);
  Mat mat = srccv.getGrey();
  greycv.copyTo(mat);
  image(source, 0, 0);
  image(greycv, source.width, 0);
  mat.release();
}
```

In the program, you use the CVImage instance greycv to keep the grayscale image after the conversion by the getGrey() method.

Conversion to a Black-and-White Image

The grayscale image you obtained in the previous section usually contains 256 levels of gray tone. In some applications, you may want to have just two levels, simply black and white. In this case, you can use the following methods to further convert the grayscale image into a black-and-white one. The exercise, Chapter05_03, will show you how to use the Processing filter() function to do so. The size of the sample image in this exercise is 600×600 pixels.

```
PImage source, grey, bw;

void setup() {
  size(1800, 600);
  source = loadImage("sample01.jpg");
  grey = createImage(source.width, source.height, ARGB);
  bw = createImage(source.width, source.height, ARGB);
  noLoop();
}

void draw() {
  background(0);
  arrayCopy(source.pixels, grey.pixels);
  grey.updatePixels();
  grey.filter(GRAY);
  arrayCopy(grey.pixels, bw.pixels);
  bw.updatePixels();
  bw.filter(THRESHOLD, 0.5);
  image(source, 0, 0);
  image(grey, source.width, 0);
  image(bw, source.width+grey.width, 0);
}
```

I often refer to the black-and-white conversion as *thresholding*. A pixel with a grayscale value higher than a threshold will be considered as white and black when its grayscale value is lower than the threshold. The function you use here is bw.filter(THRESHOLD, 0.5), where the number 0.5 is the threshold value. Figure 5-2 shows the display window.

Figure 5-2. *Black-and-white image conversion with thresholding*

The image on the left side is the original photograph. The middle one is the grayscale version after the first filter() function. The one on the right side is the black-and-white image after the second filter() function, this time with the option THRESHOLD. The next exercise, Chapter05_04, will illustrate a version done in OpenCV:

```
PImage source;
CVImage srccv, bwcv;

void setup() {
  size(1800, 600);
  System.loadLibrary(Core.NATIVE_LIBRARY_NAME);
  source = loadImage("sample04.jpg");
  srccv = new CVImage(source.width, source.height);
  bwcv = new CVImage(source.width, source.height);
  srccv.copyTo(source);
  noLoop();
}

void draw() {
  background(0);
  Mat grey = srccv.getGrey();
  Mat bw = new Mat();
  Imgproc.threshold(grey, bw, 127, 255, Imgproc.THRESH_BINARY);
  bwcv.copyTo(bw);
  srccv.copyTo(grey);
  image(source, 0, 0);
  image(srccv, source.width, 0);
  image(bwcv, source.width+srccv.width, 0);
  grey.release();
  bw.release();
}
```

The following is the OpenCV function to perform the threshold operation:

```
Imgproc.threshold(grey, bw, 127, 255, Imgproc.THRESH_BINARY);
```

In the function, the first number, 127, is the midpoint within the 0 to 255 range. It is the threshold value. The second number, 255, is the maximum number for the grayscale level.

Morphological Operations

Morphological operations in image processing are the transformations that modify the shape of a pattern in an image. In this section, I cover only the erode and dilate operations. The following exercise, Chapter05_05, shows how you can do them in Processing:

```
PImage source, grey, bw, dilate, erode;

void setup() {
  size(1800, 600);
  source = loadImage("sample02.jpg");
  grey = createImage(source.width, source.height, ARGB);
  bw = createImage(source.width, source.height, ARGB);
  dilate = createImage(source.width, source.height, ARGB);
  erode = createImage(source.width, source.height, ARGB);
  noLoop();
}

void draw() {
  background(0);
  arrayCopy(source.pixels, grey.pixels);
  grey.updatePixels();
  grey.filter(GRAY);
  arrayCopy(grey.pixels, bw.pixels);
  bw.updatePixels();
  bw.filter(THRESHOLD, 0.5);
  arrayCopy(bw.pixels, erode.pixels);
  arrayCopy(bw.pixels, dilate.pixels);
  erode.updatePixels();
  dilate.updatePixels();
  dilate.filter(DILATE);
  erode.filter(ERODE);
  image(bw, 0, 0);
  image(erode, bw.width, 0);
  image(dilate, bw.width+erode.width, 0);
}
```

The resulting display contains three images, as shown in Figure 5-3. The left one is the black-and-white image from the THRESHOLD filter. The middle one is the ERODE version. The right one is the DILATE version.

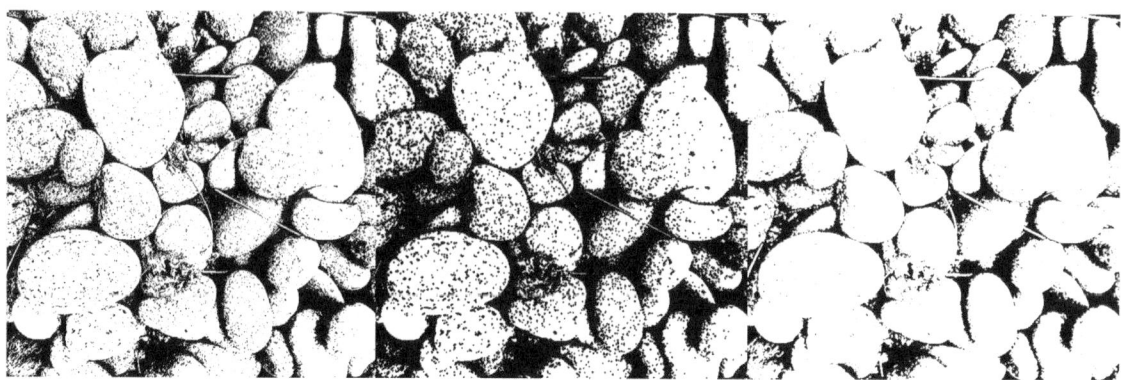

Figure 5-3. *Erode and dilate filters in Processing*

The ERODE filter reduces the number of white areas, while the DILATE filter increases the number of white areas. For applications that would like to remove the dark, tiny noise patterns, the DILATE filter would be a good choice to start with. For an OpenCV version, please refer to the following exercise, Chapter05_06:

```
PImage source;
CVImage srccv, bwcv, erodecv, dilatecv;

void setup() {
  size(1800, 600);
  System.loadLibrary(Core.NATIVE_LIBRARY_NAME);
  source = loadImage("sample02.jpg");
  srccv = new CVImage(source.width, source.height);
  bwcv = new CVImage(source.width, source.height);
  erodecv = new CVImage(source.width, source.height);
  dilatecv = new CVImage(source.width, source.height);
  srccv.copyTo(source);
  noLoop();
}

void draw() {
  background(0);
  Mat grey = srccv.getGrey();
  Mat bw = new Mat();
  Imgproc.threshold(grey, bw, 127, 255, Imgproc.THRESH_BINARY);
  Mat erode = new Mat();
  Mat dilate = new Mat();
  Mat elem = Imgproc.getStructuringElement(Imgproc.MORPH_RECT, new Size(3, 3));
  Imgproc.erode(bw, erode, elem);
  Imgproc.dilate(bw, dilate, elem);
  bwcv.copyTo(bw);
  erodecv.copyTo(erode);
  dilatecv.copyTo(dilate);
  image(bwcv, 0, 0);
  image(erodecv, bwcv.width, 0);
  image(dilatecv, bwcv.width+erodecv.width, 0);
  grey.release();
```

```
    bw.release();
    erode.release();
    dilate.release();
}
```

The program uses the former `Imgproc.threshold()` function to change the grayscale image into a black-and-white one first. The subsequent `Imgproc.erode()` and `Imgproc.dilate()` functions will perform, respectively, the erode and dilate morphological operations. Before working on the erode and dilate operations, you need another matrix, called `elem`, which is the *structuring element* or *kernel* describing the morphological operations. It usually comes with three shapes.

- `Imgproc.MORPH_RECT`

- `Imgproc.MORPH_CROSS`

- `Imgproc.MORPH_ELLIPSE`

The content of `elem` with different shape parameters is shown here:

MORPH_RECT (3×3)		
1	1	1
1	1	1
1	1	1

MORPH_CROSS (3×3)		
0	1	0
1	1	1
0	1	0

MORPH_ELLIPSE (3×3)		
0	1	0
1	1	1
0	1	0

You will find that the MORPH_CROSS and MORPH_ELLIPSE effects are identical when the size is 3×3. For a larger size, they will be different. MORPH_CROSS will have 1 only in the middle row and column, while the MORPH_ELLIPSE will approximate a circular shape with 1. The filter operation will scan through the source image with the matrix `elem`. Only those pixels with the value 1 in `elem` will be collected for calculation. The DILATE filter will replace the original image pixel with the maximum value among the neighborhood pixels defined in `elem`. The ERODE filter will replace the original image pixel with the minimum value among the neighborhood. You can find details of the three shapes in the OpenCV documentation at http://docs.opencv.org/3.1.0/d4/d86/group__imgproc__filter.html#gac2db39b56866583a95a5680313c314ad. For the `Size()` parameter, the larger the size, the more obvious the transformation effect. In general, it is a square with a pair of odd numbers.

Blur Operations

To further reduce the noise or unnecessary details in an image, you can consider using a blurring effect. Both Processing and OpenCV have a blur filter or functions. The next exercise, Chapter05_07, uses the blur filter in Processing to perform the operation:

```
PImage source, blur;

void setup() {
  size(1200, 600);
  source = loadImage("sample03.jpg");
  blur = createImage(source.width, source.height, ARGB);
  noLoop();
}

void draw() {
  background(0);
  arrayCopy(source.pixels, blur.pixels);
  blur.updatePixels();
  blur.filter(BLUR, 3);
  image(source, 0, 0);
  image(blur, source.width, 0);
}
```

The program is straightforward. It uses the filter() function with the BLUR option. The number after the option is the amount of blur. The larger the number, the more blurred the image will be. Figure 5-4 shows the resulting display window from the program.

Figure 5-4. *Blur filter in Processing*

For OpenCV, there are a few blur functions. In the next exercise, Chapter05_08, you will explore a number of them and compare the results. It uses the blur(), medianBlur(), and GaussianBlur() functions in the imgproc module of OpenCV. The first blur() function is the local averaging operation where the new image pixel is the average value of its neighborhood pixels. The GaussianBlur() function puts a higher weight on the closer pixels when calculating the average value, which is more effective to remove visible noise. The medianBlur() function employs the median instead of the average to calculate the new pixel value, which is more effective to preserve edges/boundaries while removing noise.

```
PImage source;
CVImage srccv, blurcv, mediancv, gaussiancv;

void setup() {
  size(1800, 600);
  System.loadLibrary(Core.NATIVE_LIBRARY_NAME);
  source = loadImage("sample03.jpg");
  srccv = new CVImage(source.width, source.height);
  blurcv = new CVImage(source.width, source.height);
  mediancv = new CVImage(source.width, source.height);
  gaussiancv = new CVImage(source.width, source.height);
  srccv.copyTo(source);
  noLoop();
}

void draw() {
  background(0);
  Mat mat = srccv.getBGR();
  Mat blur = new Mat();
  Mat median = new Mat();
  Mat gaussian = new Mat();
  Imgproc.medianBlur(mat, median, 9);
  Imgproc.blur(mat, blur, new Size(9, 9));
  Imgproc.GaussianBlur(mat, gaussian, new Size(9, 9), 0);
  blurcv.copyTo(blur);
  mediancv.copyTo(median);
  gaussiancv.copyTo(gaussian);
  image(blurcv, 0, 0);
  image(mediancv, blurcv.width, 0);
  image(gaussiancv, blurcv.width+mediancv.width, 0);
  mat.release();
  blur.release();
  median.release();
  gaussian.release();
}
```

The blurred images from the three functions are displayed side by side, as shown in Figure 5-5.

Figure 5-5. *Three blurring functions in OpenCV*

To conclude this section, you will combine the operations to build a practical application to convert the live webcam image into a binary black-and-white image for later processing. The first version is written in pure Processing for the exercise, Chapter05_09, shown here:

```
import processing.video.*;

Capture cap;

void setup() {
  size(1280, 480);
  cap = new Capture(this, width/2, height);
  cap.start();
}

void draw() {
  if (!cap.available())
    return;
  background(0);
  cap.read();
  PImage tmp = createImage(cap.width, cap.height, ARGB);
  arrayCopy(cap.pixels, tmp.pixels);
  tmp.filter(GRAY);
  tmp.filter(BLUR, 2);
  tmp.filter(THRESHOLD, 0.25);
  tmp.filter(DILATE);

  image(cap, 0, 0);
  image(tmp, cap.width, 0);
  text(nf(round(frameRate), 2), 10, 20);
}
```

In the program, you combine the blur, grayscale, threshold, and erode operations. For a pure Processing implementation, the performance is not good. You add the text() function to display the current frame rate on the screen for comparison. Figure 5-6 shows the Processing display window.

Figure 5-6. *Image preparation in Processing*

For an OpenCV implementation, in the exercise Chapter05_10, you also combine the image operations into one single program with the live webcam image as input. The performance is much better than the pure Processing version.

```
import processing.video.*;

Capture cap;
CVImage img;

void setup() {
  size(1280, 480);
  System.loadLibrary(Core.NATIVE_LIBRARY_NAME);
  cap = new Capture(this, width/2, height);
  cap.start();
  img = new CVImage(cap.width, cap.height);
}

void draw() {
  if (!cap.available())
    return;
  background(0);
  cap.read();
  img.copyTo(cap);
  Mat tmp1 = img.getGrey();
  Mat tmp2 = new Mat();
  Imgproc.GaussianBlur(tmp1, tmp2, new Size(5, 5), 0);
  Imgproc.threshold(tmp2, tmp1, 80, 255, Imgproc.THRESH_BINARY);
  Mat elem = Imgproc.getStructuringElement(Imgproc.MORPH_RECT, new Size(3, 3));
  Imgproc.dilate(tmp1, tmp2, elem);
  CVImage out = new CVImage(cap.width, cap.height);
  out.copyTo(tmp2);
  image(cap, 0, 0);
  image(out, cap.width, 0);
  tmp1.release();
  tmp2.release();
  elem.release();
  text(nf(round(frameRate), 2), 10, 20);
}
```

Figure 5-7 shows the Processing display window image. The frame rate is significantly higher than the Processing version.

Figure 5-7. *Image preparation in Processing with OpenCV*

143

Edge Detection

After understanding the steps to prepare an image, the first structure you will discover is the edge, or outline, of any objects in an image. A computer actually does not understand any image content. It can only systematically scan each pixel and its neighbors. For those pixels with a significant color difference from their neighbors, you can conclude those pixels belong to the outline that may separate two objects or an object against its background.

Processing does not have an edge detection filter, though it is not difficult to implement. For OpenCV, you can use the famous *Canny edge detector* developed by John F. Canny in 1986. To run the edge detection, it is often beneficial to perform a blur operation to remove the noise and convert the color image to grayscale. The next exercise, Chapter05_11, will illustrate the steps:

```
import processing.video.*;

Capture cap;
CVImage img;

void setup() {
  size(1280, 480);
  System.loadLibrary(Core.NATIVE_LIBRARY_NAME);
  cap = new Capture(this, width/2, height);
  cap.start();
  img = new CVImage(cap.width, cap.height);
}

void draw() {
  if (!cap.available())
    return;
  background(0);
  cap.read();
  img.copyTo(cap);
  Mat tmp1 = img.getGrey();
  Mat tmp2 = new Mat();
  Imgproc.GaussianBlur(tmp1, tmp2, new Size(7, 7), 1.5, 1.5);
  Imgproc.Canny(tmp2, tmp1, 10, 30);
  CVImage out = new CVImage(cap.width, cap.height);
  out.copyTo(tmp1);
  image(cap, 0, 0);
  image(out, cap.width, 0);
  text(nf(round(frameRate), 2), 10, 20);
  tmp1.release();
  tmp2.release();
}
```

The following is the major function for the edge detection:

```
Imgproc.Canny(tmp2, tmp1, 10, 30);
```

The image tmp2 is the blurred grayscale image. The image tmp1 is the one to contain the edge image. The function has two threshold values. The first number is the lower threshold. If a pixel's gradient value is below the lower threshold, it will be rejected. The second number is the upper threshold. If the pixel's gradient value is larger than the upper threshold, it will be accepted as an edge pixel. If the pixel's gradient value is between the two threshold values, it will be accepted as edge only if it is connected to another pixel that is above the upper threshold. It is also recommended by Canny that the second one is between two to three times the value of the first one. The larger the values, the fewer edges that will be detected in the image. Figure 5-8 shows the detection result.

Figure 5-8. *Canny edge detection*

For comparison, you can also convert the grayscale image to a black-and-white image with the threshold() function. After that, you can perform edge detection with the black-and-white image. The next exercise, Chapter05_12, demonstrates this approach:

```
import processing.video.*;

Capture cap;
CVImage img;

void setup() {
  size(1280, 480);
  System.loadLibrary(Core.NATIVE_LIBRARY_NAME);
  cap = new Capture(this, width/2, height);
  cap.start();
  img = new CVImage(cap.width, cap.height);
}

void draw() {
  if (!cap.available())
    return;
  background(0);
  cap.read();
  img.copyTo(cap);
  Mat tmp1 = img.getGrey();
  Mat tmp2 = new Mat();
  Imgproc.GaussianBlur(tmp1, tmp2, new Size(7, 7), 1.5, 1.5);
  Imgproc.threshold(tmp2, tmp1, 110, 255, Imgproc.THRESH_BINARY);
  Imgproc.Canny(tmp1, tmp2, 10, 30);
  CVImage out = new CVImage(cap.width, cap.height);
  out.copyTo(tmp2);
```

```
    img.copyTo(tmp1);
    image(img, 0, 0);
    image(out, img.width, 0);
    text(nf(round(frameRate), 2), 10, 20);
    tmp1.release();
    tmp2.release();
}
```

The resulting image is more abstract, as shown in Figure 5-9. There will be fewer details and noise in the final image.

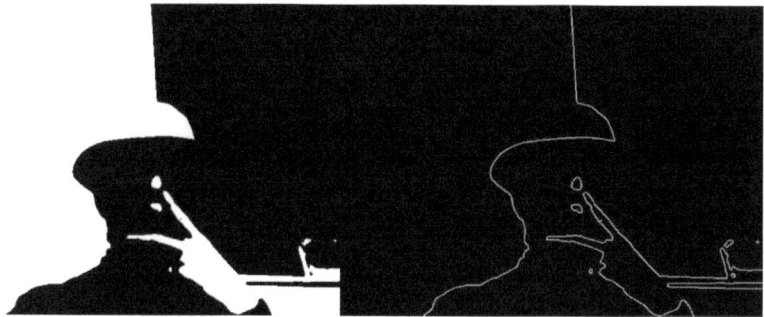

Figure 5-9. *Canny edge detection with black-and-white image*

Line Detection

Besides detecting the edge or boundary of shapes in an image, you can detect straight line segments, using the Hough line transform in OpenCV. The official OpenCV documentation has details about the mathematics behind the Hough line transform; you can find the documentation at http://docs.opencv.org/3.1.0/d9/db0/tutorial_hough_lines.html. The following exercise, Chapter05_13, is a simple implementation in Processing:

```
import processing.video.*;

Capture cap;
CVImage img;

void setup() {
    size(1280, 480);
    System.loadLibrary(Core.NATIVE_LIBRARY_NAME);
    cap = new Capture(this, width/2, height);
    cap.start();
    img = new CVImage(cap.width, cap.height);
    noStroke();
}

void draw() {
    if (!cap.available())
        return;
```

```
background(0);
cap.read();
img.copyTo(cap);
Mat tmp1 = img.getGrey();
Mat tmp2 = new Mat();
Imgproc.Canny(tmp1, tmp2, 50, 150);
MatOfPoint2f lines = new MatOfPoint2f();
Imgproc.HoughLines(tmp2, lines, 1, PI/180, 100);
CVImage out = new CVImage(cap.width, cap.height);
out.copyTo(tmp2);
image(cap, 0, 0);
image(out, cap.width, 0);
Point [] points = lines.toArray();
pushStyle();
noFill();
stroke(255);
for (Point p : points) {
  double rho = p.x;
  double theta = p.y;
  double a = cos((float)theta);
  double b = sin((float)theta);
  PVector pt1, pt2;
  double x0 = rho*a;
  double y0 = rho*b;
  pt1 = new PVector((float)(x0 + cap.width*(-b)), (float)(y0 + cap.width*(a)));
  pt2 = new PVector((float)(x0 - cap.width*(-b)), (float)(y0 - cap.width*(a)));
  line(pt1.x, pt1.y, pt2.x, pt2.y);
}
popStyle();
text(nf(round(frameRate), 2), 10, 20);
tmp1.release();
tmp2.release();
lines.release();
}
```

The main command for the line detection is the `Imgproc.HoughLines()` function. The first parameter is the black-and-white image after the Canny edge detection. The second parameter is the output matrix storing all the detected line information. Since it is a 1×N two-channel matrix, you use the subclass `MatOfPoint2f` for convenience's sake. The rest of the parameters will determine the accuracy of detection. From high-school algebra, you probably understand a line can be represented by the following:

```
y = m * x + c
```

In the `HoughLines()` function, the same line is represented by another formula.

```
rho = x * cos (theta) + y * sin(theta)
```

Here, `rho` is the perpendicular distance from the origin of the image to the line, and `theta` is the angle formed by the perpendicular line and the horizontal x-axis. The `HoughLines()` function keeps a 2D array; the first dimension is the value of `rho`, measured in pixels, and the second dimension is the value of `theta` measured in degrees.

The third parameter is the pixel resolution for the measurement of rho. The value 1 in this example indicates the resolution for rho is 1 pixel. A larger value will usually generate more lines with less accuracy. The fourth parameter is the angle resolution for the measurement of theta. The value PI/180 in this example indicates the resolution for theta is 1 degree. The fifth parameter determines how well the lines will be detected. In this example, only those lines with more than 100 points passing through will be reported. After the line detection, you convert the lines matrix into an array of Point. Each member in the array will be a line. You use the calculation inside the for loop to compute the two endpoints of each line, and finally the line() function draws the line in white.

Figure 5-10 shows the Processing window. The detected lines are drawn over the live webcam image.

Figure 5-10. *Hough line transform detection*

OpenCV has another function for line detection called HoughLinesP() that is more efficient and friendlier to use. It will return the two endpoints of each line segment. The following exercise, Chapter05_14, illustrates the use of this function:

```
import processing.video.*;

Capture cap;
CVImage img;

void setup() {
  size(1280, 480);
  System.loadLibrary(Core.NATIVE_LIBRARY_NAME);
  cap = new Capture(this, width/2, height);
  cap.start();
  img = new CVImage(cap.width, cap.height);
}

void draw() {
  if (!cap.available())
    return;
  background(0);
  cap.read();
  img.copyTo(cap);
  Mat tmp1 = img.getGrey();
  Mat tmp2 = new Mat();
  Imgproc.Canny(tmp1, tmp2, 50, 150);
  Mat lines = new Mat();
```

```
Imgproc.HoughLinesP(tmp2, lines, 1, PI/180, 80, 30, 10);
CVImage out = new CVImage(cap.width, cap.height);
out.copyTo(tmp2);
image(out, cap.width, 0);
pushStyle();
fill(100);
rect(0, 0, cap.width, cap.height);
noFill();
stroke(0);
for (int i=0; i<lines.rows(); i++) {
  double [] pts = lines.get(i, 0);
  float x1 = (float)pts[0];
  float y1 = (float)pts[1];
  float x2 = (float)pts[2];
  float y2 = (float)pts[3];
  line(x1, y1, x2, y2);
}
popStyle();
text(nf(round(frameRate), 2), 10, 20);
tmp1.release();
tmp2.release();
lines.release();
}
```

For the parameters of the HoughLinesP() function, the first one is the image matrix. The second parameter is the output matrix lines storing all the line segment information. The third parameter, 1, is the pixel resolution, while the fourth one, PI/180, is the angle resolution in degrees. The fifth parameter, 80, is the threshold value. The sixth parameter, 30, is the minimum line length. The seventh parameter, 10, is the maximum line gap. The output, lines, is a one-dimensional matrix, with only one column and multiple rows. In the for loop inside the draw() function, you loop through all the rows from lines. Each element is actually another array of size 4. The first two of them are the x and y positions of the first endpoint. The third and fourth elements of the array are the x and y positions of the second endpoint. With the two endpoints, you use the line() function to draw a straight line between them. Figure 5-11 shows the resulting image.

Figure 5-11. *Hough line transform detection*

In the next exercise, Chapter05_15, you will modify the previous one using a common technique often employed in creative image processing. For every line segment, you calculate its midpoint and sample the pixel color information. Using this color, you change the stroke color of that line segment. The result will resemble the color sketching technique in drawing.

```
import processing.video.*;

Capture cap;
CVImage img;

void setup() {
  size(1280, 480);
  System.loadLibrary(Core.NATIVE_LIBRARY_NAME);
  cap = new Capture(this, width/2, height);
  cap.start();
  img = new CVImage(cap.width, cap.height);
}

void draw() {
  if (!cap.available())
    return;
  background(0);
  cap.read();
  img.copyTo(cap);
  Mat tmp1 = img.getGrey();
  Mat tmp2 = new Mat();
  Imgproc.Canny(tmp1, tmp2, 20, 60);
  Mat lines = new Mat();
  Imgproc.HoughLinesP(tmp2, lines, 1, PI/180, 70, 30, 10);
  image(cap, 0, 0);
  pushStyle();
  noFill();
  for (int i=0; i<lines.rows(); i++) {
    double [] pts = lines.get(i, 0);
    float x1 = (float)pts[0];
    float y1 = (float)pts[1];
    float x2 = (float)pts[2];
    float y2 = (float)pts[3];
    int mx = (int)constrain((x1+x2)/2, 0, cap.width-1);
    int my = (int)constrain((y1+y2)/2, 0, cap.height-1);
    color c = cap.pixels[my*cap.width+mx];
    stroke(c);
    strokeWeight(random(1, 5));
    line(x1+cap.width, y1, x2+cap.width, y2);
  }
  popStyle();
  text(nf(round(frameRate), 2), 10, 20);
  tmp1.release();
  tmp2.release();
  lines.release();
}
```

Note that you also introduce a strokeWeight(random(1, 5)) command to use a different stroke thickness for the line segments. Figure 5-12 shows the output display.

Figure 5-12. *Line detection as drawing*

OpenCV has a LineSegmentDetector class implementing Rafael Grompone von Gioi's line segment detector. This method will first detect image gradient directions in a very small area, such as 2×2 pixels. Similar directions are concatenated together to determine whether it can be a line segment. The next exercise, Chapter05_16, re-creates the previous exercise using the new method:

```
import processing.video.*;

Capture cap;
CVImage img;
LineSegmentDetector line;

void setup() {
  size(1280, 480);
  System.loadLibrary(Core.NATIVE_LIBRARY_NAME);
  cap = new Capture(this, width/2, height);
  cap.start();
  img = new CVImage(cap.width, cap.height);
  line = Imgproc.createLineSegmentDetector();
}

void draw() {
  if (!cap.available())
    return;
  background(0);
  cap.read();
  img.copyTo(cap);
  Mat tmp1 = img.getGrey();
  Mat lines = new Mat();
  line.detect(tmp1, lines);
  pushStyle();
  for (int i=0; i<lines.rows(); i++) {
    double [] pts = lines.get(i, 0);
    float x1 = (float)pts[0];
    float y1 = (float)pts[1];
```

```
    float x2 = (float)pts[2];
    float y2 = (float)pts[3];
    int mx = (int)constrain((x1+x2)/2, 0, cap.width-1);
    int my = (int)constrain((y1+y2)/2, 0, cap.height-1);
    color col = cap.pixels[my*cap.width+mx];
    stroke(col);
    strokeWeight(random(1, 3));
    line(x1+cap.width, y1, x2+cap.width, y2);
  }
  popStyle();
  image(cap, 0, 0);
  text(nf(round(frameRate), 2), 10, 20);
  tmp1.release();
  lines.release();
}
```

You first define the global variable `line` as an instance of the `LineSegmentDetector`. In the `setup()` function, you initialize the instance using the static function `Imgproc.createLineSegmentDetector()` with the default settings. In the `draw()` function, the detection is simple. It is done using the `line.detect()` method, with the input matrix, `tmp1`, and the output result, `lines`, as parameters. The structure of the `lines` matrix is similar to the previous exercise. Each entry contains the two endpoints' x and y positions. The result display looks different from that of the previous exercise, as shown in Figure 5-13.

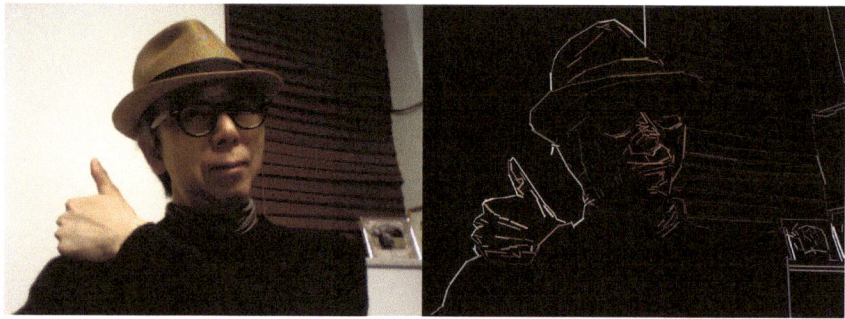

Figure 5-13. *Line detection with the OpenCV LineSegmentDetector*

Circle Detection

Similar to line detection, the OpenCV image-processing module, `imgproc`, also includes a circle detection method using the Hough circle transform, `HoughCircles()`. In the next exercise, `Chapter05_17`, you will explore this function to detect circular shapes from the prepared image from the live webcam:

```
import processing.video.*;

Capture cap;
CVImage img;

void setup() {
  size(1280, 480);
  System.loadLibrary(Core.NATIVE_LIBRARY_NAME);
```

```
  cap = new Capture(this, width/2, height);
  cap.start();
  img = new CVImage(cap.width, cap.height);
}

void draw() {
  if (!cap.available())
    return;
  background(0);
  cap.read();
  img.copyTo(cap);
  Mat tmp1 = img.getGrey();
  Mat tmp2 = new Mat();
  Imgproc.GaussianBlur(tmp1, tmp2, new Size(9, 9), 1);
  Imgproc.Canny(tmp2, tmp1, 100, 200);
  CVImage out = new CVImage(cap.width, cap.height);
  out.copyTo(tmp1);
  MatOfPoint3f circles = new MatOfPoint3f();
  Imgproc.HoughCircles(tmp1, circles, Imgproc.HOUGH_GRADIENT, 1, tmp1.rows()/8, 200, 45, 0, 0);
  Point3 [] points = circles.toArray();
  image(cap, 0, 0);
  image(out, cap.width, 0);
  pushStyle();
  noStroke();
  fill(0, 0, 255, 100);
  for (Point3 p : points) {
    ellipse((float)p.x, (float)p.y, (float)(p.z*2), (float)(p.z*2));
  }
  popStyle();
  text(nf(round(frameRate), 2), 10, 20);
  tmp1.release();
  tmp2.release();
  circles.release();
}
```

The program prepares the image first by changing it to grayscale, then by applying the Gaussian blur filter, and finally by detecting the edges. The Canny edge image is then sent to the HoughCircles() function for circle detection. The first parameter, tmp1, is the input image. The second parameter, circles, is the output result. The third parameter, Imgproc.HOUGH_GRADIENT, is the only option for circle detection. The fourth parameter is the inverse ratio of resolution. It is normally 1. The fifth parameter, tmp1.rows()/8, is the minimum distance between circles being detected. The sixth parameter, 200, is the upper threshold of the internal Canny edge detector. The seventh parameter, 45, is the threshold of center detection. The smaller the value, the more circles it will detect. The rest of the parameters are the minimum and maximum values for the radius. They default to 0. The result, circles, is a one-dimensional matrix. You use a MatOfPoint3f to store its value. Each entry will contain an array of three values, corresponding to the circle center (x, y positions) and the radius. The for loop goes through all the circles and displays them in a semitransparent blue color. Figure 5-14 shows the resulting image.

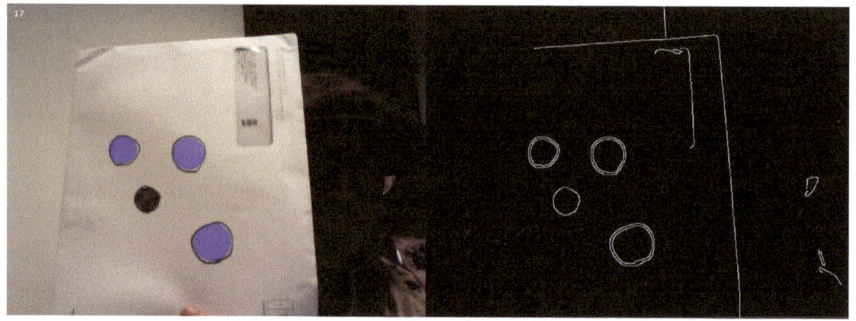

Figure 5-14. *Hough circle transform for circle detection*

You can play around with the circle detection program by overdoing the detection. In the following exercise, Chapter05_18, you purposely put a small value in the seventh parameter of the HoughCircles() function such that it generates a lot of false detection. Here is the source of the program:

```
import processing.video.*;

Capture cap;
CVImage img;

void setup() {
  size(1280, 480);
  System.loadLibrary(Core.NATIVE_LIBRARY_NAME);
  cap = new Capture(this, width/2, height);
  cap.start();
  img = new CVImage(cap.width, cap.height);
}

void draw() {
  if (!cap.available())
    return;
  background(0);
  cap.read();
  img.copyTo(cap);
  MatOfPoint3f circles = new MatOfPoint3f();
  Imgproc.HoughCircles(img.getGrey(), circles, Imgproc.HOUGH_GRADIENT, 1, img.height/10,
  200, 20, 0, 0);
  Point3 [] points = circles.toArray();
  pushStyle();
  noStroke();
  for (Point3 p : points) {
    int x1 = constrain((int)p.x, 0, cap.width-1);
    int y1 = constrain((int)p.y, 0, cap.height-1);
    color col = cap.pixels[y1*cap.width+x1];
    fill(color(red(col), green(col), blue(col), 160));
    ellipse(x1+cap.width, y1, (float)(p.z*2), (float)(p.z*2));
  }
```

```
  popStyle();
  image(cap, 0, 0);
  text(nf(round(frameRate), 2), 10, 20);
  circles.release();
}
```

You also remove the preparation steps with a hope to generate more circles. Within the `for` loop, you use the former technique to color the circle. In this version, you also use a semitransparent color for each circle. Figure 5-15 shows the resulting display.

Figure 5-15. *Drawing with Hough circle transform*

The image is an abstract rendering of the original webcam image. You can recognize the similarity in terms of color use and the position of the circles. For the shapes, you can hardly relate them with the original.

Contours Processing

In previous sections, you employed the OpenCV image-processing module, `imgproc`, to identify specific shapes from a digital image. In *contours processing*, you use the same module to identify more general outlines of the graphical shapes. It involves finding the contours and ways to interpret the contour information. Since the functions will work only on binary images, you have to prepare the images so that they contain only black-and-white information. I will cover the following steps in contours processing:

- Finding the contours
- Bounding box
- Minimum area rectangle
- Convex hull
- Polygon approximation
- Testing a point in contour
- Checking intersection

Finding the Contours

In the next exercise, Chapter05_19, the program first blurs the grayscale image and then extracts the edges with the Canny() function, before sending it to the findContours() function:

```
import processing.video.*;
import java.util.ArrayList;
import java.util.Iterator;

Capture cap;
CVImage img;

void setup() {
  size(1280, 480);
  System.loadLibrary(Core.NATIVE_LIBRARY_NAME);
  cap = new Capture(this, width/2, height);
  cap.start();
  img = new CVImage(cap.width, cap.height);
}

void draw() {
  if (!cap.available())
    return;
  background(0);
  cap.read();
  img.copyTo(cap);
  Mat tmp1 = img.getGrey();
  Mat tmp2 = new Mat();
  Imgproc.blur(tmp1, tmp2, new Size(3, 3));
  Imgproc.Canny(tmp2, tmp1, 50, 100);
  ArrayList<MatOfPoint> contours = new ArrayList<MatOfPoint>();
  Mat hierarchy = new Mat();
  Imgproc.findContours(tmp1, contours, hierarchy,
    Imgproc.RETR_LIST, Imgproc.CHAIN_APPROX_SIMPLE);
  image(cap, 0, 0);
  pushStyle();
  noFill();
  stroke(255, 255, 0);
  Iterator<MatOfPoint> it = contours.iterator();
  while (it.hasNext()) {
    Point [] pts = it.next().toArray();
    for (int i=0; i<pts.length-1; i++) {
      Point p1 = pts[i];
      Point p2 = pts[i+1];
      line((float)p1.x+cap.width, (float)p1.y, (float)p2.x+cap.width, (float)p2.y);
    }
  }
  popStyle();
  text(nf(round(frameRate), 2), 10, 20);
  tmp1.release();
  tmp2.release();
}
```

In the findContours() function, the first parameter is the black-and-white image. The second parameter is the output contours data structure. The third parameter is the hierarchy information keeping track of the relationship of the outer edges and the inner holes. The fourth parameter, Imgproc.RETR_LIST, retrieves contours information without keeping track of the hierarchy relationship. The fifth parameter, Imgproc.CHAIN_APPROX_SIMPLE, compresses the contour line segments into two endpoints only. You will use other options in later exercises. The major output, contours, is a Java ArrayList of MatOfPoint. Each MatOfPoint is converted into an array of Point. The for loop draws a line segment from one Point to the next. Figure 5-16 shows the resulting image.

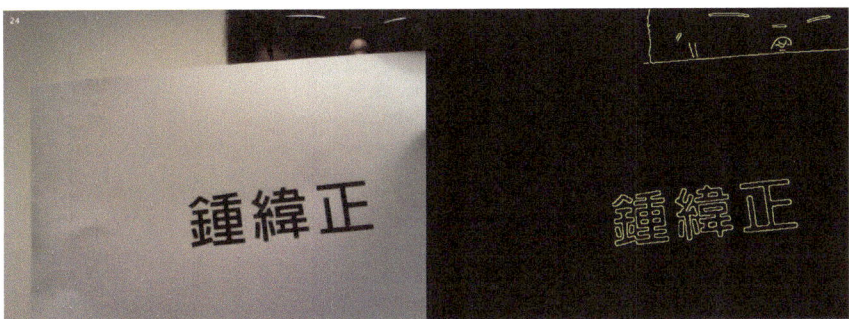

Figure 5-16. *Contours processing with black-and-white Canny image*

Instead of using a Canny edge detected image, the next exercise, Chapter05_20, uses a black-and-white image prepared by the threshold() function:

```
import processing.video.*;
import java.util.ArrayList;

Capture cap;
CVImage img;

void setup() {
  size(1280, 480);
  System.loadLibrary(Core.NATIVE_LIBRARY_NAME);
  cap = new Capture(this, width/2, height);
  cap.start();
  img = new CVImage(cap.width, cap.height);
}

void draw() {
  if (!cap.available())
    return;
  background(0);
  cap.read();
  img.copyTo(cap);
  Mat tmp1 = img.getGrey();
  Mat tmp2 = new Mat();
  Imgproc.blur(tmp1, tmp2, new Size(5, 5));
  Imgproc.threshold(tmp2, tmp1, 80, 255, Imgproc.THRESH_BINARY);
  ArrayList<MatOfPoint> contours = new ArrayList<MatOfPoint>();
```

```
Mat hierarchy = new Mat();
tmp1 = tmp2.clone();
Imgproc.findContours(tmp1, contours, hierarchy,
  Imgproc.RETR_LIST, Imgproc.CHAIN_APPROX_SIMPLE);
CVImage out = new CVImage(cap.width, cap.height);
out.copyTo(tmp1);
image(out, 0, 0);
pushStyle();
noFill();
stroke(255, 255, 0);
for (MatOfPoint ps : contours) {
  Point [] pts = ps.toArray();
  for (int i=0; i<pts.length-1; i++) {
    Point p1 = pts[i];
    Point p2 = pts[i+1];
    line((float)p1.x+cap.width, (float)p1.y, (float)p2.x+cap.width, (float)p2.y);
  }
}
popStyle();
text(nf(round(frameRate), 2), 10, 20);
tmp1.release();
tmp2.release();

}
```

The exercise employs the `threshold()` function to convert the gray image into pure black-and-white. The `findContours()` function can immediately perform contour tracing on top of the black-and-white image. In the two exercises, I also demonstrate the different ways to traverse the Java `List` of `MatOfPoint` using both a `for` loop and `iterator`. Figure 5-17 shows the resulting image.

Figure 5-17. *Contours processing with threshold image*

In the coming exercise, Chapter05_21, you use another option in the `findContours()` function to retrieve only the external outlines without returning those inner holes. You replace the original option `Imgproc.RETR_LIST` with `Imgproc.RETR_EXTERNAL`. The rest remains the same. The new statement is as follows:

```
Imgproc.findContours(tmp2, contours, hierarchy, Imgproc.RETR_EXTERNAL, Imgproc.CHAIN_APPROX_
SIMPLE);
```

As shown in Figure 5-18, the inner contours of the Chinese characters are not visible with the new option.

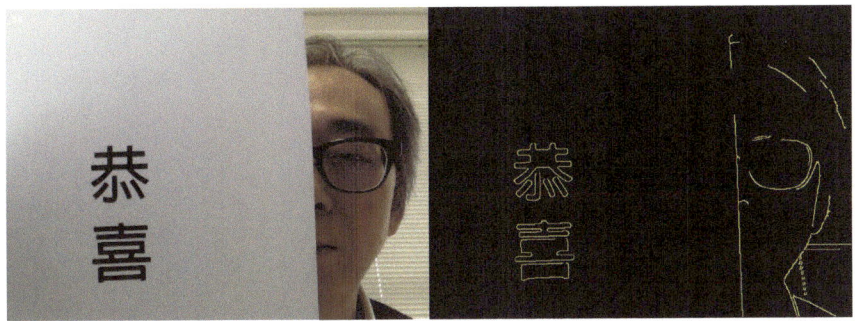

Figure 5-18. *Contours processing with the RETR_EXTERNAL option*

You will now further explore other options in the contour retrieve mode. The next exercise, Chapter05_22, will use a more complex one, RETR_CCOMP. It organizes all contours into two levels. All external boundaries will be in the top level. The holes will be in the second level. For any contours inside a hole will also be in the top level. In the exercise, you can make use of such information to fill the external contours and holes with two different colors. The source image size used in the program is 600×600 pixels.

```
import java.util.ArrayList;

CVImage cvimg;
PImage img;

void setup() {
  size(1200, 600);
  System.loadLibrary(Core.NATIVE_LIBRARY_NAME);
  img = loadImage("chinese.png");
  cvimg = new CVImage(img.width, img.height);
  noLoop();
}

void draw() {
  background(0);
  cvimg.copyTo(img);
  Mat tmp1 = new Mat();
  Imgproc.blur(cvimg.getGrey(), tmp1, new Size(3, 3));
  ArrayList<MatOfPoint> contours = new ArrayList<MatOfPoint>();
  Mat hierarchy = new Mat();
  Imgproc.findContours(tmp1, contours, hierarchy,
    Imgproc.RETR_CCOMP, Imgproc.CHAIN_APPROX_SIMPLE);
  image(img, 0, 0);
  pushStyle();
  stroke(255);
  for (int i=0; i<contours.size(); i++) {
    Point [] pts = contours.get(i).toArray();
    int parent = (int)hierarchy.get(0, i)[3];
    // parent -1 implies it is the outer contour.
    if (parent == -1) {
```

```
      fill(200);
    } else {
      fill(100);
    }
    beginShape();
    for (Point p : pts) {
      vertex((float)p.x+img.width, (float)p.y);
    }
    endShape(CLOSE);
  }
  popStyle();
  tmp1.release();
  hierarchy.release();

}
```

Besides changing the retrieve mode to RETR_CCOMP, you use the hierarchy matrix. It is a one-dimensional matrix. Each column corresponds to one entry in the contours matrix, with the same index arrangement. Each entry in the hierarchy is an array with four values. Each value is an index to the entry in the contours matrix. The mapping of the index is as follows:

- hierarchy.get(0, i)[0]: The next sibling contour

- hierarchy.get(0, i)[1]: The previous sibling contour

- hierarchy.get(0, i)[2]: The first child contour

- hierarchy.get(0, i)[3]: The parent contour

A value of -1 in the index indicates the corresponding entry is not available. If you take a look at the for loop inside the draw() function, the statement inspects the parent index of the current contour at position i.

```
int parent = (int)hierarchy.get(0, i)[3];
```

If it does not have any parent (-1), you color it with a lighter gray (if it does, you color it with darker gray). Figure 5-19 shows the resulting image. The Chinese characters on the left are from the original image. The image on the right is the rendering of the contours with two shades of gray tone.

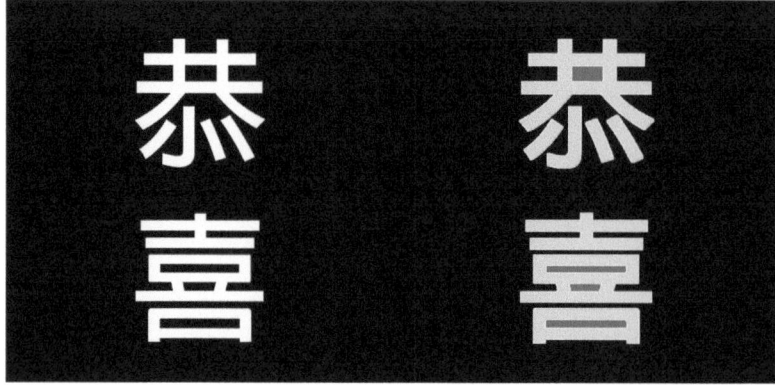

Figure 5-19. *Contours processing with option RETR_CCOMP*

There is also one more retrieve mode, RETR_TREE, where it will store in the hierarchy matrix the complete tree relationship of parent and children for each contour. Owing to its complexity, I will not cover it in this book.

After you detect the contours of the graphical shapes, drawing the contours will not be your only concern. You may want to determine the interaction among moving graphical shapes or to check overlapping regions. In the coming sections, you will investigate how you can make sense of the contour information detected from the image.

Bounding Box

The first information you can obtain from the contour information is its bounding box. You use the boundingRect() function from the OpenCV image-processing module. The input parameter is one contour, as maintained by a MatOfPoint class instance. The output is the OpenCV rectangle class, Rect.

```
import processing.video.*;
import java.util.ArrayList;
import java.util.Iterator;

Capture cap;
CVImage img;

void setup() {
  size(1280, 480);
  System.loadLibrary(Core.NATIVE_LIBRARY_NAME);
  cap = new Capture(this, width/2, height);
  cap.start();
  img = new CVImage(cap.width, cap.height);
}

void draw() {
  if (!cap.available())
    return;
  background(0);
  cap.read();
  img.copyTo(cap);
  Mat tmp1 = img.getGrey();
  Mat tmp2 = new Mat();
  Imgproc.blur(tmp1, tmp2, new Size(3, 3));
  Imgproc.Canny(tmp2, tmp1, 80, 160);
  ArrayList<MatOfPoint> contours = new ArrayList<MatOfPoint>();
  Mat hierarchy = new Mat();
  Imgproc.findContours(tmp1, contours, hierarchy,
    Imgproc.RETR_LIST, Imgproc.CHAIN_APPROX_SIMPLE);
  image(cap, 0, 0);
  pushStyle();
  noStroke();
  Iterator<MatOfPoint> it = contours.iterator();
  while (it.hasNext()) {
    Rect r = Imgproc.boundingRect(it.next());
    int cx = (int)(r.x + r.width/2);
    int cy = (int)(r.y + r.height/2);
    cx = constrain(cx, 0, cap.width-1);
```

```
    cy = constrain(cy, 0, cap.height-1);
    color col = cap.pixels[cy*cap.width+cx];
    fill(color(red(col), green(col), blue(col), 200));
    rect((float)r.x+cap.width, (float)r.y, (float)r.width, (float)r.height);
  }
  popStyle();
  text(nf(round(frameRate), 2), 10, 20);
  tmp1.release();
  tmp2.release();
}
```

In this program, Chapter05_23, once you obtain each of the bounding box's data as a Rect, you use the Processing function rect() to draw the rectangle. The Rect class contains four attributes: x, y, width, and height. You also obtain the color information from the center of the rectangle and use it to color the rectangle with transparency. The result is an abstract rendering of the original image, as shown in Figure 5-20.

Figure 5-20. *Bounding rectangle for contours*

Minimum Area Rectangle

The OpenCV image-processing module has another function, minAreaRect(), to compute the minimum-area bounding rectangle of the contour. In the next exercise, Chapter05_24, you will obtain the minimum area's rotated rectangles for the contours. The result is a rotated rectangle of the class RotatedRect.

```
import processing.video.*;
import java.util.ArrayList;
import java.util.Iterator;

Capture cap;
CVImage img;

void setup() {
  size(1280, 480);
  System.loadLibrary(Core.NATIVE_LIBRARY_NAME);
  cap = new Capture(this, width/2, height);
  cap.start();
  img = new CVImage(cap.width, cap.height);
}
```

```
void draw() {
  if (!cap.available())
    return;
  background(0);
  cap.read();
  img.copyTo(cap);
  Mat tmp1 = img.getGrey();
  Mat tmp2 = new Mat();
  Imgproc.blur(tmp1, tmp2, new Size(3, 3));
  Imgproc.Canny(tmp2, tmp1, 100, 200);
  ArrayList<MatOfPoint> contours = new ArrayList<MatOfPoint>();
  Mat hierarchy = new Mat();
  Imgproc.findContours(tmp1, contours, hierarchy,
    Imgproc.RETR_LIST, Imgproc.CHAIN_APPROX_SIMPLE);
  image(cap, 0, 0);
  pushStyle();
  rectMode(CENTER);
  noFill();
  strokeWeight(2);
  Iterator<MatOfPoint> it = contours.iterator();
  while (it.hasNext()) {
    RotatedRect r = Imgproc.minAreaRect(new MatOfPoint2f(it.next().toArray()));
    int cx = constrain((int)r.center.x, 0, cap.width-1);
    int cy = constrain((int)r.center.y, 0, cap.height-1);
    color col = cap.pixels[cy*cap.width+cx];
    stroke(col);
    Point [] pts = new Point[4];
    r.points(pts);
    beginShape();
    for (int i=0; i<pts.length; i++) {
      vertex((float)pts[i].x+cap.width, (float)pts[i].y);
    }
    endShape(CLOSE);
  }
  popStyle();
  text(nf(round(frameRate), 2), 10, 20);
  tmp1.release();
  tmp2.release();
}
```

The minAreaRect() function accepts a parameter in the format of MatOfPoint2f. Each member from the contours output is an instance of MatOfPoint. In this case, you have to convert it to the proper class, MatOfPoint2f, before it can be used in the minAreaRect() function. The following statement can perform the conversion:

```
new MatOfPoint2f(it.next().toArray())
```

The RotatedRect instance, r, has the property center that maintains the center position of the rotated rectangle. You use the center point to find out the color information for the drawing of the rectangle. To draw the rectangle, you use the points() method to compute the four corner points of the rotated rectangle. The result is a Point array, pts. With the four corner points, you can use the beginShape() and endShape(CLOSE) methods to draw the rectangle, by specifying the vertices. Figure 5-21 shows the output image.

Figure 5-21. *Minimum-area rectangle of contour*

Convex Hull

In addition to the bounding box, you can use OpenCV to find the convex hull of the contour information. The function that you use is convexHull(). It takes the MatOfPoint contour information and outputs a MatOfInt matrix, hull. The output is actually a Point array of the indices to the contour. In principle, the number of entries in the hull is less than the Point array, pts, because it contains only the points making up the convex shape.

```
import java.util.ArrayList;
import java.util.Iterator;

CVImage cv;
PImage img;

void setup() {
  size(1200, 600);
  background(50);
  System.loadLibrary(Core.NATIVE_LIBRARY_NAME);
  img = loadImage("chinese.png");
  cv = new CVImage(img.width, img.height);
  noLoop();
}

void draw() {
  cv.copyTo(img);
  Mat tmp1 = cv.getGrey();
  Mat tmp2 = new Mat();
  Imgproc.blur(tmp1, tmp2, new Size(3, 3));
  Imgproc.Canny(tmp2, tmp1, 100, 200);
  ArrayList<MatOfPoint> contours = new ArrayList<MatOfPoint>();
  Mat hierarchy = new Mat();
  Imgproc.findContours(tmp1, contours, hierarchy,
    Imgproc.RETR_LIST, Imgproc.CHAIN_APPROX_SIMPLE);
  image(img, 0, 0);
  pushStyle();
  noFill();
  stroke(250);
  Iterator<MatOfPoint> it = contours.iterator();
```

```
while (it.hasNext()) {
  MatOfInt hull = new MatOfInt();
  MatOfPoint mPt = it.next();
  Point [] pts = mPt.toArray();
  Imgproc.convexHull(mPt, hull);
  int [] indices = hull.toArray();
  beginShape();
  for (int i=0; i<indices.length; i++) {
    vertex((float)pts[indices[i]].x+img.width, (float)pts[indices[i]].y);
  }
  endShape(CLOSE);
  hull.release();
  mPt.release();
}
popStyle();
tmp1.release();
tmp2.release();
}
```

In this program, Chapter05_25, you use the Chinese characters for testing. The result will be more obvious. Within the while loop, you go through each contour and create a closed shape using the vertices from the hull array. Figure 5-22 shows the resulting image for reference. The characters on the left side are the originals, while the figures on the right side are convex hulls from the contours.

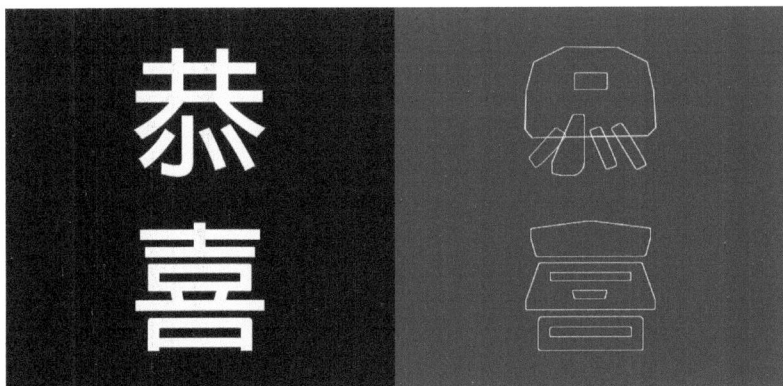

Figure 5-22. *Convex hull processing in OpenCV*

Polygon Approximation

In addition to using the convex hull to simplify a contour, OpenCV provides other methods to streamline a contour. The next exercise, Chapter05_26, introduces a way to approximate a polygon for a given contour. The function is approxPolyDP().

```
import processing.video.*;
import java.util.ArrayList;
import java.util.Iterator;
```

```
Capture cap;
CVImage img;

void setup() {
  size(1280, 480);
  System.loadLibrary(Core.NATIVE_LIBRARY_NAME);
  cap = new Capture(this, width/2, height);
  cap.start();
  img = new CVImage(cap.width, cap.height);
}

void draw() {
  if (!cap.available())
    return;
  background(0);
  cap.read();
  img.copyTo(cap);
  Mat tmp1 = img.getGrey();
  Mat tmp2 = new Mat();
  Imgproc.blur(tmp1, tmp2, new Size(3, 3));
  Imgproc.Canny(tmp2, tmp1, 100, 200);
  ArrayList<MatOfPoint> contours = new ArrayList<MatOfPoint>();
  Mat hierarchy = new Mat();
  Imgproc.findContours(tmp1, contours, hierarchy,
    Imgproc.RETR_LIST, Imgproc.CHAIN_APPROX_SIMPLE);
  image(cap, 0, 0);
  pushStyle();
  noFill();
  Iterator<MatOfPoint> it = contours.iterator();
  while (it.hasNext()) {
    strokeWeight(random(5));
    stroke(255, random(160, 256));
    MatOfPoint2f poly = new MatOfPoint2f();
    Imgproc.approxPolyDP(new MatOfPoint2f(it.next().toArray()), poly, 3, true);
    Point [] pts = poly.toArray();
    beginShape();
    for (int i=0; i<pts.length; i++) {
      vertex((float)pts[i].x+cap.width, (float)pts[i].y);
    }
    endShape(CLOSE);
  }
  popStyle();
  text(nf(round(frameRate), 2), 10, 20);
  tmp1.release();
  tmp2.release();
}
```

Within the while loop, you pass each of the contours to the approxPolyDP() function. The first parameter is the contour information converted to MatOfPoint2f. The second parameter, poly, is the output polygon information stored as another MatOfPoint2f. The third parameter is the approximation accuracy. A smaller value will have a closer approximation. The true value in the fourth parameter shows that the approximated curve is closed. Note that you also vary the stroke weight and stroke color to simulate a hand-drawn animation effect. Figure 5-23 shows the resulting image.

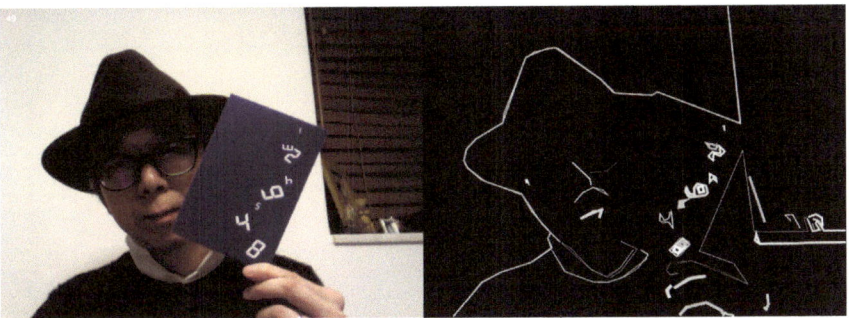

Figure 5-23. *Polygon approximation*

Testing a Point in Contour

The next exercise, Chapter05_27, is an interactive one because you can use the mouse to change the fill() color of the contours. Within the draw() function, before you draw each contour, you perform a test to see if the current mouse position, mouseX and mouseY, is inside it, by using the function pointPolygonTest(). As you are using the right side of the window, you have to subtract the mouseX value by half of the window size, i.e., cap.width. To use the pointPolygonTest() function, you first convert your current contour information, mp, by converting it from MatOfPoint to MatOfPoint2f and pass it as the first parameter. The second parameter is the mouse position stored in a Point object instance. The third Boolean parameter indicates whether you want to return the distance data. For this exercise, you use false to return an indicator to show whether the point is inside or outside the contour. A positive value indicates that the point is inside the contour, a negative value is outside, and zero is just on an edge.

```
import processing.video.*;
import java.util.ArrayList;
import java.util.Iterator;

Capture cap;
CVImage img;

void setup() {
  size(1280, 480);
  System.loadLibrary(Core.NATIVE_LIBRARY_NAME);
  cap = new Capture(this, width/2, height);
  cap.start();
  img = new CVImage(cap.width, cap.height);
}
```

```
void draw() {
  if (!cap.available())
    return;
  background(250);
  cap.read();
  img.copyTo(cap);
  Mat tmp1 = img.getGrey();
  Mat tmp2 = new Mat();
  Imgproc.blur(tmp1, tmp2, new Size(3, 3));
  Imgproc.Canny(tmp2, tmp1, 80, 160);
  ArrayList<MatOfPoint> contours = new ArrayList<MatOfPoint>();
  Mat hierarchy = new Mat();
  Imgproc.findContours(tmp1, contours, hierarchy,
    Imgproc.RETR_LIST, Imgproc.CHAIN_APPROX_SIMPLE);
  image(cap, 0, 0);
  pushStyle();
  stroke(50);
  Iterator<MatOfPoint> it = contours.iterator();
  while (it.hasNext()) {
    MatOfPoint mp = it.next();
    Point [] pts = mp.toArray();
    boolean inside = true;
    if (mouseX < cap.width) {
      noFill();
    } else {
      int mx = constrain(mouseX-cap.width, 0, cap.width-1);
      int my = constrain(mouseY, 0, cap.height-1);
      double result = Imgproc.pointPolygonTest(new MatOfPoint2f(pts),
        new Point(mx, my), false);
      if (result > 0) {
        fill(255, 0, 0);
      } else {
        noFill();
      }
    }
    beginShape();
    for (int i=0; i<pts.length; i++) {
      vertex((float)pts[i].x+cap.width, (float)pts[i].y);
    }
    endShape(CLOSE);
  }
  popStyle();
  text(nf(round(frameRate), 2), 10, 20);
  tmp1.release();
  tmp2.release();
  hierarchy.release();
}
```

In this program, you set the fill() color to red when the mouse position is inside the contour. Otherwise, it will be noFill(). Figure 5-24 shows the moment when the mouse position is inside the hole formed by the fingers.

Figure 5-24. *Testing whether a point is inside a contour with pointPolygonTest*

Checking Intersection

Before moving on to the general shape-matching section, I will summarize the use of contour processing with one more exercise, Chapter05_28. In this exercise, you will refer to the use of RotatedRect in the former exercise, Chapter05_24, and perform the detection between a fixed rectangular region and the rotated rectangles generated from the live webcam image on the screen.

```
import processing.video.*;
import java.util.ArrayList;
import java.util.Iterator;

Capture cap;
CVImage img;
float minArea, maxArea;
RotatedRect rRect;

void setup() {
  size(1280, 480);
  System.loadLibrary(Core.NATIVE_LIBRARY_NAME);
  cap = new Capture(this, width/2, height);
  cap.start();
  img = new CVImage(cap.width, cap.height);
  minArea = 50;
  maxArea = 6000;
  // This is the fixed rectangular region of size 200x200.
  rRect = new RotatedRect(new Point(cap.width/2, cap.height/2),
    new Size(200, 200), 0);
  rectMode(CENTER);
}

void draw() {
  if (!cap.available())
    return;
  background(0);
  cap.read();
  img.copyTo(cap);
  Mat tmp1 = img.getGrey();
  Mat tmp2 = new Mat();
```

```
Imgproc.blur(tmp1, tmp2, new Size(3, 3));
Imgproc.Canny(tmp2, tmp1, 100, 200);
ArrayList<MatOfPoint> contours = new ArrayList<MatOfPoint>();
Mat hierarchy = new Mat();
Imgproc.findContours(tmp1, contours, hierarchy,
  Imgproc.RETR_LIST, Imgproc.CHAIN_APPROX_SIMPLE);
// Draw the fixed rectangular region.
pushStyle();
fill(255, 20);
stroke(0, 0, 255);
rect((float)rRect.center.x+cap.width,
  (float)rRect.center.y, (float)rRect.size.width,
  (float)rRect.size.height);
popStyle();

pushStyle();
Iterator<MatOfPoint> it = contours.iterator();
while (it.hasNext()) {
  MatOfPoint ctr = it.next();
  float area = (float)Imgproc.contourArea(ctr);
  // Exclude the large and small rectangles
  if (area < minArea || area > maxArea)
    continue;
  // Obtain the rotated rectangles from each contour.
  RotatedRect r = Imgproc.minAreaRect(new MatOfPoint2f(ctr.toArray()));
  Point [] pts = new Point[4];
  r.points(pts);
  stroke(255, 255, 0);
  noFill();
  // Draw the rotated rectangles.
  beginShape();
  for (int i=0; i<pts.length; i++) {
    vertex((float)pts[i].x+cap.width, (float)pts[i].y);
  }
  endShape(CLOSE);
  // Compute the intersection between the fixed region and
  // each rotated rectangle.
  MatOfPoint2f inter = new MatOfPoint2f();
  int rc = Imgproc.rotatedRectangleIntersection(r, rRect, inter);
  //  Skip the cases with no intersection.
  if (rc == Imgproc.INTERSECT_NONE)
    continue;
  // Obtain the convex hull of the intersection polygon.
  MatOfInt idx = new MatOfInt();
  MatOfPoint mp = new MatOfPoint(inter.toArray());
  Imgproc.convexHull(mp, idx);
  int [] idArray = idx.toArray();
  Point [] ptArray = mp.toArray();
  // Fill the intersection area.
  noStroke();
  fill(255, 100);
```

```
    beginShape();
    for (int i=0; i<idArray.length; i++) {
      Point p = ptArray[idArray[i]];
      vertex((float)p.x+cap.width, (float)p.y);
    }
    endShape(CLOSE);
    inter.release();
    idx.release();
    mp.release();
  }
  popStyle();
  image(cap, 0, 0);
  text(nf(round(frameRate), 2), 10, 20);
  tmp1.release();
  tmp2.release();
  hierarchy.release();
}
```

The program first defines a fixed region using a RotatedRect instance, rRect. It position is at the center of the video capture screen with the size of 200×200 pixels. In the draw() function, you first retrieve all the contours from the webcam image. For each contour, you screen out those with a size either too small or too large. For the remaining ones, you compute the minimum-area rotated rectangles stored in the variable r. With each rotated rectangle r, you check it against the fixed region rRect with this statement:

```
int rc = Imgproc.rotatedRectangleIntersection(r, rRect, inter);
```

If there is intersection between them, the vertex information will be in the MatOfPoint2f variable inter. The return code, rc, will actually tell you the type of interaction that occurred. The possible values for rc are as follows:

- Imgproc.INTERSECT_NONE (no overlapping area)
- Imgproc.INTERSECT_PARTIAL (with overlapping area)
- Imgproc.INTERSECT_FULL (one rectangle inside the other)

You can find a detailed description of the check at http://docs.opencv.org/3.1.0/d3/dc0/group__imgproc__shape.html. For those cases with intersection, you try to draw the overlapping area with a semitransparent fill color. Nevertheless, you find that the order of vertices returned from the variable, inter, does not guarantee a convex shape. In the program, you add a few lines to find the convex hull from the vertices in inter before you draw them on the screen. Figure 5-25 shows the sample output display from the program.

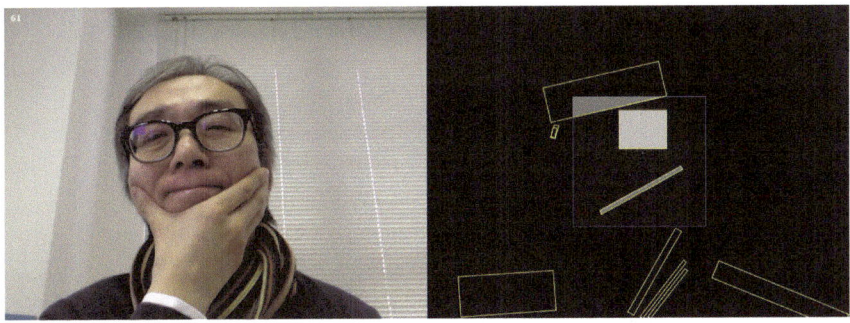

Figure 5-25. *Finding intersection between rotated rectangles*

Shape Detection

In this last section of this chapter, I introduce the shape-matching function, matchShapes(), in the OpenCV image-processing module. The working mechanism for the exercise, Chapter05_29, is to build a shape template that you would like to match the live webcam image with. In this case, you will use the Chinese character shown in Figure 5-26. You can also create your own patterns. Any white shapes on top of a black background will usually work well. The size of this pattern image is 640×480 pixels.

Figure 5-26. *Sample Chinese character to match with*

The program will load the image from the data folder and build the contour with the findContours() function you learned about in the previous sections. Since you have prior knowledge of this character that it contains only one contour, you just store the first contour in a MatOfPoint variable. The prepareChar() function in the following source code performs this function:

```
import processing.video.*;
import java.util.ArrayList;
import java.util.Iterator;

Capture cap;
PImage img;
CVImage cv;
MatOfPoint ch;
float maxVal;

void setup() {
  size(1280, 480);
  System.loadLibrary(Core.NATIVE_LIBRARY_NAME);
  cap = new Capture(this, width/2, height);
  cap.start();
  img = loadImage("chinese.png");
  ch = prepareChar(img);
  cv = new CVImage(cap.width, cap.height);
  maxVal = 5;
}

MatOfPoint prepareChar(PImage i) {
  CVImage chr = new CVImage(i.width, i.height);
  chr.copyTo(i);
  Mat tmp1 = chr.getGrey();
  Mat tmp2 = new Mat();
  Imgproc.blur(tmp1, tmp2, new Size(3, 3));
  Imgproc.threshold(tmp2, tmp1, 127, 255, Imgproc.THRESH_BINARY);
```

```
  Mat hierarchy = new Mat();
  ArrayList<MatOfPoint> contours = new ArrayList<MatOfPoint>();
  Imgproc.findContours(tmp1, contours, hierarchy,
    Imgproc.RETR_LIST, Imgproc.CHAIN_APPROX_SIMPLE);
  tmp1.release();
  tmp2.release();
  hierarchy.release();
  return contours.get(0);
}

void draw() {
  if (!cap.available())
    return;
  background(0);
  cap.read();
  cv.copyTo(cap);
  Mat tmp1 = cv.getGrey();
  Mat tmp2 = new Mat();
  Imgproc.blur(tmp1, tmp2, new Size(3, 3));
  Imgproc.Canny(tmp2, tmp1, 100, 200);
  ArrayList<MatOfPoint> contours = new ArrayList<MatOfPoint>();
  Mat hierarchy = new Mat();
  Imgproc.findContours(tmp1, contours, hierarchy,
    Imgproc.RETR_LIST, Imgproc.CHAIN_APPROX_SIMPLE);
  Iterator<MatOfPoint> it = contours.iterator();
  pushStyle();
  while (it.hasNext()) {
    MatOfPoint cont = it.next();
    double val = Imgproc.matchShapes(ch, cont, Imgproc.CV_CONTOURS_MATCH_I1, 0);
    if (val > maxVal)
      continue;
    RotatedRect r = Imgproc.minAreaRect(new MatOfPoint2f(cont.toArray()));
    Point ctr = r.center;
    noStroke();
    fill(255, 200, 0);
    text((float)val, (float)ctr.x+cap.width, (float)ctr.y);
    Point [] pts = cont.toArray();
    noFill();
    stroke(100);
    beginShape();
    for (int i=0; i<pts.length; i++) {
      vertex((float)pts[i].x+cap.width, (float)pts[i].y);
    }
    endShape(CLOSE);
  }
  popStyle();
  image(cap, 0, 0);
  text(nf(round(frameRate), 2), 10, 20);
  tmp1.release();
  tmp2.release();
  hierarchy.release();
}
```

173

Within the draw() function, you go through each contour from the live webcam image. You use the matchShapes() function to perform the matching. The first two parameters are the Chinese character contour and each of the live webcam image contours. The rest are the matching method and a dummy parameter. The return value, val, indicates how close the matching is; the smaller the value, the better. You also exclude those contours with a return value larger than the threshold maxVal. You employ the minAreaRect() function to find out the center of the contour in order to display the matching value on the screen. The rest of the program is similar to those in previous sections to draw each contour.

In the test shown in Figure 5-27, the sample characters are not the same as the stored one. The matching values range from 1.5 to 3.5.

Figure 5-27. *Shape-matching test with other characters*

In the next test, shown in Figure 5-28, one out of the three characters is the correct one. The matching value for the correct character is around 0.6.

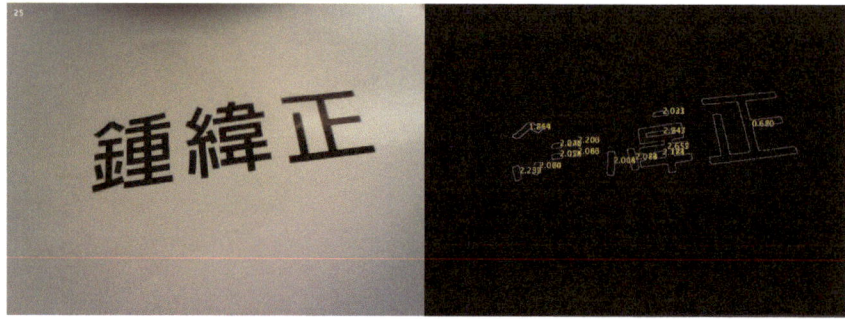

Figure 5-28. *Shape-matching test with one correct character*

In the next test, shown in Figure 5-29, you use the same three characters but with an upside-down orientation. The matching value for the correct character is around 0.4.

Figure 5-29. *Shape-matching test with upside-down characters*

In the next test, shown in Figure 5-30, you use a hand-drawn character. The matching value for the sample character is around 1.0. You can explore the matching method parameter in the matchShapes() function. Different methods may produce a different range of return values. It is necessary to test and experiment to find the one suitable for the application.

Figure 5-30. *Shape-matching test with hand-drawn character*

Conclusion

In this chapter, you began some computer vision tasks to identify and analyze structural elements in digital images. You start by preparing your images and extracting the edges. From the edge information, you detect geometrical elements such as straight lines and circles. Through the tasks with general contours processing, you developed a simple application to detect more complex shapes in a live webcam video stream. In the next chapter, I will introduce the ideas of detecting and analyzing motion from prerecorded or live videos.

CHAPTER 6

■ ■ ■

Understanding Motion

In the previous chapter, you learned how to make sense of the content within one frame of an image. In this chapter, you will start to understand motion across multiple frames of digital video or a live webcam stream. As a simple explanation, you identify motion whenever there are differences between two consecutive frames. In computer vision, you try to use various methods to make sense of those differences in order to understand phenomena such as the movement direction and foreground-background separation. To begin the chapter, I will introduce existing approaches that digital artists have been using to work with moving images in Processing. The topics I will cover are as follows:

- Effects with moving images
- Frame differencing
- Background removal
- Optical flow
- Motion history

Effects with Moving Images

In the 1990s, multimedia designers mainly employed the software Director to create interactive content, delivered through the CD-ROM platform. Digital video materials at that time consisted mainly of prerecorded content. Nevertheless, Director is capable of extending its functionalities with extras or plug-ins. One of these extras is TrackThemColors, developed by Daniel Rozin. The extras enable Director to capture and analyze digital images captured from a webcam. Around 1999, John Maeda's Reactive Books series, *Mirror Mirror*, also used video input as an interactive feature. In addition, Josh Nimoy's Myron library (consisting of WebCamXtra and JMyron) provided access to webcams from Director, Java, and Processing. The library was named after the Myron Krueger, the great American computer researcher and artist who created the early form of augmented reality applications with a live video stream in the 1970s. Another reference is the freeze-frame motion study from the great English photographer Eadweard Muybridge, where he displayed a sequence of still photographs to illustrate continuous movement, such as a horse running.

With the use of the video library in Processing, you have a consistent set of functions to work with moving images. Media artists and designers have been exploring ways to generate creative visual effects in Processing with moving images. The following sections will implement a number of common effects in Processing to illustrate the creative concepts behind such effects. I will cover the following:

- Mosaic effect
- Slit-scan photography
- Scrolling effect
- Visualization in 3D

© Bryan WC Chung 2017
B. WC. Chung, *Pro Processing for Images and Computer Vision with OpenCV*,
DOI 10.1007/978-1-4842-2775-6_6

Mosaic Effect

The first exercise, Chapter06_01, is a modified version of the mosaic effect you completed in Chapter 3. Instead of using a single solid color for each cell in the grid, you will create a smaller version of the original image, in this case, the live webcam video stream, for each cell. The effect has been used in a lot of digital art and advertising materials. The following is the program source:

```
// Mosaic effect
import processing.video.*;

final int CELLS = 40;
Capture cap;
PImage img;
int idx;
int rows, cols;

void setup() {
  size(960, 720);
  background(0);
  cap = new Capture(this, 640, 480);
  cap.start();
  rows = CELLS;
  cols = CELLS;
  img = createImage(width/cols, height/rows, ARGB);
  idx = 0;
}

void draw() {
  if (!cap.available())
    return;
  cap.read();
  img.copy(cap, 0, 0, cap.width, cap.height,
    0, 0, img.width, img.height);
  int px = idx % cols;
  int py = idx / cols;
  int ix = px*cap.width/cols;
  int iy = py*cap.height/rows;
  color col = cap.pixels[iy*cap.width+ix];
  tint(col);
  image(img, px*img.width, py*img.height);
  idx++;
  idx %= (rows*cols);
}
```

Within the draw() function, each frame of the program will copy a snapshot of the webcam video image to a smaller PImage called img. It will go through the whole screen from left to right and from top to bottom to paste the latest frame onto each cell of the grid. Before it pastes the img, it uses the tint() function to alter the color, reflecting the color information from the top-left corner of that cell. As a result, the final display will resemble the live image while each cell is a separate frame in time. Figure 6-1 shows a sample of the display screen.

Figure 6-1. *Mosaic with live camera input*

Slit-Scan Effect

Slit-scan is a photographic technique to expose only a slit of an image at a time. For digital image processing, you can rework it to include only one line of pixels at a time. For the next exercise, Chapter06_02, you will copy only one vertical line of pixels from each frame of the webcam live stream. This is a common technique to generate still image from moving images. Golan Levin provides a comprehensive information catalog of slit-scan artwork at http://www.flong.com/texts/lists/slit_scan/. The following listing is the source of the exercise:

```
// Slit-scan effect
import processing.video.*;

Capture cap;
PImage img;
int idx, mid;

void setup() {
  size(1280, 480);
  background(0);
  cap = new Capture(this, width/2, height);
  cap.start();
  img = createImage(1, cap.height, ARGB);
  idx = 0;
  mid = cap.width/2;
}

void draw() {
  if (!cap.available())
    return;
  cap.read();
  img.copy(cap, mid, 0, 1, cap.height,
    0, 0, img.width, img.height);
  image(img, idx, 0);
  idx++;
  idx %= width;
}
```

The program is simple. In the draw( ) function, you take a vertical line of pixels in the center of the capture video and copy it to a horizontally moving location, indicated by idx. In this case, each vertical line on the screen represents a separate moment in time, moving from left to right. Figure 6-2 shows the resulting image.

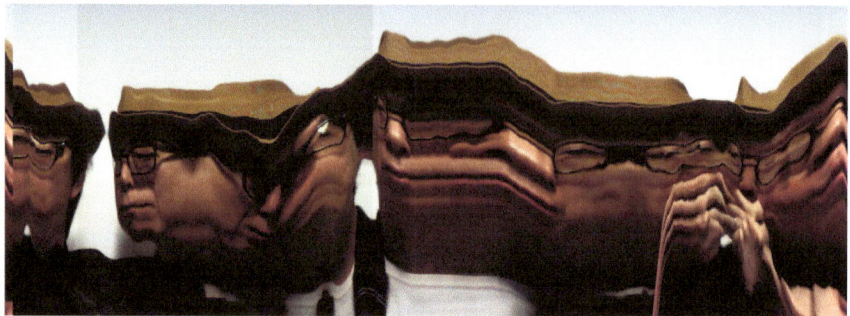

Figure 6-2. *Slit-scan effect with Processing*

Scrolling Effect

Again, back in the 1990s, the English multimedia art group Antirom (http://www.antirom.com/) made popular the scrolling effect of a filmstrip. In the age of Flash, the Japanese designer Yugop Nakamura also experimented heavily with the scrolling strip as an interface element. The idea behind this is simple. First you construct a long strip of multiple images, similar to an analog filmstrip. The images are usually still snapshots of a continuous movement. Then you animate the filmstrip with a scrolling movement, either horizontally or vertically. When the scrolling speed reaches a certain threshold, each cell in the filmstrip seems to animate by itself, producing an effect similar to early cinema. You will implement a Processing version in the following exercise, Chapter06_03:

```
// Scrolling effect
import processing.video.*;

// Processing modes for the draw() function
public enum Mode {
  WAITING, RECORDING, PLAYING
}

final int FPS = 24;
Capture cap;
Mode mode;
PShape [] shp;
PImage [] img;
PShape strip;
int dispW, dispH;
int recFrame;
float px, vx;

void setup() {
  size(800, 600, P3D);
  background(0);
  cap = new Capture(this, 640, 480);
```

```
  cap.start();
  // Frame size of the film strip
  dispW = 160;
  dispH = 120;
  // Position and velocity of the film strip
  px = 0;
  vx = 0;
  prepareShape();
  mode = Mode.WAITING;
  recFrame = 0;
  frameRate(FPS);
  noStroke();
  fill(255);
}

void prepareShape() {
  // Film strip shape
  strip = createShape(GROUP);
  // Keep 24 frames in the PImage array
  img = new PImage[FPS];
  int extra = ceil(width/dispW);
  // Keep 5 more frames to compensate for the
  // continuous scrolling effect
  shp = new PShape[FPS+extra];
  for (int i=0; i<FPS; i++) {
    img[i] = createImage(dispW, dispH, ARGB);
    shp[i] = createShape(RECT, 0, 0, dispW, dispH);
    shp[i].setStroke(false);
    shp[i].setFill(color(255));
    shp[i].setTexture(img[i]);
    shp[i].translate(i*img[i].width, 0);
    strip.addChild(shp[i]);
  }
  // The 5 extra frames are the same as the
  // first 5 ones.
  for (int i=FPS; i<shp.length; i++) {
    shp[i] = createShape(RECT, 0, 0, dispW, dispH);
    shp[i].setStroke(false);
    shp[i].setFill(color(255));
    int j = i % img.length;
    shp[i].setTexture(img[j]);
    shp[i].translate(i*img[j].width, 0);
    strip.addChild(shp[i]);
  }
}

void draw() {
  switch (mode) {
  case WAITING:
    waitFrame();
    break;
  case RECORDING:
```

```
      recordFrame();
      break;
    case PLAYING:
      playFrame();
      break;
  }
}

void waitFrame() {
  // Display to live webcam image while waiting
  if (!cap.available())
    return;
  cap.read();
  background(0);
  image(cap, (width-cap.width)/2, (height-cap.height)/2);
}

void recordFrame() {
  // Record each frame into the PImage array
  if (!cap.available())
    return;
  if (recFrame >= FPS) {
    mode = Mode.PLAYING;
    recFrame = 0;
    println("Finish recording");
    return;
  }
  cap.read();
  img[recFrame].copy(cap, 0, 0, cap.width, cap.height,
    0, 0, img[recFrame].width, img[recFrame].height);
  int sw = 80;
  int sh = 60;
  int tx = recFrame % (width/sw);
  int ty = recFrame / (width/sw);
  image(img[recFrame], tx*sw, ty*sh, sw, sh);
  recFrame++;
}

void playFrame() {
  background(0);
  // Compute the scrolling speed
  vx = (width/2 - mouseX)*0.6;
  px += vx;
  // Check for 2 boundary conditions
  if (px < (width-strip.getWidth())) {
    px = width - strip.getWidth() - px;
  } else if (px > 0) {
    px = px - strip.getWidth() + width;
  }
  shape(strip, px, 250);
}
```

```
void mousePressed() {
  // Press mouse button to record
  if (mode != Mode.RECORDING) {
    mode = Mode.RECORDING;
    recFrame = 0;
    background(0);
    println("Start recording");
  }
}
```

The program has three states, represented by the enum type mode. The first one is the WAITING state where the live webcam is displayed on the screen. Once the user presses the mouse button, the program proceeds to the RECORDING state. In this state, it records 24 frames into the PImage array called img. The user also gets the feedback of the layout of 24 small frames on the screen within that second. After the recording, it moves on to the PLAYING state, where a long horizontal filmstrip is displayed. It will scroll either left or right depending on the mouse location. The user can also alter the scrolling speed by moving the mouse toward the left or right margin. To create the illusion that the filmstrip scrolls in a continuous loop, you add 5 more extra frames to the end of the original 24 frames. These five frames make up of the width of the display screen (800 pixels). When the filmstrip scrolls beyond its boundaries, you simply place the other end of the strip within the screen window, as shown in the playFrame() function. The whole filmstrip is kept in the strip PShape consisting of the 29 frames in the shp array. Figure 6-3 shows a sample screenshot for reference.

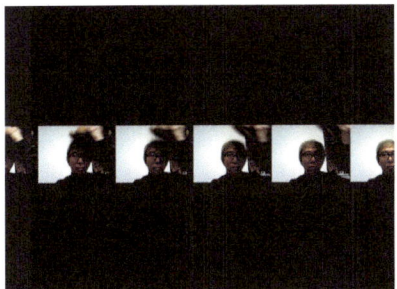

Figure 6-3. *Scrolling effect of filmstrip*

Visualization in 3D

You can further extend your experiments into the three-dimensional space. In the next exercise, Chapter06_04, you will display a collection of 24 frames together in the Processing display window. The program will visualize 24 consecutive frames simultaneously in a translucent block of 24 picture frames, rotating slowly in the three-dimensional space.

```
// 3D effect
import processing.video.*;

final int FPS = 24;
final int CAPW = 640;
final int CAPH = 480;
```

```
Capture cap;
PImage [] img;
PShape [] shp;
int idx;
float angle;
int dispW, dispH;

void setup() {
  size(800, 600, P3D);
  cap = new Capture(this, CAPW, CAPH, FPS);
  cap.start();
  idx = 0;
  angle = 0;
  frameRate(FPS);
  // Keep the 24 frames in each img array member
  img = new PImage[FPS];
  // Keep the 24 images in a separate PShape
  shp = new PShape[FPS];
  dispW = cap.width;
  dispH = cap.height;
  for (int i=0; i<FPS; i++) {
    img[i] = createImage(dispW, dispH, ARGB);
    shp[i] = createShape(RECT, 0, 0, dispW, dispH);
    shp[i].setStroke(false);
    shp[i].setFill(color(255, 255, 255, 80));
    shp[i].setTint(color(255, 255, 255, 80));
    shp[i].setTexture(img[i]);
  }
}

void draw() {
  if (!cap.available())
    return;
  background(0);
  lights();
  cap.read();
  // Copy the latest capture image into the
  // array member with index - idx
  img[idx].copy(cap, 0, 0, cap.width, cap.height,
    0, 0, img[idx].width, img[idx].height);
  pushMatrix();
  translate(width/2, height/2, -480);
  rotateY(radians(angle));
  translate(-dispW/2, -dispH/2, -480);
  displayAll();
  popMatrix();
```

```
  // Loop through the array with the idx
  idx++;
  idx %= FPS;
  angle += 0.5;
  angle %= 360;
  text(nf(round(frameRate), 2), 10, 20);
}

void displayAll() {
  // Always display the first frame of
  // index - idx
  pushMatrix();
  int i = idx - FPS + 1;
  if (i < 0)
    i += FPS;
  for (int j=0; j<FPS; j++) {
    shape(shp[i], 0, 0);
    i++;
    i %= FPS;
    translate(0, 0, 40);
  }
  popMatrix();
}
```

Each rectangular picture frame corresponds to one out of the 24 frames in a second. The one on top is always the latest frame. You can actually see the motion propagate down to other frames, one by one. Since the frames are translucent, you can see through them as the motion sinks downward. I have used this effect in my artwork *Movement in Time, Part 1* (http://www.magicandlove.com/blog/artworks/movement-in-time-v-1/). With this effect, a cinematic jump cut will turn into a smooth transition. The trick is in the displayAll() function. The variable idx represents the latest frame. The oldest frame will then be calculated from the following statement, with an additional adjustment because of the negative value:

```
int i = idx - FPS + 1;
```

The for loop afterward will display each frame in the correct order. To keep all 24 frames in a second, you use two arrays, img and shp. The array img stores each video frame as a PImage, which will be used as a texture mapped on top of each member of the array shp, as PShape. The draw() function manages the rotation of the whole picture-frame block, as shown in Figure 6-4.

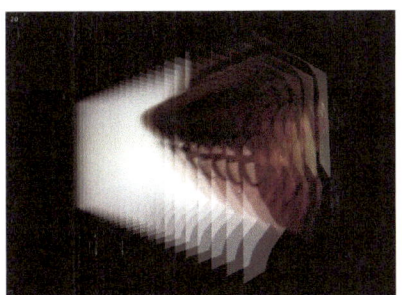

Figure 6-4. *Video frames in 3D*

Frame Differencing

Now that you have seen a number of examples that work with frames in moving images, you can proceed to understand how motion is detected in computer vision. The basic principle is that you can realize motion only when there are changes across two picture frames. By comparing two frames, you can tell briefly what type of motion has happened between these two frames. The way to compare two frames is to use the blend() function, covered in Chapter 3, in Processing. In the next exercise, Chapter06_05, you will implement frame differencing between the live webcam stream and a static image:

```
// Difference between video and background
import processing.video.*;

final int CAPW = 640;
final int CAPH = 480;

Capture cap;
PImage back, img, diff;
int dispW, dispH;

void setup() {
  size(800, 600);
  cap = new Capture(this, CAPW, CAPH);
  cap.start();
  dispW = width/2;
  dispH = height/2;
  back = createImage(dispW, dispH, ARGB);
  img = createImage(dispW, dispH, ARGB);
  diff = createImage(dispW, dispH, ARGB);
}

void draw() {
  if (!cap.available())
    return;
  background(0);
  cap.read();
  // Get the difference image.
  diff.copy(cap, 0, 0, cap.width, cap.height,
    0, 0, img.width, img.height);
  diff.filter(GRAY);
  diff.blend(back, 0, 0, back.width, back.height,
    0, 0, diff.width, diff.height, DIFFERENCE);
  // Obtain the threshold binary image.
  img.copy(diff, 0, 0, diff.width, diff.height,
    0, 0, img.width, img.height);
  img.filter(THRESHOLD, 0.4);
  image(cap, 0, 0, dispW, dispH);
  image(back, dispW, 0, dispW, dispH);
  image(diff, 0, dispH, dispW, dispH);
  image(img, dispW, dispH, dispW, dispH);
  text(nf(round(frameRate), 2), 10, 20);
}
```

```
void mousePressed() {
  // Update the background image.
  back.copy(cap, 0, 0, cap.width, cap.height,
    0, 0, back.width, back.height);
  back.filter(GRAY);
}
```

In this program, you can press the mouse button to record a static image from the webcam live stream and store it as a background frame in the PImage variable called back. In each frame, within the draw() function, it compares the current frame with the background using the blend() function and stores the difference in the PImage variable diff. A threshold filter is further applied to generate the binary PImage called img. In the Processing display window, you show the current video frame in the top-left corner, the background image in the top-right corner, the difference image in the bottom-left corner, and the threshold binary image in the bottom-right corner. In the threshold image, the white regions indicate where the motion occurs. Figure 6-5 shows a sample screenshot for reference.

Figure 6-5. *Frame difference between live video and background*

For applications that are unable to obtain a static background image, you can consider comparing two consecutive frames to obtain the difference. The following exercise, Chapter06_06, demonstrates the pure Processing implementation to obtain the difference across two frames:

```
// Difference between consecutive frames
import processing.video.*;

final int CNT = 2;
// Capture size
final int CAPW = 640;
final int CAPH = 480;

Capture cap;
// Keep two frames to use alternately with
// array indices (prev, curr).
PImage [] img;
int prev, curr;
// Display image size
int dispW, dispH;
```

```
void setup() {
  size(800, 600);
  dispW = width/2;
  dispH = height/2;
  cap = new Capture(this, CAPW, CAPH);
  cap.start();
  img = new PImage[CNT];
  for (int i=0; i<img.length; i++) {
    img[i] = createImage(dispW, dispH, ARGB);
  }
  prev = 0;
  curr = 1;
}

void draw() {
  if (!cap.available())
    return;
  background(0);
  cap.read();
  // Copy video image to current frame.
  img[curr].copy(cap, 0, 0, cap.width, cap.height,
    0, 0, img[curr].width, img[curr].height);
  // Display current and previous frames.
  image(img[curr], 0, 0, dispW, dispH);
  image(img[prev], dispW, 0, dispW, dispH);
  PImage tmp = createImage(dispW, dispH, ARGB);
  arrayCopy(img[curr].pixels, tmp.pixels);
  tmp.updatePixels();
  // Create the difference image.
  tmp.blend(img[prev], 0, 0, img[prev].width, img[prev].height,
    0, 0, tmp.width, tmp.height, DIFFERENCE);
  tmp.filter(GRAY);
  image(tmp, 0, dispH, dispW, dispH);
  // Convert the difference image to binary.
  tmp.filter(THRESHOLD, 0.3);
  image(tmp, dispW, dispH, dispW, dispH);
  text(nf(round(frameRate), 2), 10, 20);
  // Swap the two array indices.
  int temp = prev;
  prev = curr;
  curr = temp;
}
```

The program keeps a PImage buffer array, img, to maintain the previous and current frames from the video stream, by swapping the two pointer indices, prev and curr. The rest of the code is similar to the former program. It uses the blend() function to retrieve the DIFFERENCE image and the THRESHOLD filter to extract the black-and-white binary image. Figure 6-6 shows a sample screenshot of the program.

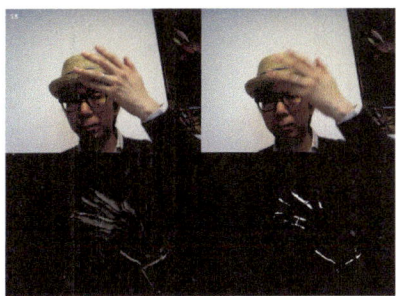

Figure 6-6. *Difference between two frames in Processing*

With the black-and-white difference image, the next step is to derive meaningful information from it. In Chapter 5, you learned how to retrieve the contour information from the white areas against the black background. In the next exercise, Chapter06_07, you will use the same technique to find out the bounding boxes of the contours identified from the black-and-white image. This program will use OpenCV. Remember to add the code folder with the OpenCV libraries and the CVImage class definition to the Processing sketch folder.

```
// Difference between 2 consecutive frames
import processing.video.*;
import java.util.ArrayList;
import java.util.Iterator;

final int CNT = 2;
// Capture size
final int CAPW = 640;
final int CAPH = 480;
// Minimum bounding box area
final float MINAREA = 200.0;

Capture cap;
// Previous and current frames in Mat format
Mat [] frames;
int prev, curr;
CVImage img;
// Display size
int dispW, dispH;

void setup() {
  size(800, 600);
  dispW = width/2;
  dispH = height/2;
  System.loadLibrary(Core.NATIVE_LIBRARY_NAME);
  cap = new Capture(this, CAPW, CAPH);
  cap.start();
  img = new CVImage(dispW, dispH);
  frames = new Mat[CNT];
  for (int i=0; i<CNT; i++) {
    frames[i] = new Mat(img.height, img.width,
      CvType.CV_8UC1, Scalar.all(0));
  }
```

```
  prev = 0;
  curr = 1;
}

void draw() {
  if (!cap.available())
    return;
  background(0);
  cap.read();
  PImage tmp0 = createImage(dispW, dispH, ARGB);
  tmp0.copy(cap, 0, 0, cap.width, cap.height,
    0, 0, tmp0.width, tmp0.height);
  // Display current frame.
  image(tmp0, 0, 0);
  img.copyTo(tmp0);
  frames[curr] = img.getGrey();
  CVImage out = new CVImage(dispW, dispH);
  out.copyTo(frames[prev]);
  // Display previous frame.
  image(out, dispW, 0, dispW, dispH);
  Mat tmp1 = new Mat();
  Mat tmp2 = new Mat();
  // Difference between previous and current frames
  Core.absdiff(frames[prev], frames[curr], tmp1);
  Imgproc.threshold(tmp1, tmp2, 90, 255, Imgproc.THRESH_BINARY);
  out.copyTo(tmp2);
  // Display threshold difference image.
  image(out, 0, dispH, dispW, dispH);
  // Obtain contours of the difference binary image
  ArrayList<MatOfPoint> contours = new ArrayList<MatOfPoint>();
  Mat hierarchy = new Mat();
  Imgproc.findContours(tmp2, contours, hierarchy,
    Imgproc.RETR_LIST, Imgproc.CHAIN_APPROX_SIMPLE);
  Iterator<MatOfPoint> it = contours.iterator();
  pushStyle();
  fill(255, 180);
  noStroke();
  while (it.hasNext()) {
    MatOfPoint cont = it.next();
    // Draw each bounding box
    Rect rct = Imgproc.boundingRect(cont);
    float area = (float)(rct.width * rct.height);
    if (area < MINAREA)
      continue;
    rect((float)rct.x+dispW, (float)rct.y+dispH,
      (float)rct.width, (float)rct.height);
  }
  popStyle();
  text(nf(round(frameRate), 2), 10, 20);
  int temp = prev;
  prev = curr;
  curr = temp;
```

```
    hierarchy.release();
    tmp1.release();
    tmp2.release();
}
```

The program is similar to the former one except that you use the OpenCV Mat instance called frames to store the previous and current frames. You also employ the Core.absdiff() function to compute the difference image and use Imgproc.threshold() to generate the black-and-white binary image. When you loop through the contours data structure, you first calculate the bounding box area to filter those contours with smaller areas. For the rest, you display the rectangles in the bottom-right corner of the display window, as shown in Figure 6-7.

Figure 6-7. *Simple tracking with frame differencing*

Background Removal

In the previous frame differencing exercise, if you observe long enough, the static background will remain black. Only the moving objects in the foreground will be white. Background removal or background subtraction in OpenCV means separating the foreground moving objects from the static background image. You do not need to provide a static background image as in the exercise, Chapter06_05. In the video module of OpenCV, the BackgroundSubtractor class will learn from a sequence of input images for generating a foreground mask by performing a subtraction between the current frame and a background model, which contains the static background of the scene. The next exercise, Chapter06_08, illustrates the basic operations of the background subtraction:

```
// Background subtraction
import processing.video.*;
import org.opencv.video.*;
import org.opencv.video.Video;

// Capture size
final int CAPW = 640;
final int CAPH = 480;

Capture cap;
CVImage img;
PImage back;
// OpenCV background subtractor
BackgroundSubtractorMOG2 bkg;
```

```
// Foreground mask
Mat fgMask;

void setup() {
  size(1280, 480);
  System.loadLibrary(Core.NATIVE_LIBRARY_NAME);
  cap = new Capture(this, CAPW, CAPH);
  cap.start();
  img = new CVImage(cap.width, cap.height);
  bkg = Video.createBackgroundSubtractorMOG2();
  fgMask = new Mat();
}

void draw() {
  if (!cap.available())
    return;
  background(0);
  cap.read();
  img.copyTo(cap);
  Mat capFrame = img.getBGRA();
  bkg.apply(capFrame, fgMask);
  CVImage out = new CVImage(fgMask.cols(), fgMask.rows());
  out.copyTo(fgMask);
  image(cap, 0, 0);
  // Display the foreground mask
  image(out, cap.width, 0);
  text(nf(round(frameRate), 2), 10, 20);
  capFrame.release();
}
```

The program uses the Gaussian mixture-based background/foreground segmentation algorithm by Zoran Zivkovic. The class definition is in the video module of OpenCV. Note the use of additional import statements to include the class definitions. The class instance is created by the Video.createBackgroundSubtractorMOG2() function. To use the object, you pass the video frame and a foreground mask Mat, fgMask, to the apply() function for each frame in the draw() function. The BackgroundSubtractor object, bkg, will learn from each frame what the static background should be and generate the foreground mask. The foreground mask, fgMask, is a black-and-white image, where the black area is the background and the white regions are the foreground objects. The program will display the original video frame on the left side and the foreground mask on the right side, as shown in Figure 6-8.

Figure 6-8. *Background subtraction in OpenCV*

With the foreground mask, you can combine it with the video frame to retrieve the foreground image from the background. The following exercise, Chapter06_09, will use this method to implement the effect, which is similar to chroma key in video production:

```
// Background subtraction
import processing.video.*;
import org.opencv.video.*;
import org.opencv.video.Video;

// Capture size
final int CAPW = 640;
final int CAPH = 480;

Capture cap;
CVImage img;
PImage back;
BackgroundSubtractorKNN bkg;
Mat fgMask;
int dispW, dispH;

void setup() {
  size(800, 600);
  dispW = width/2;
  dispH = height/2;
  System.loadLibrary(Core.NATIVE_LIBRARY_NAME);
  cap = new Capture(this, CAPW, CAPH);
  cap.start();
  img = new CVImage(dispW, dispH);
  bkg = Video.createBackgroundSubtractorKNN();
  fgMask = new Mat();
  // Background image
  back = loadImage("background.png");
}

void draw() {
  if (!cap.available())
    return;
  background(0);
  cap.read();
  PImage tmp = createImage(dispW, dispH, ARGB);
  // Resize the capture image
  tmp.copy(cap, 0, 0, cap.width, cap.height,
    0, 0, tmp.width, tmp.height);
  img.copyTo(tmp);
  Mat capFrame = img.getBGRA();
  bkg.apply(capFrame, fgMask);
  // Combine the video frame and foreground
  // mask to obtain the foreground image.
  Mat fgImage = new Mat();
  capFrame.copyTo(fgImage, fgMask);
  CVImage out = new CVImage(fgMask.cols(), fgMask.rows());
```

```
    // Display the original video capture image.
    image(tmp, 0, 0);
    // Display the static background image.
    image(back, dispW, 0);
    out.copyTo(fgMask);
    // Display the foreground mask.
    image(out, 0, dispH);
    out.copyTo(fgImage);
    // Display the foreground image on top of
    // the static background.
    image(back, dispW, dispH);
    image(out, dispW, dispH);
    text(nf(round(frameRate), 2), 10, 20);
    capFrame.release();
    fgImage.release();
}
```

In this program, you display four images. The top-left one is the live video stream. The top-right one is a static background image, stored in a PImage instance called back. The bottom-left one is the foreground mask, as shown in the previous exercise. The bottom-right one is the foreground image displayed on top of the background image. You also experiment with another background subtraction method, the K-nearest neighbor's background subtraction, BackgroundSubtractorKNN. This method is more efficient when there are fewer foreground pixels within the image. Inside the draw() function, the program defines a new variable called fgImage to store the foreground image. You copy the current video image, capFrame, to the fgImage with the foreground mask fgMask.

```
capFrame.copyTo(fgImage, fgMask);
```

In this case, only the white areas in the mask will be copied. Figure 6-9 shows the overall resulting image.

Figure 6-9. *Background subtraction and foreground extraction*

In addition to the foreground image, the OpenCV BackgroundSubtractor can also retrieve the background image with the getBackgroundImage() function. The next exercise, Chapter06_10, will demonstrate its usage.

```
// Background subtraction
import processing.video.*;
import org.opencv.video.*;
import org.opencv.video.Video;
```

```
// Capture size
final int CAPW = 640;
final int CAPH = 480;

Capture cap;
CVImage img;
PImage back;
BackgroundSubtractorKNN bkg;
// Foreground mask object
Mat fgMask;
int dispW, dispH;

void setup() {
  size(800, 600);
  dispW = width/2;
  dispH = height/2;
  System.loadLibrary(Core.NATIVE_LIBRARY_NAME);
  cap = new Capture(this, CAPW, CAPH);
  cap.start();
  img = new CVImage(dispW, dispH);
  bkg = Video.createBackgroundSubtractorKNN();
  fgMask = new Mat();
  // Background image
  back = loadImage("background.png");
}

void draw() {
  if (!cap.available())
    return;
  background(0);
  cap.read();
  PImage tmp = createImage(dispW, dispH, ARGB);
  // Resize the capture image
  tmp.copy(cap, 0, 0, cap.width, cap.height,
    0, 0, tmp.width, tmp.height);
  img.copyTo(tmp);
  Mat capFrame = img.getBGR();
  bkg.apply(capFrame, fgMask);
  // Background image object
  Mat bkImage = new Mat();
  bkg.getBackgroundImage(bkImage);
  CVImage out = new CVImage(fgMask.cols(), fgMask.rows());
  // Display the original video capture image.
  image(tmp, 0, 0);
  out.copyTo(bkImage);
  // Display the background image.
  image(out, dispW, 0);
  out.copyTo(fgMask);
  // Display the foreground mask.
  image(out, 0, dispH);
  // Obtain the foreground image with the PImage
  // mask method.
```

195

```
    tmp.mask(out);
    // Display the forground image on top of
    // the static background.
    image(back, dispW, dispH);
    image(tmp, dispW, dispH);
    text(nf(round(frameRate), 2), 10, 20);
    capFrame.release();
}
```

Inside the draw() function, you define a new Mat variable called bkImage and use the getBackgroundImage(bkImage) method to pass the background image matrix to the bkImage variable. The program also explains another way to perform the mask operation using the Processing PImage class's mask() method. Figure 6-10 shows a sample screenshot.

Figure 6-10. *Background image retrieval*

Optical Flow

OpenCV has another approach to find out the motion details in moving images: the optical flow features in the video module. To put it in simple terms, *optical flow* is the analysis of how the pixels move across two consecutive frames, as illustrated in Figure 6-11.

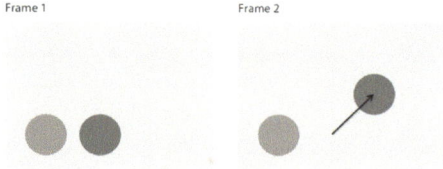

Figure 6-11. *Optical flow*

From Frame 2, you can scan each pixel one by one and try to match it with the pixels in Frame 1, around the original neighborhood. If you find a match, you can claim that the pixel in Frame 1 flows to the new position in Frame 2. The arrow you identified for that pixel will be the optical flow information. To work with optical flow, you can assume the following: that the pixel intensities of a moving object do not change much between consecutive frames, that neighboring pixels have similar motion, and that the object does not move too fast.

In the OpenCV implementation, there are two types of optical flow analysis: *sparse* and *dense*. In this chapter, you will study the dense optical flow first. The sparse optical flow involves feature point identification, which is the topic for the next chapter. In general, dense optical flow is the calculation of optical flow information for each single pixel in the image. It is resource intensive. Normally, you reduce the size of the video frame to enhance the performance. The first optical flow exercise, Chapter06_11, will implement the dense optical flow algorithm based on the 2003 "Two-Frame Motion Estimation Based on Polynomial Expansion" paper by Gunnar Farneback.

```
// Dense optical flow
import processing.video.*;
import org.opencv.video.*;
import org.opencv.video.Video;

// Capture size
final int CAPW = 640;
final int CAPH = 480;

Capture cap;
CVImage img;
float scaling;
int w, h;
Mat last;

void setup() {
  size(1280, 480);
  System.loadLibrary(Core.NATIVE_LIBRARY_NAME);
  cap = new Capture(this, CAPW, CAPH);
  cap.start();
  scaling = 10;
  w = floor(CAPW/scaling);
  h = floor(CAPH/scaling);
  img = new CVImage(w, h);
  last = new Mat(h, w, CvType.CV_8UC1);
}

void draw() {
  if (!cap.available())
    return;
  background(0);
  cap.read();
  img.copy(cap, 0, 0, cap.width, cap.height,
    0, 0, img.width, img.height);
  img.copyTo();
  Mat grey = img.getGrey();
  Mat flow = new Mat(last.size(), CvType.CV_32FC2);
  Video.calcOpticalFlowFarneback(last, grey, flow,
    0.5, 3, 10, 2, 7, 1.5, Video.OPTFLOW_FARNEBACK_GAUSSIAN);
  grey.copyTo(last);
  drawFlow(flow);
  image(cap, 0, 0);
  grey.release();
  flow.release();
  text(nf(round(frameRate), 2), 10, 20);
}
```

```
void drawFlow(Mat f) {
  // Draw the flow data.
  pushStyle();
  noFill();
  stroke(255);
  for (int y=0; y<f.rows(); y++) {
    float py = y*scaling;
    for (int x=0; x<f.cols(); x++) {
      double [] pt = f.get(y, x);
      float dx = (float)pt[0];
      float dy = (float)pt[1];
      // Skip areas with no flow.
      if (dx == 0 && dy == 0)
        continue;
      float px = x*scaling;
      dx *= scaling;
      dy *= scaling;
      line(px+cap.width, py, px+cap.width+dx, py+dy);
    }
  }
  popStyle();
}
```

Figure 6-12 shows the resulting screenshot.

Figure 6-12. *Farneback dense optical flow*

Instead of drawing the flow line in white, you can retrieve the color information from the video capture frame and color the lines in the original color. In this case, you can easily generate an interactive rendering of the live webcam image, as shown in Figure 6-13.

Figure 6-13. *Dense optical flow in color*

In this version, Chapter06_12, the only changes you need to make is in the drawFlow() function. Instead of using the stroke(255) function outside the for loops, you compute the pixel color and assign it to the stroke() function. You have used this technique in previous chapters.

```
void drawFlow(Mat f) {
  // Draw the flow data.
  pushStyle();
  noFill();
  for (int y=0; y<f.rows(); y++) {
    int py = (int)constrain(y*scaling, 0, cap.height-1);
    for (int x=0; x<f.cols(); x++) {
      double [] pt = f.get(y, x);
      float dx = (float)pt[0];
      float dy = (float)pt[1];
      // Skip areas with no flow.
      if (dx == 0 && dy == 0)
        continue;
      int px = (int)constrain(x*scaling, 0, cap.width-1);
      color col = cap.pixels[py*cap.width+px];
      stroke(col);
      dx *= scaling;
      dy *= scaling;
      line(px+cap.width, py, px+cap.width+dx, py+dy);
    }
  }
  popStyle();
}
```

In addition to using the optical flow information to render the webcam image, you can use it for interaction design. For example, you can define a virtual hotspot on the display screen together with the live image from the webcam. When you wave a hand across the virtual hotspot, you can trigger an event for the program, such as playing back a short sound clip. It is quite common to design such an air drum kit or piano in interaction design. The following exercise, Chapter06_13, will implement such a virtual hotspot using optical flow information. To simplify the program, you will define an additional class, Region, to encapsulate the code to implement the hotspot. The following is the definition of Region:

```
import java.awt.Rectangle;
import java.lang.reflect.Method;

// The class to define the hotspot.
class Region {
  // Threshold value to trigger the callback function.
  final float FLOW_THRESH = 20;
  Rectangle rct;      // area of the hotspot
  Rectangle screen;   // area of the live capture
  float scaling;      // scaling factor for optical flow size
  PVector flowInfo;   // flow information within the hotspot
  PApplet parent;
  Method func;        // callback function
  boolean touched;

  public Region(PApplet p, Rectangle r, Rectangle s, float f) {
    parent = p;
    // Register the callback function named regionTriggered.
    try {
      func = p.getClass().getMethod("regionTriggered",
        new Class[]{this.getClass()});
    }
    catch (Exception e) {
      println(e.getMessage());
    }
    screen = s;
    rct = (Rectangle)screen.createIntersection(r);
    scaling = f;
    flowInfo = new PVector(0, 0);
    touched = false;
  }

  void update(Mat f) {
    Rect sr = new Rect(floor(rct.x/scaling), floor(rct.y/scaling),
      floor(rct.width/scaling), floor(rct.height/scaling));
    // Obtain the submatrix - region of interest.
    Mat flow = f.submat(sr);
    flowInfo.set(0, 0);
    // Accumulate the optical flow vectors.
    for (int y=0; y<flow.rows(); y++) {
      for (int x=0; x<flow.cols(); x++) {
        double [] vec = flow.get(y, x);
        PVector item = new PVector((float)vec[0], (float)vec[1]);
        flowInfo.add(item);
```

```
      }
    }
    flow.release();
    // When the magnitude of total flow is larger than a
    // threshold, trigger the callback.
    if (flowInfo.mag()>FLOW_THRESH) {
      touched = true;
      try {
        func.invoke(parent, this);
      }
      catch (Exception e) {
        println(e.getMessage());
      }
    } else {
      touched = false;
    }
  }

  void drawBox() {
    // Draw the hotspot rectangle.
    pushStyle();
    if (touched) {
      stroke(255, 200, 0);
      fill(0, 100, 255, 160);
    } else {
      stroke(160);
      noFill();
    }
    rect((float)(rct.x+screen.x), (float)(rct.y+screen.y),
      (float)rct.width, (float)rct.height);
    popStyle();
  }

  void drawFlow(Mat f, PVector o) {
    // Visualize flow inside the region on
    // the right hand side screen.
    Rect sr = new Rect(floor(rct.x/scaling), floor(rct.y/scaling),
      floor(rct.width/scaling), floor(rct.height/scaling));
    Mat flow = f.submat(sr);
    pushStyle();
    noFill();
    stroke(255);
    for (int y=0; y<flow.rows(); y++) {
      float y1 = y*scaling+rct.y + o.y;
      for (int x=0; x<flow.cols(); x++) {
        double [] vec = flow.get(y, x);
        float x1 = x*scaling+rct.x + o.x;
        float dx = (float)(vec[0]*scaling);
        float dy = (float)(vec[1]*scaling);
        line(x1, y1, x1+dx, y1+dy);
      }
    }
```

```
    popStyle();
    flow.release();
  }

  float getFlowMag() {
    // Get the flow vector magnitude.
    return flowInfo.mag();
  }

  void writeMsg(PVector o, String m) {
    // Display message on screen.
    int px = round(o.x + rct.x);
    int py = round(o.y + rct.y);
    text(m, px, py-10);
  }
}
```

In the class definition of Region, you use a Java Rectangle called rct to define the hotspot area. Another Rectangle is the video capture window, called screen. You use the Java Rectangle instead of the OpenCV Rect because it provides you with an additional method to compute the intersection between two rectangles for fear that the definition of rct will be outside screen, as demonstrated in the following statement:

```
rct = (Rectangle)screen.createIntersection(r);
```

In the constructor of Region, you also use the Java Method class to register the method regionTriggered from the main program. In the update() method, you receive the optical flow matrix from the parameter f. Since you downsample the video capture image by the amount given in scaling, to compute the optical flow, you also need to downsample the Region rectangle by the same amount. After that, you calculate the submatrix within the original optical flow matrix using the Region rectangle with the following statement:

```
Mat flow = f.submat(sr);
```

In the two nested for loops, you accumulate all the flow vectors into the variable flowInfo. If its magnitude is greater than a threshold, you can conclude that something is moving in front of the camera and thus invoke the callback function, regionTriggered, in the main program. The other methods are straightforward. They simply draw the rectangle and the flow lines.

For the main program, you have defined two hotspots for testing. In the draw() function, after you compute the optical flow information, you loop through the regions array to update and draw the necessary information. As a callback function, you have defined a function called regionTriggered. The hotspot that causes the trigger will be passed to the callback as a Region object instance. It first retrieves the magnitude of all the flow vectors inside the region and then calls the method writeMsg() to display the number on top of the region.

```
// Interaction design with optical flow
import processing.video.*;
import org.opencv.video.*;
import org.opencv.video.Video;
import java.awt.Rectangle;

// Capture size
final int CAPW = 640;
final int CAPH = 480;
```

```
Capture cap;
CVImage img;
float scaling;
int w, h;
Mat last;
Region [] regions;
// Flag to indicate if it is the first frame.
boolean first;
// Offset to the right hand side display.
PVector offset;

void setup() {
  size(1280, 480);
  System.loadLibrary(Core.NATIVE_LIBRARY_NAME);
  cap = new Capture(this, CAPW, CAPH);
  cap.start();
  scaling = 20;
  w = floor(CAPW/scaling);
  h = floor(CAPH/scaling);
  img = new CVImage(w, h);
  last = new Mat(h, w, CvType.CV_8UC1);
  Rectangle screen = new Rectangle(0, 0, cap.width, cap.height);
  // Define 2 hotspots.
  regions = new Region[2];
  regions[0] = new Region(this, new Rectangle(100, 100, 100, 100),
    screen, scaling);
  regions[1] = new Region(this, new Rectangle(500, 200, 100, 100),
    screen, scaling);
  first = true;
  offset = new PVector(cap.width, 0);
}

void draw() {
  if (!cap.available())
    return;
  background(0);
  cap.read();
  img.copy(cap, 0, 0, cap.width, cap.height,
    0, 0, img.width, img.height);
  img.copyTo();
  Mat grey = img.getGrey();
  if (first) {
    grey.copyTo(last);
    first = false;
    return;
  }
  Mat flow = new Mat(last.size(), CvType.CV_32FC2);
  Video.calcOpticalFlowFarneback(last, grey, flow,
    0.5, 3, 10, 2, 7, 1.5, Video.OPTFLOW_FARNEBACK_GAUSSIAN);
  grey.copyTo(last);
  image(cap, 0, 0);
  drawFlow(flow);
```

203

```
  // Update the hotspots with the flow matrix.
  // Draw the hotspot rectangle.
  // Draw also the flow on the right hand side display.
  for (Region rg : regions) {
    rg.update(flow);
    rg.drawBox();
    rg.drawFlow(flow, offset);
  }
  grey.release();
  flow.release();
  text(nf(round(frameRate), 2), 10, 20);
}

void drawFlow(Mat f) {
  // Draw the flow data.
  pushStyle();
  noFill();
  stroke(255);
  for (int y=0; y<f.rows(); y++) {
    int py = (int)constrain(y*scaling, 0, cap.height-1);
    for (int x=0; x<f.cols(); x++) {
      double [] pt = f.get(y, x);
      float dx = (float)pt[0];
      float dy = (float)pt[1];
      // Skip areas with no flow.
      if (dx == 0 && dy == 0)
        continue;
      int px = (int)constrain(x*scaling, 0, cap.width-1);
      dx *= scaling;
      dy *= scaling;
      line(px, py, px+dx, py+dy);
    }
  }
  popStyle();
}

void regionTriggered(Region r) {
  // Callback function from the Region class.
  // It displays the flow magnitude number on
  // top of the hotspot rectangle.
  int mag = round(r.getFlowMag());
  r.writeMsg(offset, nf(mag, 3));
}
```

Figure 6-14 shows a sample screenshot for reference. Note that one of the hotspots is activated by waving in front of the webcam. It is filled with semitransparent color and with the optical flow magnitude value shown on the right of the display.

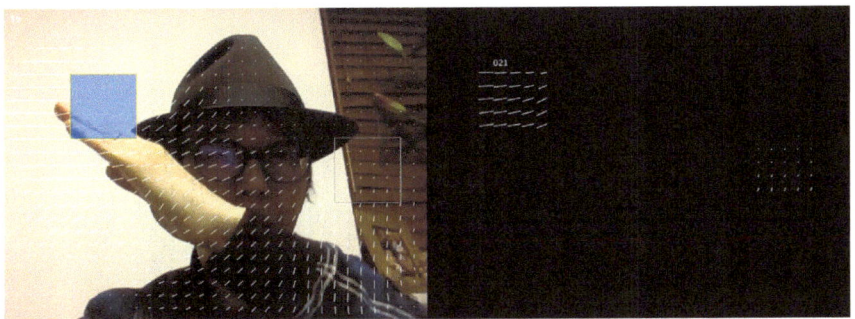

Figure 6-14. *Virtual hotspots with optical flow interaction*

Motion History

In the optical flow analysis, notice that the function uses just two frames to compute the flow information. OpenCV provides other functions that accumulate more frames to analyze the motion history in detail. Nevertheless, starting from version 3.0, the functions are no longer in the standard distribution of OpenCV. It is now distributed in the extra modules of the opencv_contrib repository at https://github.com/opencv/opencv_contrib. This is the reason that in Chapter 1 you built the OpenCV library with the extra module optflow. The following are the functions related to motion history:

- calcGlobalOrientation

- calcMotionGradient

- segmentMotion

- updateMotionHistory

The next exercise, Chapter06_14, is based on the motempl.cpp sample in the opencv_contrib distribution. Since it is slightly complicated, you will build it up step-by-step. I will review the technique to compare two consecutive frames to create the threshold difference image that was covered in the previous section of the chapter.

```
// Display threshold difference image.
import processing.video.*;
import org.opencv.core.*;
import org.opencv.imgproc.Imgproc;

final int CNT = 2;
Capture cap;
CVImage img;
Mat [] buf;
Mat silh;
int last;

void setup() {
  size(1280, 480);
  background(0);
  System.loadLibrary(Core.NATIVE_LIBRARY_NAME);
  println(Core.VERSION);
  cap = new Capture(this, width/2, height);
```

```
    cap.start();
    img = new CVImage(cap.width, cap.height);
    last = 0;
    // Two frames buffer for comparison
    buf = new Mat[CNT];
    for (int i=0; i<CNT; i++) {
      buf[i] = Mat.zeros(cap.height, cap.width,
        CvType.CV_8UC1);
    }
    // Threshold difference image
    silh = new Mat(cap.height, cap.width, CvType.CV_8UC1,
      Scalar.all(0));
}

void draw() {
  if (!cap.available())
    return;
  background(0);
  cap.read();
  img.copy(cap, 0, 0, cap.width, cap.height,
    0, 0, img.width, img.height);
  img.copyTo();
  Mat grey = img.getGrey();
  grey.copyTo(buf[last]);
  int idx1, idx2;
  idx1 = last;
  idx2 = (last + 1) % buf.length;
  last = idx2;
  silh = buf[idx2];
  // Create the threshold difference image between two frames.
  Core.absdiff(buf[idx1], buf[idx2], silh);
  Imgproc.threshold(silh, silh, 30, 255, Imgproc.THRESH_BINARY);
  CVImage out = new CVImage(cap.width, cap.height);
  out.copyTo(silh);
  image(img, 0, 0);
  image(out, cap.width, 0);
  text(nf(round(frameRate), 2), 10, 20);
  grey.release();
}
```

The program uses a Mat array called buf to maintain the two consecutive frames from the webcam. Basically, it makes use of the Core.absdiff() and Imgproc.threshold() functions to compute the threshold difference image for each frame in the draw() function. Figure 6-15 shows a sample screenshot.

Figure 6-15. *Threshold difference image*

The result is like what you did in Figure 6-6 with Processing. Since the threshold difference image contains information with just two frames, the next step, Chapter06_15, is to accumulate a few of these images to construct a motion history image.

```
// Display motion history image.
import processing.video.*;
import org.opencv.core.*;
import org.opencv.imgproc.Imgproc;
import org.opencv.optflow.Optflow;
import java.lang.System;

final int CNT = 2;
// Motion history duration is 5 seconds.
final double MHI_DURATION = 5;
Capture cap;
CVImage img;
Mat [] buf;
Mat mhi, silh, mask;
int last;
double time0;

void setup() {
  size(1280, 480);
  background(0);
  System.loadLibrary(Core.NATIVE_LIBRARY_NAME);
  println(Core.VERSION);
  cap = new Capture(this, width/2, height);
  cap.start();
  img = new CVImage(cap.width, cap.height);
  last = 0;
  // Maintain two buffer frames.
  buf = new Mat[CNT];
  for (int i=0; i<CNT; i++) {
    buf[i] = Mat.zeros(cap.height, cap.width,
      CvType.CV_8UC1);
  }
```

```
  // Initialize the threshold difference image.
  silh = new Mat(cap.height, cap.width, CvType.CV_8UC1,
    Scalar.all(0));
  // Initialize motion history image.
  mhi = Mat.zeros(cap.height, cap.width, CvType.CV_32FC1);
  mask = Mat.zeros(cap.height, cap.width, CvType.CV_8UC1);
  // Store timestamp when program starts to run.
  time0 = System.nanoTime();
}

void draw() {
  if (!cap.available())
    return;
  background(0);
  cap.read();
  img.copy(cap, 0, 0, cap.width, cap.height,
    0, 0, img.width, img.height);
  img.copyTo();
  Mat grey = img.getGrey();
  grey.copyTo(buf[last]);
  int idx1, idx2;
  idx1 = last;
  idx2 = (last + 1) % buf.length;
  last = idx2;
  silh = buf[idx2];
  // Get current timestamp in seconds.
  double timestamp = (System.nanoTime() - time0)/1e9;
  // Create binary threshold image from two frames.
  Core.absdiff(buf[idx1], buf[idx2], silh);
  Imgproc.threshold(silh, silh, 30, 255, Imgproc.THRESH_BINARY);
  // Update motion history image from the threshold.
  Optflow.updateMotionHistory(silh, mhi, timestamp, MHI_DURATION);
  mhi.convertTo(mask, CvType.CV_8UC1,
    255.0/MHI_DURATION,
    (MHI_DURATION - timestamp)*255.0/MHI_DURATION);
  // Display the greyscale motion history image.
  CVImage out = new CVImage(cap.width, cap.height);
  out.copyTo(mask);
  image(img, 0, 0);
  image(out, cap.width, 0);
  text(nf(round(frameRate), 2), 10, 20);
  grey.release();
}
```

After you obtain the threshold difference image of the silhouette, silh, you use the OpenCV extra module, optflow, to create the motion history image with the function Optflow.updateMotionHistory(). The first parameter is the input silhouette image. The second parameter is the output motion history image. The third parameter is the current timestamp in seconds. The last parameter is the maximum duration (measured in seconds) of motion details you intend to maintain, which is five seconds in this case. The motion history image, mhi, is then converted back to 8 bits, called mask, for display. The bright areas are the recent movement, and they will fade to black when there are no more movements. Figure 6-16 shows a sample screenshot.

Figure 6-16. *Motion history image*

The next step, Chapter06_16, will further analyze the motion history image to find out the motion gradient. That is in which direction the pixels are moving between frames. The optical flow module provides another function, calcMotionGradient(), to compute the motion direction for each pixel in the motion history image.

```
// Display global motion direction.
import processing.video.*;
import org.opencv.core.*;
import org.opencv.imgproc.Imgproc;
import org.opencv.optflow.Optflow;
import java.lang.System;

final int CNT = 2;
// Define motion history duration.
final double MHI_DURATION = 5;
final double MAX_TIME_DELTA = 0.5;
final double MIN_TIME_DELTA = 0.05;
Capture cap;
CVImage img;
Mat [] buf;
Mat mhi, mask, orient, silh;
int last;
double time0;

void setup() {
  size(1280, 480);
  background(0);
  System.loadLibrary(Core.NATIVE_LIBRARY_NAME);
  println(Core.VERSION);
  cap = new Capture(this, width/2, height);
  cap.start();
  img = new CVImage(cap.width, cap.height);
  last = 0;
  // Image buffer with two frames.
  buf = new Mat[CNT];
  for (int i=0; i<CNT; i++) {
    buf[i] = Mat.zeros(cap.height, cap.width, CvType.CV_8UC1);
  }
```

```
  // Motion history image
  mhi = Mat.zeros(cap.height, cap.width, CvType.CV_32FC1);
  // Threshold difference image
  silh = Mat.zeros(cap.height, cap.width, CvType.CV_8UC1);
  mask = Mat.zeros(cap.height, cap.width, CvType.CV_8UC1);
  orient = Mat.zeros(cap.height, cap.width, CvType.CV_32FC1);
  // Program start time
  time0 = System.nanoTime();
  smooth();
}

void draw() {
  if (!cap.available())
    return;
  background(0);
  cap.read();
  img.copy(cap, 0, 0, cap.width, cap.height,
    0, 0, img.width, img.height);
  img.copyTo();
  Mat grey = img.getGrey();
  grey.copyTo(buf[last]);
  int idx1, idx2;
  idx1 = last;
  idx2 = (last + 1) % buf.length;
  last = idx2;
  silh = buf[idx2];
  // Get current time in seconds.
  double timestamp = (System.nanoTime() - time0)/1e9;
  // Compute difference with threshold.
  Core.absdiff(buf[idx1], buf[idx2], silh);
  Imgproc.threshold(silh, silh, 30, 255, Imgproc.THRESH_BINARY);
  // Update motion history image.
  Optflow.updateMotionHistory(silh, mhi, timestamp, MHI_DURATION);
  mhi.convertTo(mask, CvType.CV_8UC1,
    255.0/MHI_DURATION,
    (MHI_DURATION - timestamp)*255.0/MHI_DURATION);
  // Display motion history image in 8bit greyscale.
  CVImage out = new CVImage(cap.width, cap.height);
  out.copyTo(mask);
  image(img, 0, 0);
  image(out, cap.width, 0);
  // Compute overall motion gradient.
  Optflow.calcMotionGradient(mhi, mask, orient,
    MAX_TIME_DELTA, MIN_TIME_DELTA, 3);
  // Calculate motion direction of whole frame.
  double angle = Optflow.calcGlobalOrientation(orient, mask,
    mhi, timestamp, MHI_DURATION);
  // Skip cases with too little motion.
  double count = Core.norm(silh, Core.NORM_L1);
  if (count > (cap.width*cap.height*0.1)) {
    pushStyle();
    noFill();
```

```
    stroke(255, 0, 0);
    float radius = min(cap.width, cap.height)/2.0;
    ellipse(cap.width/2+cap.width, cap.height/2, radius*2, radius*2);
    stroke(0, 0, 255);
    // Draw the main direction of motion.
    line(cap.width/2+cap.width, cap.height/2,
      cap.width/2+cap.width+radius*cos(radians((float)angle)),
      cap.height/2+radius*sin(radians((float)angle)));
    popStyle();
  }
  fill(0);
  text(nf(round(frameRate), 2), 10, 20);
  grey.release();
}
```

Inside the draw() function, the statement takes the motion history image, mhi, and produces two output images.

```
Optflow.calcMotionGradient(mhi, mask, orient, MAX_TIME_DELTA, MIN_TIME_DELTA, 3);
```

The first one, mask, indicates which pixels have valid motion gradient information. The second one, orient, shows the motion direction angle in degrees for each pixel. Note that the output Mat, called mask, will overwrite the original content from the previous steps. The next statement calculates the average motion direction from the results of the previous statement:

```
double angle = Optflow.calcGlobalOrientation(orient, mask, mhi, timestamp, MHI_DURATION);
```

It will return the motion angle measured in degrees, with a value from 0 to 360. The program also skips those cases when there is too little motion on the screen. In the end, the program draws a big circle and a straight line from the circle center toward the direction of the motion detected. Figure 6-17 shows a sample screenshot with a blue line pointing to the motion direction.

Figure 6-17. *Global motion direction*

211

Once you have the global motion direction, you can use it for gestural interaction. The next exercise, Chapter06_17, demonstrates a simple usage of the motion direction, as obtained from the variable angle:

```
// Gestural interaction demo
import processing.video.*;
import org.opencv.core.*;
import org.opencv.imgproc.Imgproc;
import org.opencv.optflow.Optflow;
import java.lang.System;

final int CNT = 2;
// Define motion history duration.
final double MHI_DURATION = 3;
final double MAX_TIME_DELTA = 0.5;
final double MIN_TIME_DELTA = 0.05;
Capture cap;
CVImage img;
Mat [] buf;
Mat mhi, mask, orient, silh;
int last;
double time0;
float rot, vel, drag;

void setup() {
  // Three dimensional scene
  size(640, 480, P3D);
  background(0);
  // Disable depth test.
  hint(DISABLE_DEPTH_TEST);
  System.loadLibrary(Core.NATIVE_LIBRARY_NAME);
  println(Core.VERSION);
  cap = new Capture(this, width, height);
  cap.start();
  img = new CVImage(cap.width, cap.height);
  last = 0;
  // Image buffer with two frames.
  buf = new Mat[CNT];
  for (int i=0; i<CNT; i++) {
    buf[i] = Mat.zeros(cap.height, cap.width, CvType.CV_8UC1);
  }
  // Motion history image
  mhi = Mat.zeros(cap.height, cap.width, CvType.CV_32FC1);
  // Threshold difference image
  silh = Mat.zeros(cap.height, cap.width, CvType.CV_8UC1);
  mask = Mat.zeros(cap.height, cap.width, CvType.CV_8UC1);
  orient = Mat.zeros(cap.height, cap.width, CvType.CV_32FC1);
  // Program start time
  time0 = System.nanoTime();
  smooth();
  // Rotation of the cube in Y direction
  rot = 0;
```

```
  // Rotation velocity
  vel = 0;
  // Damping force
  drag = 0.9;
}

void draw() {
  if (!cap.available())
    return;
  background(0);
  cap.read();
  img.copy(cap, 0, 0, cap.width, cap.height,
    0, 0, img.width, img.height);
  img.copyTo();
  Mat grey = img.getGrey();
  grey.copyTo(buf[last]);
  int idx1, idx2;
  idx1 = last;
  idx2 = (last + 1) % buf.length;
  last = idx2;
  silh = buf[idx2];
  // Get current time in seconds.
  double timestamp = (System.nanoTime() - time0)/1e9;
  // Compute difference with threshold.
  Core.absdiff(buf[idx1], buf[idx2], silh);
  Imgproc.threshold(silh, silh, 30, 255, Imgproc.THRESH_BINARY);
  // Update motion history image.
  Optflow.updateMotionHistory(silh, mhi, timestamp, MHI_DURATION);
  mhi.convertTo(mask, CvType.CV_8UC1,
    255.0/MHI_DURATION,
    (MHI_DURATION - timestamp)*255.0/MHI_DURATION);
  // Display motion history image in 8bit greyscale.
  CVImage out = new CVImage(cap.width, cap.height);
  out.copyTo(mask);
  image(img, 0, 0);
  // Compute overall motion gradient.
  Optflow.calcMotionGradient(mhi, mask, orient,
    MAX_TIME_DELTA, MIN_TIME_DELTA, 3);
  // Calculate motion direction of whole frame.
  double angle = Optflow.calcGlobalOrientation(orient, mask,
    mhi, timestamp, MHI_DURATION);
  // Skip cases with too little motion.
  double count = Core.norm(silh, Core.NORM_L1);
  if (count > (cap.width*cap.height*0.1)) {
    // Moving to the right
    if (angle < 10 || (360 - angle) < 10) {
      vel -= 0.02;
      // Moving to the left
    } else if (abs((float)angle-180) < 20) {
      vel += 0.02;
    }
  }
```

213

```
  // Slow down the velocity
  vel *= drag;
  // Update the rotation angle
  rot += vel;
  fill(0);
  text(nf(round(frameRate), 2), 10, 20);
  // Draw the cube.
  pushMatrix();
  pushStyle();
  fill(255, 80);
  stroke(255);
  translate(cap.width/2, cap.height/2, 0);
  rotateY(rot);
  box(200);
  popStyle();
  popMatrix();
  grey.release();
}
```

The structure of the program remains the same. You add a 3D scene with a semitransparent cube in the center of the screen. When you move horizontally in front of the webcam, you spin the cube along its *y*-axis. You treat the motion as an acceleration force to alter the velocity of spinning. Figure 6-18 shows a screenshot of the program.

Figure 6-18. *Gestural interaction with motion direction*

Besides retrieving the global motion direction, you can segment the motion gradient image to identify individual motion regions. The next exercise, Chapter06_18, will show how you can use the function segmentMotion() to split the overall motion information into separate areas:

```
// Motion history with motion segment
import processing.video.*;
import org.opencv.core.*;
import org.opencv.imgproc.Imgproc;
import org.opencv.optflow.Optflow;
import java.lang.System;
import java.util.ArrayList;
```

```
final int CNT = 2;
// Minimum region area to display
final float MIN_AREA = 300;
// Motion history duration
final double MHI_DURATION = 3;
final double MAX_TIME_DELTA = 0.5;
final double MIN_TIME_DELTA = 0.05;

Capture cap;
CVImage img;
Mat [] buf;
Mat mhi, mask, orient, segMask, silh;
int last;
double time0, timestamp;

void setup() {
  size(1280, 480);
  background(0);
  System.loadLibrary(Core.NATIVE_LIBRARY_NAME);
  println(Core.VERSION);
  cap = new Capture(this, width/2, height);
  cap.start();
  img = new CVImage(cap.width, cap.height);
  last = 0;
  buf = new Mat[CNT];
  for (int i=0; i<CNT; i++) {
    buf[i] = Mat.zeros(cap.height, cap.width, CvType.CV_8UC1);
  }
  // Motion history image
  mhi = Mat.zeros(cap.height, cap.width, CvType.CV_32FC1);
  mask = Mat.zeros(cap.height, cap.width, CvType.CV_8UC1);
  orient = Mat.zeros(cap.height, cap.width, CvType.CV_32FC1);
  segMask = Mat.zeros(cap.height, cap.width, CvType.CV_32FC1);
  // Threshold difference image
  silh = Mat.zeros(cap.height, cap.width, CvType.CV_8UC1);
  // Program start time
  time0 = System.nanoTime();
  timestamp = 0;
  smooth();
}

void draw() {
  if (!cap.available())
    return;
  background(0);
  cap.read();
  img.copy(cap, 0, 0, cap.width, cap.height,
    0, 0, img.width, img.height);
  img.copyTo();
  Mat grey = img.getGrey();
  grey.copyTo(buf[last]);
```

215

```
    int idx1, idx2;
    idx1 = last;
    idx2 = (last + 1) % buf.length;
    last = idx2;
    silh = buf[idx2];
    double timestamp = (System.nanoTime() - time0)/1e9;
    // Create threshold difference image.
    Core.absdiff(buf[idx1], buf[idx2], silh);
    Imgproc.threshold(silh, silh, 30, 255, Imgproc.THRESH_BINARY);
    // Update motion history image.
    Optflow.updateMotionHistory(silh, mhi, timestamp, MHI_DURATION);
    // Convert motion history to 8bit image.
    mhi.convertTo(mask, CvType.CV_8UC1,
      255.0/MHI_DURATION,
      (MHI_DURATION - timestamp)*255.0/MHI_DURATION);
    // Display motion history image in greyscale.
    CVImage out = new CVImage(cap.width, cap.height);
    out.copyTo(mask);
    // Calculate overall motion gradient.
    Optflow.calcMotionGradient(mhi, mask, orient,
      MAX_TIME_DELTA, MIN_TIME_DELTA, 3);
    // Segment general motion into different regions.
    MatOfRect regions = new MatOfRect();
    Optflow.segmentMotion(mhi, segMask, regions,
      timestamp, MAX_TIME_DELTA);
    image(img, 0, 0);
    image(out, cap.width, 0);
    // Plot individual motion areas.
    plotMotion(regions.toArray());
    pushStyle();
    fill(0);
    text(nf(round(frameRate), 2), 10, 20);
    popStyle();
    grey.release();
    regions.release();
}

void plotMotion(Rect [] rs) {
    pushStyle();
    fill(0, 0, 255, 80);
    stroke(255, 255, 0);
    for (Rect r : rs) {
        // Skip regions of small area.
        float area = r.width*r.height;
        if (area < MIN_AREA)
            continue;
        // Obtain submatrices from motion images.
        Mat silh_roi = silh.submat(r);
        Mat mhi_roi = mhi.submat(r);
        Mat orient_roi = orient.submat(r);
        Mat mask_roi = mask.submat(r);
```

```
  // Calculate motion direction of that region.
  double angle = Optflow.calcGlobalOrientation(orient_roi,
    mask_roi, mhi_roi, timestamp, MHI_DURATION);
  // Skip regions with little motion.
  double count = Core.norm(silh_roi, Core.NORM_L1);
  if (count < (r.width*r.height*0.05))
    continue;
  PVector center = new PVector(r.x + r.width/2,
    r.y + r.height/2);
  float radius = min(r.width, r.height)/2.0;
  ellipse(center.x, center.y, radius*2, radius*2);
  line(center.x, center.y,
    center.x+radius*cos(radians((float)angle)),
    center.y+radius*sin(radians((float)angle)));
  silh_roi.release();
  mhi_roi.release();
  orient_roi.release();
  mask_roi.release();
  }
  popStyle();
}
```

After you finish the statement to calculate the motion gradient image, you segment the motion information with the following statement:

```
Optflow.segmentMotion(mhi, segMask, regions, timestamp, MAX_TIME_DELTA);
```

The major input is the motion history image, mhi. In this case, you do not have a segment mask. The second parameter, segMask, is just an empty image. The result of the operation will be stored in the MatOfRect variable regions. You wrote the function plotMotion() to go through each Rect from regions. In the function, it skips the regions with areas too small to use. You use the same calcGlobalOrientation() function to find out the motion direction. The only difference is that you use a submatrix as a *region of interest* for each of the images mhi, orient, and mask. The rest is the same as what you did in the exercise Chapter06_16. Figure 6-19 shows a sample screenshot for reference.

Figure 6-19. *Segment motion demonstration*

Each circle on the left side of the image is the motion segment region. The size of the circle is defined by the shorter side of the region's width and height. The straight line inside the circle points to the motion direction from the center.

Conclusion

In this chapter, you investigated how to work creatively with motion to generate visual effects. In addition, you also learned how to identify motion from a sequence of frames and how such information can be used for interface design with gestural interactions. In the next chapter, you will continue your study of motion by first identifying points of interest and then track them across image frames to understand more about the movement.

CHAPTER 7

Feature Detection and Matching

This chapter continues the exploration of motion from the previous chapter with more sophisticated tracking methods. In the previous chapter, you compared and analyzed the whole image between frames to identify movement information. As a result, the motion details tracked from these methods are general, without making use of the specific structural elements in the image. In this chapter, you will first investigate how to locate the points of interest for detection. The common term for them is *feature points*. Then you will try to track how these feature points move between frames. The functions are mainly provided in the features2d module in OpenCV. In addition to the feature points, you will explore how to detect facial features and people using the objdetect module. The following are the topics covered in this chapter:

- Corner detection

- Sparse optical flow

- Feature detection

- Feature matching

- Face detection

- People detection

Corner Detection

In previous chapters, you learned that, in the imgproc module, the Canny() function can effectively detect edges in a digital image. In this chapter, you will go a step further to detect corner points in a digital image. The concept is like edge detection. As shown in Figure 7-1, corner points are those pixels that have significant changes in color in different directions.

© Bryan WC Chung 2017
B. WC. Chung, *Pro Processing for Images and Computer Vision with OpenCV*,
DOI 10.1007/978-1-4842-2775-6_7

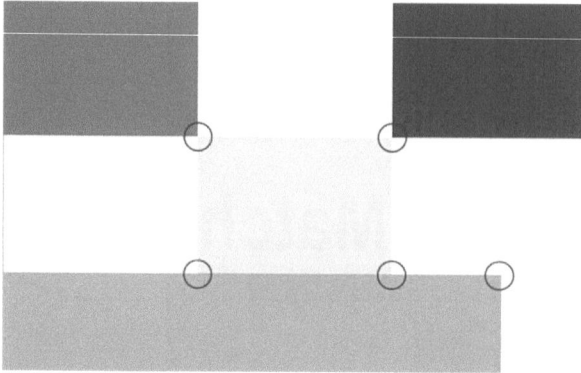

Figure 7-1. *Corner detection*

The first exercise, Chapter07_01, demonstrates the Harris corner detection method created by Chris Harris and Mike Stephens in 1988. To speed up the execution, you will scale down the original webcam image by a scaling factor of 10 in this exercise. After the corner detection, you normalize the result matrix to 8-bit resolution and loop through it to identify the corner pixels with values higher than the threshold.

```
// Harris corner detection
import processing.video.*;
import org.opencv.core.*;
import org.opencv.imgproc.Imgproc;

// Threshold value for a corner
final int THRESH = 140;
Capture cap;
CVImage img;
// Scale down the image for detection.
float scaling;
int w, h;

void setup() {
  size(640, 480);
  background(0);
  scaling = 10;
  System.loadLibrary(Core.NATIVE_LIBRARY_NAME);
  println(Core.VERSION);
  cap = new Capture(this, width, height);
  cap.start();
  w = floor(cap.width/scaling);
  h = floor(cap.height/scaling);
  img = new CVImage(w, h);
  smooth();
}
```

```
void draw() {
  if (!cap.available())
    return;
  background(0);
  cap.read();
  img.copy(cap, 0, 0, cap.width, cap.height,
    0, 0, img.width, img.height);
  img.copyTo();
  Mat grey = img.getGrey();
  // Output matrix of corner information
  Mat corners = Mat.zeros(grey.size(), CvType.CV_32FC1);
  Imgproc.cornerHarris(grey, corners, 2, 3, 0.04,
    Core.BORDER_DEFAULT);
  // Normalize the corner information matrix.
  Mat cor_norm = Mat.zeros(grey.size(), CvType.CV_8UC1);
  Core.normalize(corners, cor_norm, 0, 255,
    Core.NORM_MINMAX, CvType.CV_8UC1);
  image(cap, 0, 0);
  pushStyle();
  noFill();
  stroke(255, 0, 0);
  strokeWeight(2);
  // Draw each corner with value greater than threshold.
  for (int y=0; y<cor_norm.rows(); y++) {
    for (int x=0; x<cor_norm.cols(); x++) {
      if (cor_norm.get(y, x)[0] < THRESH)
        continue;
      ellipse(x*scaling, y*scaling, 10, 10);
    }
  }
  fill(0);
  text(nf(round(frameRate), 2), 10, 20);
  popStyle();
  grey.release();
  corners.release();
  cor_norm.release();
}
```

The major function is the cornerHarris() function from the imgproc module. The first parameter is the input grayscale image, grey. The second parameter is the output matrix, corners, that indicates how likely each pixel will be a corner point. The technical explanation of the rest of the parameters is beyond the scope of this book. If you're interested, you can find the official OpenCV tutorial at http://docs.opencv.org/3.1.0/d4/d7d/tutorial_harris_detector.html. The third parameter is the 2×2 neighborhood size for calculating the gradient (change of pixel intensity). The fourth parameter is the 3×3 aperture size of the Sobel derivative, as shown in the OpenCV documentation at http://docs.opencv.org/3.1.0/d2/d2c/tutorial_sobel_derivatives.html. The fifth parameter is the Harris detector parameter, shown in the previously mentioned Harris detector tutorial, and the last parameter is the border type indicator. Figure 7-2 shows a sample run of the program.

Figure 7-2. *Harris corner detection*

Sparse Optical Flow

You learned how to use the dense optical flow feature in Chapter 6. In this section, I will explain how you can use the sparse optical flow for motion detection. In dense optical flow, you inspect and trace all the pixels from a downsampled image, whereas in sparse optical flow, you inspect only a selected number of pixels. Those are the points you are interested in tracking, called *feature points*. In general, they are the corner points. The following are the steps you need to follow:

1. Identify the feature points.

2. Improve the accuracy of the points.

3. Calculate the optical flow of the points.

4. Visualize the flow information.

Identify the Feature Points

The next exercise, Chapter07_02, will use the function goodFeaturesToTrack() developed by Jianbo Shi and Carlo Tomasi in 1994. The function returns the most prominent corners in a digital image.

```
// Feature points detection
import processing.video.*;
import org.opencv.core.*;
import org.opencv.imgproc.Imgproc;

Capture cap;
CVImage img;

void setup() {
  size(1280, 480);
  background(0);
  System.loadLibrary(Core.NATIVE_LIBRARY_NAME);
  println(Core.VERSION);
  cap = new Capture(this, width/2, height);
  cap.start();
```

```
  img = new CVImage(cap.width, cap.height);
  smooth();
}

void draw() {
  if (!cap.available())
    return;
  background(0);
  cap.read();
  img.copy(cap, 0, 0, cap.width, cap.height,
    0, 0, img.width, img.height);
  img.copyTo();
  Mat grey = img.getGrey();
  MatOfPoint corners = new MatOfPoint();
  // Identify the good feature points.
  Imgproc.goodFeaturesToTrack(grey, corners,
    100, 0.01, 10);
  Point [] points = corners.toArray();
  pushStyle();
  noStroke();
  // Draw each feature point according to its
  // original color of the pixel.
  for (Point p : points) {
    int x = (int)constrain((float)p.x, 0, cap.width-1);
    int y = (int)constrain((float)p.y, 0, cap.height-1);
    color c = cap.pixels[y*cap.width+x];
    fill(c);
    ellipse(x+cap.width, y, 10, 10);
  }
  image(img, 0, 0);
  fill(0);
  text(nf(round(frameRate), 2), 10, 20);
  popStyle();
  grey.release();
  corners.release();
}
```

Inside the draw() function, after you obtain the grayscale image, you pass it to the goodFeaturesToTrack() function. It will return the feature point information in the MatOfPoint variable called corners. The remaining three parameters are the maximum number of points detected, the quality level for detection, and the minimum distance between each feature point. After you convert the corners variable into the array of Point called points, you loop through it to draw each corner as a circle, with the color taken from the original video capture image. Figure 7-3 shows a sample screenshot of the program.

Figure 7-3. *Good features to track*

Improve the Accuracy

After you obtain the list of feature points, you can use an OpenCV function to enhance the accuracy of the position of the points. Even though you are working on a digital image with pixels at an integer position, the corners can occur at positions between two adjacent pixels. That is at subpixel position. The following exercise, Chapter07_03, explores this function, cornerSubPix(), to enhance the accuracy of the corner point position:

```
// Feature points detection with subpixel accuracy
import processing.video.*;
import org.opencv.core.*;
import org.opencv.imgproc.Imgproc;

Capture cap;
CVImage img;
TermCriteria term;
int w, h;
float xRatio, yRatio;

void setup() {
  size(800, 600);
  background(0);
  System.loadLibrary(Core.NATIVE_LIBRARY_NAME);
  println(Core.VERSION);
  w = 640;
  h = 480;
  xRatio = (float)width/w;
  yRatio = (float)height/h;
  cap = new Capture(this, w, h);
  cap.start();
  img = new CVImage(cap.width, cap.height);
  term = new TermCriteria(TermCriteria.COUNT | TermCriteria.EPS,
    20, 0.03);
  smooth();
}
```

```
void draw() {
  if (!cap.available())
    return;
  background(200);
  cap.read();
  img.copy(cap, 0, 0, cap.width, cap.height,
    0, 0, img.width, img.height);
  img.copyTo();
  Mat grey = img.getGrey();
  MatOfPoint corners = new MatOfPoint();
  // Detect the initial feature points.
  Imgproc.goodFeaturesToTrack(grey, corners,
    100, 0.01, 10);
  MatOfPoint2f c2 = new MatOfPoint2f(corners.toArray());
  Imgproc.cornerSubPix(grey, c2,
    new Size(5, 5),
    new Size(-1, -1), term);
  Point [] points = corners.toArray();
  pushStyle();
  noFill();
  stroke(100);
  // Display the original points.
  for (Point p : points) {
    ellipse((float)p.x*xRatio, (float)p.y*yRatio, 20, 20);
  }
  points = c2.toArray();
  stroke(0);
  // Display the more accurate points.
  for (Point p : points) {
    ellipse((float)p.x*xRatio, (float)p.y*yRatio, 20, 20);
  }
  fill(0);
  text(nf(round(frameRate), 2), 10, 20);
  popStyle();
  grey.release();
  corners.release();
  c2.release();
}
```

In the program, you use a bigger sketch canvas size and a smaller video capture size to reveal the difference between the old (pixel-level) and new (subpixel-level) corners position. In the draw() function, after the goodFeaturesToTrack() function, you get a list of feature points in the MatOfPoint variable called corners. The new function, cornerSubPix(), will use the same inputs, the grey image and the corners matrix. The corners will be used as both the input and the output to store the new feature points with subpixel accuracy. To enable the enhanced accuracy, the input corners must be in a new floating-point format of MatOfPoint2f. For the cornerSubPix() function, the third parameter, Size(5, 5), is half the search window size. The fourth one, Size(-1, -1), is half the size of the zone in the search window that no search is done. The negative values indicate no such zone. The last one, term, is the termination criteria for the iterative process. It determines when an iterative process, such as the cornerSubPix() will end, either the maximum count 20 is reached or the desired accuracy of 0.03 pixel is achieved. In this example, you specify it in the setup() function with a maximum count 20 and the desired accuracy of 0.03 pixel. Figure 7-4 shows a screenshot of the running program. The gray circles indicate the pixel-level corners, while the black circles indicate the subpixel-level corners.

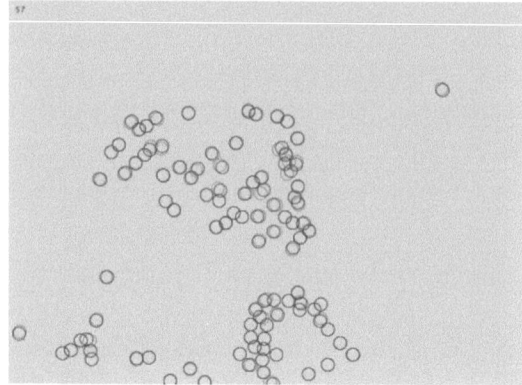

Figure 7-4. *Subpixel accuracy feature points*

Calculate the Optical Flow

After you have the accurate positions of the feature points, the next program, Chapter07_04, will track the flow of such feature points. The main function is calcOpticalFlowPyrLK() from the video module of OpenCV. It is the implementation based on the 2000 paper "Pyramidal Implementation of the Lucas Kanade Feature Tracker" by Jean-Yves Bouguet.

```
// Sparse optical flow
import processing.video.*;
import org.opencv.core.*;
import org.opencv.video.Video;
import org.opencv.imgproc.Imgproc;

final int CNT = 2;
// Threshold to recalculate the feature points
final int MIN_PTS = 20;
// Number of points to track
final int TRACK_PTS = 150;

Capture cap;
CVImage img;
TermCriteria term;
// Keep the old and new frames in greyscale.
Mat [] grey;
// Keep the old and new feature points.
MatOfPoint2f [] points;
// Keep the last index of the buffer.
int last;
// First run of the program
boolean first;

void setup() {
  size(1280, 480);
  background(0);
  System.loadLibrary(Core.NATIVE_LIBRARY_NAME);
```

```
    println(Core.VERSION);
    cap = new Capture(this, width/2, height);
    cap.start();
    img = new CVImage(cap.width, cap.height);
    term = new TermCriteria(TermCriteria.COUNT | TermCriteria.EPS,
        20, 0.03);
    // Initialize the image and keypoint buffers.
    grey = new Mat[CNT];
    points = new MatOfPoint2f[CNT];
    for (int i=0; i<CNT; i++) {
        grey[i] = Mat.zeros(cap.height, cap.width, CvType.CV_8UC1);
        points[i] = new MatOfPoint2f();
    }
    last = 0;
    first = true;
    smooth();
}

void draw() {
    if (!cap.available())
        return;
    background(0);
    cap.read();
    img.copy(cap, 0, 0, cap.width, cap.height,
        0, 0, img.width, img.height);
    img.copyTo();
    if (first) {
        // Initialize feature points in first run.
        findFeatures(img.getGrey());
        first = false;
        return;
    }
    int idx1, idx2;
    idx1 = last;
    idx2 = (idx1 + 1) % grey.length;
    last = idx2;
    grey[idx2] = img.getGrey();
    // Keep status and error of running the
    // optical flow function.
    MatOfByte status = new MatOfByte();
    MatOfFloat err = new MatOfFloat();
    Video.calcOpticalFlowPyrLK(grey[idx1], grey[idx2],
        points[idx1], points[idx2], status, err);
    Point [] pts = points[idx2].toArray();
    byte [] statArr = status.toArray();
    pushStyle();
    noStroke();
    int count = 0;
    for (int i=0; i<pts.length; i++) {
        // Skip error cases.
        if (statArr[i] == 0)
            continue;
```

227

```
    int x = (int)constrain((float)pts[i].x, 0, cap.width-1);
    int y = (int)constrain((float)pts[i].y, 0, cap.height-1);
    color c = cap.pixels[y*cap.width+x];
    fill(c);
    ellipse(x+cap.width, y, 10, 10);
    count++;
  }
  // Re-initialize feature points when valid points
  // drop down to the threshold.
  if (count < MIN_PTS)
    findFeatures(img.getGrey());
  image(img, 0, 0);
  fill(0);
  text(nf(round(frameRate), 2), 10, 20);
  popStyle();
  status.release();
  err.release();
}

void findFeatures(Mat g) {
  // Find feature points given the greyscale image g.
  int idx1, idx2;
  idx1 = last;
  idx2 = (idx1 + 1) % grey.length;
  last = idx2;
  grey[idx2] = g;
  MatOfPoint pt = new MatOfPoint();
  // Calculate feature points at pixel level.
  Imgproc.goodFeaturesToTrack(grey[idx2], pt,
    TRACK_PTS, 0.01, 10);
  points[idx2] = new MatOfPoint2f(pt.toArray());
  // Recalculate feature points at subpixel level.
  Imgproc.cornerSubPix(grey[idx2], points[idx2],
    new Size(10, 10),
    new Size(-1, -1), term);
  grey[idx2].copyTo(grey[idx1]);
  points[idx2].copyTo(points[idx1]);
  pt.release();
}

void keyPressed() {
  if (keyCode == 32) {
    // Press SPACE to initialize feature points.
    findFeatures(img.getGrey());
  }
}
```

Regarding the data structures, the program maintains two consecutive frames in grayscale stored in the array variable called grey. It also needs to keep two consecutive feature point lists stored in the MatOfPoint2f array called points. You use the integer variable last to keep track of which index in the array is the last image frame data. The boolean variable, first, indicates whether it is the first time to run the draw() loop. In the case of the first run, it will find the feature points by calling findFeatures() and update both the previous and current frame information. The function findFeatures() is the same as what you did in the previous exercise, Chapter07_03.

In the draw() function, you update the index idx1 to the last frame and idx2 to the current frame. After the update, you use the major function Video.calcOpticalFlowPyrLK() to compute the optical flow information between the last frame and current frame. The four input parameters to the functions are the previous frame, current frame, previous frame feature points, and current frame feature points. There are two outputs from the function. The first one is a MatOfByte variable, status, that returns 1 when the corresponding flow is found and 0 otherwise. The second output is the error measure that is not used in the current exercise. The for loop will then go through all the valid flow and draw tiny circles at the current frame feature points. The program also counts the valid flow data, and if the number drops below the threshold, MIN_PTS, it will initiate the findFeatures() function to recalculate the feature points for the current video image. Figure 7-5 is a sample screenshot of the program.

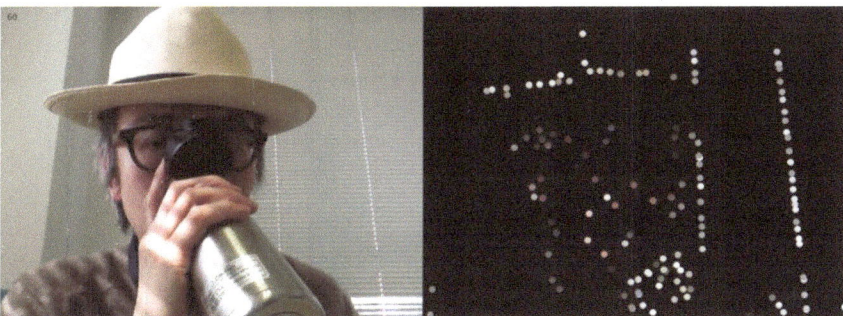

Figure 7-5. *Optical flow visualization*

Visualize the Flow Information

Instead of drawing the current feature points on the screen, you can generate a more creative visualization of the optical flow information. The next example, Chapter07_05, is an interactive animation of flow information. The logic is simple. You connect each pair of feature points from the previous position to its current position.

```
// Optical flow animation
import processing.video.*;
import org.opencv.core.*;
import org.opencv.video.Video;
import org.opencv.imgproc.Imgproc;

final int CNT = 2;
final int TRACK_PTS = 200;
final int MAX_DIST = 100;
```

```
Capture cap;
CVImage img;
TermCriteria term;
// Keep two consecutive frames and feature
// points list.
Mat [] grey;
MatOfPoint2f [] points;
int last;
boolean first;

void setup() {
  size(1280, 480);
  background(0);
  System.loadLibrary(Core.NATIVE_LIBRARY_NAME);
  println(Core.VERSION);
  cap = new Capture(this, width/2, height);
  cap.start();
  img = new CVImage(cap.width, cap.height);
  term = new TermCriteria(TermCriteria.COUNT | TermCriteria.EPS,
    20, 0.03);
  grey = new Mat[CNT];
  points = new MatOfPoint2f[CNT];
  for (int i=0; i<CNT; i++) {
    grey[i] = Mat.zeros(cap.height, cap.width, CvType.CV_8UC1);
    points[i] = new MatOfPoint2f();
  }
  last = 0;
  first = true;
  smooth();
}

void draw() {
  if (!cap.available())
    return;
  fillBack();
  cap.read();
  img.copy(cap, 0, 0, cap.width, cap.height,
    0, 0, img.width, img.height);
  img.copyTo();

  if (first) {
    findFeatures(img.getGrey());
    first = false;
    return;
  }
  int idx1, idx2;
  idx1 = last;
  idx2 = (idx1 + 1) % grey.length;
  last = idx2;
  grey[idx2] = img.getGrey();
  MatOfByte status = new MatOfByte();
  MatOfFloat err = new MatOfFloat();
```

```
Video.calcOpticalFlowPyrLK(grey[idx1], grey[idx2],
  points[idx1], points[idx2], status, err);
// pt1 - last feature points list
// pt2 - current feature points list
Point [] pt1 = points[idx1].toArray();
Point [] pt2 = points[idx2].toArray();
byte [] statArr = status.toArray();
PVector p1 = new PVector(0, 0);
PVector p2 = new PVector(0, 0);
pushStyle();
stroke(255, 200);
noFill();
for (int i=0; i<pt2.length; i++) {
  if (statArr[i] == 0)
    continue;
  // Constrain the points inside the video frame.
  p1.x = (int)constrain((float)pt1[i].x, 0, cap.width-1);
  p1.y = (int)constrain((float)pt1[i].y, 0, cap.height-1);
  p2.x = (int)constrain((float)pt2[i].x, 0, cap.width-1);
  p2.y = (int)constrain((float)pt2[i].y, 0, cap.height-1);
  // Discard the flow with great distance.
  if (p1.dist(p2) > MAX_DIST)
    continue;
  line(p1.x+cap.width, p1.y, p2.x+cap.width, p2.y);
}
// Find new feature points for each frame.
findFeatures(img.getGrey());
image(img, 0, 0);
fill(0);
text(nf(round(frameRate), 2), 10, 20);
popStyle();
status.release();
err.release();
}

void findFeatures(Mat g) {
  grey[last] = g;
  MatOfPoint pt = new MatOfPoint();
  Imgproc.goodFeaturesToTrack(grey[last], pt,
    TRACK_PTS, 0.01, 10);
  points[last] = new MatOfPoint2f(pt.toArray());
  Imgproc.cornerSubPix(grey[last], points[last],
    new Size(5, 5),
    new Size(-1, -1), term);
  pt.release();
}

void fillBack() {
  // Set background color with transparency.
  pushStyle();
  noStroke();
  fill(0, 0, 0, 80);
```

```
  rect(cap.width, 0, cap.width, cap.height);
  popStyle();
}
```

To create a motion blur effect, you do not clear the background color to black completely. In the fillBack() function, you fill the background with a rectangle of semitransparent color to create the motion trail of the lines. Figure 7-6 shows a screenshot of the animation.

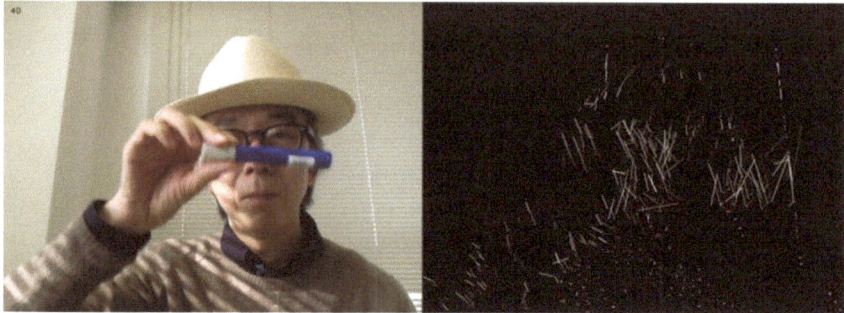

Figure 7-6. *Optical flow animation*

In creative coding, you often do not have correct and definite answers. In most cases, you just keep on asking the "what if?" question. Starting from the previous exercise, you can ask, what if you do not clear the screen to black? What if you pick up color for the lines from the video image? What if you use a different stroke weight? The next exercise, Chapter07_06, illustrates the ideas by accumulating the flow animation into a form of gesture painting. You can easily associate the effects to action paintings from painters such as Jackson Pollock.

```
// Optical flow drawing
import processing.video.*;
import org.opencv.core.*;
import org.opencv.video.Video;
import org.opencv.imgproc.Imgproc;

final int CNT = 2;
final int TRACK_PTS = 150;
final int MAX_DIST = 100;

Capture cap;
CVImage img;
TermCriteria term;
Mat [] grey;
MatOfPoint2f [] points;
int last;
boolean first;

void setup() {
  size(1280, 480);
  background(0);
  System.loadLibrary(Core.NATIVE_LIBRARY_NAME);
```

```
  println(Core.VERSION);
  cap = new Capture(this, width/2, height);
  cap.start();
  img = new CVImage(cap.width, cap.height);
  term = new TermCriteria(TermCriteria.COUNT | TermCriteria.EPS,
    20, 0.03);
  // Initialize the buffers for the 2 images and 2 keypoint lists.
  grey = new Mat[CNT];
  points = new MatOfPoint2f[CNT];
  for (int i=0; i<CNT; i++) {
    grey[i] = Mat.zeros(cap.height, cap.width, CvType.CV_8UC1);
    points[i] = new MatOfPoint2f();
  }
  last = 0;
  first = true;
  smooth();
}

void draw() {
  // Note that we do not clear the background.
  if (!cap.available())
    return;
  cap.read();
  img.copy(cap, 0, 0, cap.width, cap.height,
    0, 0, img.width, img.height);
  img.copyTo();

  if (first) {
    findFeatures(img.getGrey());
    first = false;
    return;
  }
  int idx1, idx2;
  idx1 = last;
  idx2 = (idx1 + 1) % grey.length;
  last = idx2;
  grey[idx2] = img.getGrey();
  MatOfByte status = new MatOfByte();
  MatOfFloat err = new MatOfFloat();
  Video.calcOpticalFlowPyrLK(grey[idx1], grey[idx2],
    points[idx1], points[idx2], status, err);
  Point [] pt2 = points[idx2].toArray();
  Point [] pt1 = points[idx1].toArray();
  byte [] statArr = status.toArray();
  PVector p1 = new PVector(0, 0);
  PVector p2 = new PVector(0, 0);
  pushStyle();
  noFill();
  for (int i=0; i<pt2.length; i++) {
    if (statArr[i] == 0)
      continue;
```

```
    p1.x = (int)constrain((float)pt1[i].x, 0, cap.width-1);
    p1.y = (int)constrain((float)pt1[i].y, 0, cap.height-1);
    p2.x = (int)constrain((float)pt2[i].x, 0, cap.width-1);
    p2.y = (int)constrain((float)pt2[i].y, 0, cap.height-1);
    if (p1.dist(p2) > MAX_DIST)
      continue;
    color c = cap.pixels[(int)p2.y*cap.width+(int)p2.x];
    stroke(red(c), green(c), blue(c), (int)random(100, 160));
    strokeWeight(random(3, 6));
    line(p1.x+cap.width, p1.y, p2.x+cap.width, p2.y);
    c = cap.pixels[(int)p1.y*cap.width+(int)p1.x];
    stroke(red(c), green(c), blue(c), (int)random(120, 240));
    strokeWeight(random(1, 4));
    line(p1.x+cap.width, p1.y, p2.x+cap.width, p2.y);
  }
  findFeatures(img.getGrey());
  image(img, 0, 0);
  fill(0);
  text(nf(round(frameRate), 2), 10, 20);
  popStyle();
  status.release();
  err.release();
}

void findFeatures(Mat g) {
  // Re-initialize the feature points.
  grey[last] = g;
  MatOfPoint pt = new MatOfPoint();
  Imgproc.goodFeaturesToTrack(grey[last], pt,
    TRACK_PTS, 0.01, 10);
  points[last] = new MatOfPoint2f(pt.toArray());
  Imgproc.cornerSubPix(grey[last], points[last],
    new Size(10, 10),
    new Size(-1, -1), term);
  pt.release();
}
```

The program is like the last one, except that you do not clear the background. Within the for loop to draw the flow data, you first pick up color from the live video image, and then you draw two lines instead of just one. The first line is a thicker one with more transparent color. The second line is thinner and more opaque. It creates a more painterly effect. Figure 7-7 contains two screenshots of the rendering with optical flow painting. My artwork *Movement in Time, Part 1* (http://www.magicandlove.com/blog/artworks/movement-in-time-v-1/) is an example of using sparse optical flow to generate gestural paintings from classic Hollywood film sequences.

Figure 7-7. *Optical flow drawing*

Feature Detection

In the previous sections, you tried to locate key feature points through the use of the Harris corner method and the goodFeaturesToTrack() function with the Shi and Tomasi method. OpenCV provides generalized key point processing for you to detect them, describe them, and match them between consecutive frames. In this section, you will first study how to identify the key points using the FeatureDetector class in the features2d module. The next exercise, Chapter07_07, will demonstrate the basic operation of the class:

```
// Features detection
import processing.video.*;
import org.opencv.core.*;
import org.opencv.imgproc.Imgproc;
import org.opencv.features2d.FeatureDetector;

final float MIN_RESP = 0.003;
Capture cap;
CVImage img;
FeatureDetector fd;

void setup() {
  size(1280, 480);
  background(0);
  System.loadLibrary(Core.NATIVE_LIBRARY_NAME);
  println(Core.VERSION);
  cap = new Capture(this, width/2, height);
  cap.start();
  img = new CVImage(cap.width, cap.height);
```

```
  // Create the instance of the class.
  fd = FeatureDetector.create(FeatureDetector.ORB);
  smooth();
}

void draw() {
  if (!cap.available())
    return;
  background(0);
  cap.read();
  img.copy(cap, 0, 0, cap.width, cap.height,
    0, 0, img.width, img.height);
  img.copyTo();
  Mat grey = img.getGrey();
  MatOfKeyPoint pt = new MatOfKeyPoint();
  // Detect keypoints from the image.
  fd.detect(grey, pt);
  image(cap, 0, 0);
  CVImage out = new CVImage(cap.width, cap.height);
  out.copyTo(grey);
  tint(255, 100);
  image(out, cap.width, 0);
  noTint();
  pushStyle();
  noFill();
  stroke(255, 200, 0);
  KeyPoint [] kps = pt.toArray();
  for (KeyPoint kp : kps) {
    // Skip the keypoints that are less likely.
    if (kp.response < MIN_RESP)
      continue;
    float x1 = (float)kp.pt.x;
    float y1 = (float)kp.pt.y;
    float x2 = x1 + kp.size*cos(radians(kp.angle))/2;
    float y2 = y1 + kp.size*sin(radians(kp.angle))/2;
    // size is the diameter of neighborhood.
    ellipse(x1+cap.width, y1, kp.size, kp.size);
    // Draw also the orientation direction.
    line(x1+cap.width, y1, x2+cap.width, y2);
  }
  fill(0);
  text(nf(round(frameRate), 2), 10, 20);
  popStyle();
  grey.release();
  pt.release();
}
```

You use the FeatureDetector class instance fd to work on the major tasks. In the setup() function, you create the instance fd with the FeatureDetector.create() function. The parameter indicates the type of detector you use. In the Java build of OpenCV 3.1, you have the following types:

AKAZE, DYNAMIC_AKAZE, GRID_AKAZE, PYRAMID_AKAZE,

BRISK, DYNAMIC_BRISK, GRID_BRISK, PYRAMID_BRISK,

FAST, DYNAMIC_FAST, GRID_FAST, PYRAMID_FAST,

GFTT, DYNAMIC_GFTT, GRID_GFTT, PYRAMID, GFTT,

HARRIS, DYNAMIC_HARRIS, GRID_HARRIS, PYRAMID_HARRIS,

MSER, DYNAMIC_MSER, GRID_MSER, PYRAMID_MSER,

ORB, DYNAMIC_ORB, GRID_ORB, PYRAMID_ORB,

SIMPLEBLOB, DYNAMIC_SIMPLEBLOB, GRID_SIMPLEBLOB, PYRAMID_SIMPLEBLOB

In the current exercise, you will use the type FeatureDetector.ORB. Detailed descriptions of the various detector types are beyond the scope of this book. Nevertheless, you can refer to Figure 7-9 later in the chapter for a comparison of various detector types.

In the draw() function, you use the method fd.detect(grey, pt) to perform the key point detection and store the result in the MatOfKeyPoint instance called pt. After you convert pt into a KeyPoint array, kps, you use a for loop to go through each KeyPoint object. For each KeyPoint, the property pt is the position of the point. The property response describes how likely it is a key point. You compare it with a threshold of MIN_RESP to skip those with smaller values. The property size is the diameter of the key point neighborhood. The property angle shows the key point orientation. You use a circle to indicate the key point and its neighborhood size and a straight line to show the direction. Figure 7-8 shows a sample screenshot. The grayscale image is displayed in darker tones to create a higher contrast with the key point circles.

Figure 7-8. *Feature detection in features2d*

Figure 7-9 shows a collection of the key points detected using different FeatureDetector types.

Figure 7-9. *Comparison of different FeatureDetector types*

You can use the key point information for creative visualization. In the next section, you will, however, study generalized feature matching in OpenCV for subsequent tracking purposes. Before you can work with feature matching, there is one more step: key point description. You will use the DescriptorExtractor class from the features2d module to compute the descriptor of the key points. The next exercise, Chapter07_08, will illustrate the use of the descriptor:

```
// Keypoint descriptor
import processing.video.*;
import org.opencv.core.*;
import org.opencv.imgproc.Imgproc;
import org.opencv.features2d.FeatureDetector;

Capture cap;
CVImage img;
FeatureDetector fd;
DescriptorExtractor de;

void setup() {
  size(1280, 480);
  background(0);
  System.loadLibrary(Core.NATIVE_LIBRARY_NAME);
  println(Core.VERSION);
  cap = new Capture(this, width/2, height);
  cap.start();
  img = new CVImage(cap.width, cap.height);
  fd = FeatureDetector.create(FeatureDetector.AKAZE);
  // Create the instance for the descriptor
  de = DescriptorExtractor.create(DescriptorExtractor.AKAZE);
  smooth();
}
```

```
void draw() {
  if (!cap.available())
    return;
  background(0);
  cap.read();
  img.copy(cap, 0, 0, cap.width, cap.height,
    0, 0, img.width, img.height);
  img.copyTo();
  Mat grey = img.getGrey();
  image(cap, 0, 0);
  CVImage out = new CVImage(cap.width, cap.height);
  out.copyTo(grey);
  tint(255, 200);
  image(out, cap.width, 0);
  noTint();
  MatOfKeyPoint pt = new MatOfKeyPoint();
  fd.detect(grey, pt);
  Mat desc = new Mat();
  // Compute the descriptor from grey and pt.
  de.compute(grey, pt, desc);
  pushStyle();
  noFill();
  stroke(255, 200, 0);
  KeyPoint [] kps = pt.toArray();
  for (KeyPoint kp : kps) {
    float x = (float)kp.pt.x;
    float y = (float)kp.pt.y;
    ellipse(x+cap.width, y, kp.size, kp.size);
  }
  popStyle();
  pt.release();
  grey.release();
  desc.release();
  fill(0);
  text(nf(round(frameRate), 2), 10, 20);
}
```

The program is like the last one. It only adds a new class, DescriptorExtractor, and its instance, de. It uses the DescriptorExtractor.create() method to create an instance in the setup() function. In the draw() function, it uses the compute() method to create the descriptor in the Mat called desc. The display in the Processing window is similar to Figure 7-8 except that you generate more key points on the screen because you do not skip those key points with a low response. For each key point in pt, there will be one entry in desc for the description of that key point. Once you have the descriptor information in desc, you are ready to proceed to matching in the next section.

Feature Matching

Feature matching usually involves two sets of information. The first set consists of the feature points and the descriptor of a known image. You can refer it as the *trained set*. The second one consists of the feature points and the descriptor coming from a new image, usually from the live capture image. You can refer it as the *query set*. The job of feature matching is to perform the feature point matching between the trained set and the query set. The purpose of doing the feature matching is to identify a known pattern from the trained set and track where that pattern moves in the query set. In the coming exercises, you will first perform a general feature matching between two snapshots from the live video stream, and in the second exercise, you interactively select a pattern in a snapshot and try to track where it moves in the live video stream.

The next exercise, Chapter07_09, is the preparation of the matching. It will display the trained snapshot image and the live query image, together with the key point information. You can press the mouse button to toggle the training action.

```
// Features matching
import processing.video.*;
import org.opencv.core.*;
import org.opencv.imgproc.Imgproc;
import org.opencv.features2d.FeatureDetector;

Capture cap;
CVImage img;
FeatureDetector fd;
DescriptorExtractor de;
// Two sets of keypoints: train, query
MatOfKeyPoint trainKp, queryKp;
// Two sets of descriptor: train, query
Mat trainDc, queryDc;
Mat grey;
// Keep if training started.
boolean trained;
// Keep the trained image.
PImage trainImg;

void setup() {
  size(1280, 480);
  background(0);
  System.loadLibrary(Core.NATIVE_LIBRARY_NAME);
  println(Core.VERSION);
  cap = new Capture(this, width/2, height);
  cap.start();
  img = new CVImage(cap.width, cap.height);
  trainImg = createImage(cap.width, cap.height, ARGB);
  fd = FeatureDetector.create(FeatureDetector.BRISK);
  de = DescriptorExtractor.create(DescriptorExtractor.BRISK);
  trainKp = new MatOfKeyPoint();
  queryKp = new MatOfKeyPoint();
  trainDc = new Mat();
  queryDc = new Mat();
  grey = Mat.zeros(cap.height, cap.width, CvType.CV_8UC1);
  trained = false;
  smooth();
}
```

```
void draw() {
  if (!cap.available())
    return;
  background(0);
  cap.read();

  if (trained) {
    image(trainImg, 0, 0);
    image(cap, trainImg.width, 0);
    img.copy(cap, 0, 0, cap.width, cap.height,
      0, 0, img.width, img.height);
    img.copyTo();
    grey = img.getGrey();
    fd.detect(grey, queryKp);
    de.compute(grey, queryKp, queryDc);
    drawTrain();
    drawQuery();
  } else {
    image(cap, 0, 0);
    image(cap, cap.width, 0);
  }
  pushStyle();
  fill(0);
  text(nf(round(frameRate), 2), 10, 20);
  popStyle();
}

void drawTrain() {
  // Draw the keypoints for the trained snapshot.
  pushStyle();
  noFill();
  stroke(255, 200, 0);
  KeyPoint [] kps = trainKp.toArray();
  for (KeyPoint kp : kps) {
    float x = (float)kp.pt.x;
    float y = (float)kp.pt.y;
    ellipse(x, y, kp.size, kp.size);
  }
  popStyle();
}

void drawQuery() {
  // Draw the keypoints for live query image.
  pushStyle();
  noFill();
  stroke(255, 200, 0);
  KeyPoint [] kps = queryKp.toArray();
  for (KeyPoint kp : kps) {
    float x = (float)kp.pt.x;
    float y = (float)kp.pt.y;
    ellipse(x+trainImg.width, y, kp.size, kp.size);
  }
```

```
  popStyle();
}

void mousePressed() {
  // Press mouse button to toggle training.
  if (!trained) {
    arrayCopy(cap.pixels, trainImg.pixels);
    trainImg.updatePixels();
    img.copy(trainImg, 0, 0, trainImg.width, trainImg.height,
      0, 0, img.width, img.height);
    img.copyTo();
    grey = img.getGrey();
    fd.detect(grey, trainKp);
    de.compute(grey, trainKp, trainDc);
    trained = true;
  } else {
    trained = false;
  }
}
```

The program is relatively straightforward. You keep two pairs of the data structure. The first pair is the MatOfKeyPoint for the trained image, trainKp, and the query image, queryKp. The second pair consists of the descriptors, trainDc and queryDC. When users press the mouse button, it will take a snapshot of the current video stream and use the image to compute the trained key points, trainKp, and the descriptor, trainDc. In the draw() function, if there is a trained image, the program will compute the query key points, queryKp, and the descriptor, queryDc, from the live video image. Both images and the key point information will be displayed in the Processing window.

Figure 7-10 shows a sample screenshot of running the program. The left image is the still image and its trained key points. The right image is the live video image and its query key points.

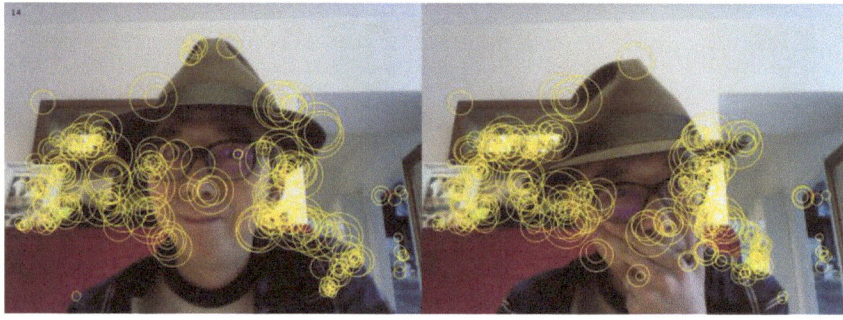

Figure 7-10. *Feature points from the trained and query images*

The next exercise, Chapter07_10, will introduce matching to identify the corresponding key points between the trained and query images.

```
// Features matching
import processing.video.*;
import java.util.Arrays;
import org.opencv.core.*;
```

```
import org.opencv.imgproc.Imgproc;
import org.opencv.features2d.FeatureDetector;
import org.opencv.features2d.DescriptorExtractor;
import org.opencv.features2d.DescriptorMatcher;

final int MAX_DIST = 200;
Capture cap;
CVImage img;
FeatureDetector fd;
DescriptorExtractor de;
MatOfKeyPoint trainKp, queryKp;
Mat trainDc, queryDc;
DescriptorMatcher match;
Mat grey;
boolean trained;
PImage trainImg;

void setup() {
  size(1280, 480);
  background(0);
  System.loadLibrary(Core.NATIVE_LIBRARY_NAME);
  println(Core.VERSION);
  cap = new Capture(this, width/2, height);
  cap.start();
  img = new CVImage(cap.width, cap.height);
  trainImg = createImage(cap.width, cap.height, ARGB);
  fd = FeatureDetector.create(FeatureDetector.ORB);
  de = DescriptorExtractor.create(DescriptorExtractor.ORB);
  match = DescriptorMatcher.create(DescriptorMatcher.BRUTEFORCE_L1);
  trainKp = new MatOfKeyPoint();
  queryKp = new MatOfKeyPoint();
  trainDc = new Mat();
  queryDc = new Mat();
  grey = Mat.zeros(cap.height, cap.width, CvType.CV_8UC1);
  trained = false;
  smooth();
}

void draw() {
  if (!cap.available())
    return;
  background(0);
  cap.read();

  if (trained) {
    image(trainImg, 0, 0);
    image(cap, trainImg.width, 0);
    img.copy(cap, 0, 0, cap.width, cap.height,
      0, 0, img.width, img.height);
    img.copyTo();
    grey = img.getGrey();
    fd.detect(grey, queryKp);
```

```
    de.compute(grey, queryKp, queryDc);
    MatOfDMatch pairs = new MatOfDMatch();
   // Perform key point matching.
    match.match(queryDc, trainDc, pairs);

    DMatch [] dm = pairs.toArray();
    KeyPoint [] tKp = trainKp.toArray();
    KeyPoint [] qKp = queryKp.toArray();
    // Connect the matched key points.
    for (DMatch d : dm) {
    // Skip those with large distance.
      if (d.distance>MAX_DIST)
        continue;
      KeyPoint t = tKp[d.trainIdx];
      KeyPoint q = qKp[d.queryIdx];
      line((float)t.pt.x, (float)t.pt.y,
        (float)q.pt.x+cap.width, (float)q.pt.y);
    }
    drawTrain();
    drawQuery();
    pairs.release();
  } else {
    image(cap, 0, 0);
    image(cap, cap.width, 0);
  }
  pushStyle();
  fill(0);
  text(nf(round(frameRate), 2), 10, 20);
  popStyle();
}

void drawTrain() {
  pushStyle();
  noFill();
  stroke(255, 200, 0);
  KeyPoint [] kps = trainKp.toArray();
  for (KeyPoint kp : kps) {
    float x = (float)kp.pt.x;
    float y = (float)kp.pt.y;
    ellipse(x, y, kp.size, kp.size);
  }
  popStyle();
}

void drawQuery() {
  pushStyle();
  noFill();
  stroke(255, 200, 0);
  KeyPoint [] kps = queryKp.toArray();
  for (KeyPoint kp : kps) {
    float x = (float)kp.pt.x;
    float y = (float)kp.pt.y;
```

```
      ellipse(x+trainImg.width, y, kp.size, kp.size);
    }
    popStyle();
}

void mousePressed() {
  if (!trained) {
    arrayCopy(cap.pixels, trainImg.pixels);
    trainImg.updatePixels();
    img.copy(trainImg, 0, 0, trainImg.width, trainImg.height,
      0, 0, img.width, img.height);
    img.copyTo();
    grey = img.getGrey();
    fd.detect(grey, trainKp);
    de.compute(grey, trainKp, trainDc);
    trained = true;
  } else {
    trained = false;
  }
}
```

Most of the code is identical to the previous program, Chapter07_09. Nevertheless, you have a few new entries in this code. In the setup() function, you have to initialize the DescriptorMatcher class instance, match, with the following statement:

```
match = DescriptorMatcher.create(DescriptorMatcher.BRUTEFORCE_L1);
```

The parameter inside the static create() method is the matching method. The following variations of the brute-force method are supported: BRUTEFORCE, BRUTEFORCE_HAMMING, BRUTEFORCE_HAMMINGLUT, BRUTEFORCE_L1, and BRUTEFORCE_SL2. If you click inside the Processing image, the following statement will be executed inside the draw() function:

```
match.match(queryDc, trainDc, pairs);
```

The match() function will perform the matching between the key point descriptor from the live image, queryDc, and the key point descriptor from the stored image on the left side, trainDc. The variable, pairs, will store all the matching key point pairs as a MatOfDMatch instance. DMatch is a data structure to maintain the matching indices of the key points, queryIdx and trainIdx, stored in the query and trained key point lists, queryKp and trainKp. The for loop afterward will enumerate all the key point matching pairs and draw the matching lines for those with the matching distance, d.distance, shorter than the threshold of MAX_DIST. Figure 7-11 shows the resulting screenshot of the execution.

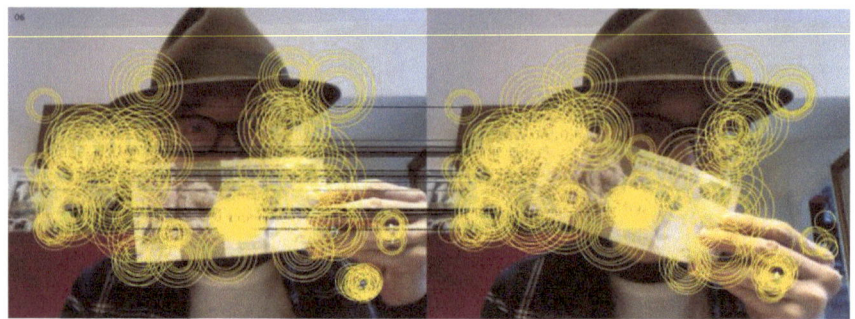

Figure 7-11. *Feature matching*

In many cases, you will not use the whole image through the webcam as the training image pattern. You may just select part of the image as the pattern you would like to track. In the next exercise, Chapter07_11, you will use the mouse to draw a rectangle to select only part of the live image for tracking purposes. This is similar to the Rectangular Marquee tool in most graphic software. You click and drag to define a rectangular area as the trained image and use only those key points inside this area to match against those in the query image from the live video. To simplify the main program, you define a separate class, Dragging, to handle the mouse interaction from here.

```
import org.opencv.core.Rect;

// Define 3 states of mouse drag action.
public enum State {
    IDLE,
    DRAGGING,
    SELECTED
}
// A class to handle the mouse drag action
public class Dragging {
  PVector p1, p2;
  Rect roi;
  State state;

  public Dragging() {
    p1 = new PVector(Float.MAX_VALUE, Float.MAX_VALUE);
    p2 = new PVector(Float.MIN_VALUE, Float.MIN_VALUE);
    roi = new Rect(0, 0, 0, 0);
    state = State.IDLE;
  }

  void init(PVector m) {
    empty(m);
    state = State.DRAGGING;
  }

  void update(PVector m) {
    p2.set(m.x, m.y);
    roi.x = (int)min(p1.x, p2.x);
    roi.y = (int)min(p1.y, p2.y);
```

```
    roi.width = (int)abs(p2.x-p1.x);
    roi.height = (int)abs(p2.y-p1.y);
  }

  void move(PVector m) {
    update(m);
  }

  void stop(PVector m) {
    update(m);
    state = State.SELECTED;
  }

  void empty(PVector m) {
    p1.set(m.x, m.y);
    p2.set(m.x, m.y);
    roi.x = (int)m.x;
    roi.y = (int)m.y;
    roi.width = 0;
    roi.height = 0;
  }

  void reset(PVector m) {
    empty(m);
    state = State.IDLE;
  }

  boolean isDragging() {
    return (state == State.DRAGGING);
  }

  boolean isSelected() {
    return (state == State.SELECTED);
  }

  boolean isIdle() {
    return (state == State.IDLE);
  }

  Rect getRoi() {
    return roi;
  }
}
```

The class defines three states of mouse interaction: IDLE, when no selection is initiated; DRAGGING, when user has clicked and started dragging the mouse; and SELECTED, when the user has released the mouse button to confirm the selection rectangle, roi. The class maintains two PVector objects: p1, the top-left corner of the selection rectangle, and p2, the bottom-right corner of the selection rectangle. When the user starts the click-drag action, the program will call the init() method. During the drag action, it will call the move() method. When user stops and releases the mouse button, it will call the stop() method. When the user clicks without any dragging, it will clear the selection by calling the reset() method. The class also provides three Boolean methods (isIdle(), isDragging(), and isSelected()) for the users to query the state of the interaction.

The main program is similar to the Chapter07_10 exercise, except that you have additional code to handle the selection interaction and the ways to eliminate the key points outside the selection rectangle.

```
// Features matching with selection
import processing.video.*;
import java.util.Arrays;
import org.opencv.core.*;
import org.opencv.imgproc.Imgproc;
import org.opencv.features2d.FeatureDetector;
import org.opencv.features2d.DescriptorExtractor;
import org.opencv.features2d.DescriptorMatcher;
import org.opencv.calib3d.Calib3d;

Capture cap;
CVImage img;
// Feature detector, extractor and matcher
FeatureDetector fd;
DescriptorExtractor de;
DescriptorMatcher match;
// Key points and descriptors for train and query
MatOfKeyPoint trainKp, queryKp;
Mat trainDc, queryDc;
// Buffer for the trained image
PImage trainImg;
// A class to work with mouse drag & selection
Dragging drag;
Mat hg;
MatOfPoint2f trainRect, queryRect;

void setup() {
  size(1280, 480);
  background(0);
  System.loadLibrary(Core.NATIVE_LIBRARY_NAME);
  println(Core.VERSION);
  cap = new Capture(this, width/2, height);
  cap.start();
  img = new CVImage(cap.width, cap.height);
  trainImg = createImage(cap.width, cap.height, ARGB);
  fd = FeatureDetector.create(FeatureDetector.ORB);
  de = DescriptorExtractor.create(DescriptorExtractor.ORB);
  match = DescriptorMatcher.create(DescriptorMatcher.BRUTEFORCE_HAMMING);
  trainKp = new MatOfKeyPoint();
  queryKp = new MatOfKeyPoint();
  trainDc = new Mat();
  queryDc = new Mat();
  hg = Mat.eye(3, 3, CvType.CV_32FC1);
  drag = new Dragging();
  smooth();
  trainRect = new MatOfPoint2f();
  queryRect = new MatOfPoint2f();
}
```

```
void draw() {
  if (!cap.available())
    return;
  background(0);
  cap.read();
  img.copy(cap, 0, 0, cap.width, cap.height,
    0, 0, img.width, img.height);
  img.copyTo();
  Mat grey = img.getGrey();
  image(trainImg, 0, 0);
  image(cap, trainImg.width, 0);

  if (drag.isDragging()) {
    drawRect(cap.width);
  } else if (drag.isSelected()) {
    drawRect(0);
    matchPoints(grey);
    drawTrain();
    drawQuery();
  }
  pushStyle();
  fill(80);
  text(nf(round(frameRate), 2), 10, 20);
  popStyle();
  grey.release();
}

void matchPoints(Mat im) {
  // Match the trained and query key points.
  fd.detect(im, queryKp);
  de.compute(im, queryKp, queryDc);
  // Skip if the trained or query descriptors are empty.
  if (!queryDc.empty() &&
    !trainDc.empty()) {
    MatOfDMatch pairs = new MatOfDMatch();
    match.match(queryDc, trainDc, pairs);
    DMatch [] dm = pairs.toArray();
    // Convert trained and query MatOfKeyPoint to array.
    KeyPoint [] tKp = trainKp.toArray();
    KeyPoint [] qKp = queryKp.toArray();
    float minDist = Float.MAX_VALUE;
    float maxDist = Float.MIN_VALUE;
    // Obtain the min and max distances of matching.
    for (DMatch d : dm) {
      if (d.distance < minDist) {
        minDist = d.distance;
      }
      if (d.distance > maxDist) {
        maxDist = d.distance;
      }
    }
```

```
float thresVal = 2*minDist;
ArrayList<Point> trainList = new ArrayList<Point>();
ArrayList<Point> queryList = new ArrayList<Point>();
pushStyle();
noFill();
stroke(255);
for (DMatch d : dm) {
  if (d.queryIdx >= qKp.length ||
    d.trainIdx >= tKp.length)
    continue;
  // Skip match data with distance larger than
  // 2 times of min distance.
  if (d.distance > thresVal)
    continue;
  KeyPoint t = tKp[d.trainIdx];
  KeyPoint q = qKp[d.queryIdx];
  trainList.add(t.pt);
  queryList.add(q.pt);
  // Draw a line for each pair of matching key points.
  line((float)t.pt.x, (float)t.pt.y,
    (float)q.pt.x+cap.width, (float)q.pt.y);
}
MatOfPoint2f trainM = new MatOfPoint2f();
MatOfPoint2f queryM = new MatOfPoint2f();
trainM.fromList(trainList);
queryM.fromList(queryList);
// Find the homography matrix between the trained
// key points and query key points.
// Proceed only with more than 5 key points.
if (trainList.size() > 5 &&
  queryList.size() > 5) {
  hg = Calib3d.findHomography(trainM, queryM, Calib3d.RANSAC, 3.0);
  if (!hg.empty()) {
    // Perform perspective transform to the
    // selection rectangle with the homography matrix.
    Core.perspectiveTransform(trainRect, queryRect, hg);
  }
  pairs.release();
  trainM.release();
  queryM.release();
  hg.release();
}
if (!queryRect.empty()) {
  // Draw the transformed selection matrix.
  Point [] out = queryRect.toArray();
  stroke(255, 255, 0);
  for (int i=0; i<out.length; i++) {
    int j = (i+1) % out.length;
    Point p1 = out[i];
    Point p2 = out[j];
    line((float)p1.x+cap.width, (float)p1.y,
      (float)p2.x+cap.width, (float)p2.y);
```

```
      }
    }
  }
  popStyle();
}

void drawRect(float ox) {
  // Draw the selection rectangle.
  pushStyle();
  noFill();
  stroke(255, 255, 0);
  rect(drag.getRoi().x+ox, drag.getRoi().y,
    drag.getRoi().width, drag.getRoi().height);
  popStyle();
}

void drawTrain() {
  // Draw the trained key points.
  pushStyle();
  noFill();
  stroke(255, 200, 0);
  KeyPoint [] kps = trainKp.toArray();
  for (KeyPoint kp : kps) {
    float x = (float)kp.pt.x;
    float y = (float)kp.pt.y;
    ellipse(x, y, 10, 10);
  }
  popStyle();
}

void drawQuery() {
  // Draw live image key points.
  pushStyle();
  noFill();
  stroke(255, 200, 0);
  KeyPoint [] kps = queryKp.toArray();
  for (KeyPoint kp : kps) {
    float x = (float)kp.pt.x;
    float y = (float)kp.pt.y;
    ellipse(x+trainImg.width, y, 10, 10);
  }
  popStyle();
}

void mouseClicked() {
  // Reset the drag rectangle.
  drag.reset(new PVector(0, 0));
}
```

```
void mousePressed() {
  // Click only on the right hand side of the window
  // to start the drag action.
  if (mouseX < cap.width || mouseX >= cap.width*2)
    return;
  if (mouseY < 0 || mouseY >= cap.height)
    return;
  drag.init(new PVector(mouseX-cap.width, mouseY));
}

void mouseDragged() {
  // Drag the selection rectangle.
  int x = constrain(mouseX, cap.width, cap.width*2-1);
  int y = constrain(mouseY, 0, cap.height-1);
  drag.move(new PVector(x-cap.width, y));
}

void mouseReleased() {
  // Finalize the selection rectangle.
  int x = constrain(mouseX, cap.width, cap.width*2-1);
  int y = constrain(mouseY, 0, cap.height-1);
  drag.stop(new PVector(x-cap.width, y));

  // Compute the trained key points and descriptor.
  arrayCopy(cap.pixels, trainImg.pixels);
  trainImg.updatePixels();
  CVImage tBGR = new CVImage(trainImg.width, trainImg.height);
  tBGR.copy(trainImg, 0, 0, trainImg.width, trainImg.height,
    0, 0, tBGR.width, tBGR.height);
  tBGR.copyTo();
  Mat temp = tBGR.getGrey();
  Mat tTrain = new Mat();
  // Detect and compute key points and descriptors.
  fd.detect(temp, trainKp);
  de.compute(temp, trainKp, tTrain);
  // Define the selection rectangle.
  Rect r = drag.getRoi();
  // Convert MatOfKeyPoint to array.
  KeyPoint [] iKpt = trainKp.toArray();
  ArrayList<KeyPoint> oKpt = new ArrayList<KeyPoint>();
  trainDc.release();
  // Select only the key points inside selection rectangle.
  for (int i=0; i<iKpt.length; i++) {
    if (r.contains(iKpt[i].pt)) {
      // Add key point to the output list.
      oKpt.add(iKpt[i]);
      trainDc.push_back(tTrain.row(i));
    }
  }
```

```
   trainKp.fromList(oKpt);
   // Compute the selection rectangle as MatOfPoint2f.
   ArrayList<Point> quad = new ArrayList<Point>();
   quad.add(new Point(r.x, r.y));
   quad.add(new Point(r.x+r.width, r.y));
   quad.add(new Point(r.x+r.width, r.y+r.height));
   quad.add(new Point(r.x, r.y+r.height));
   trainRect.fromList(quad);
   queryRect.release();
   tTrain.release();
   temp.release();
}
```

In the Processing window, there will be two images on the screen. The left one is the trained image when the user has performed a selection through the mouse drag action. The right side is the live video image. When the user wants to make a selection, the user needs to click and drag on the right live image. When the selection rectangle is confirmed, it will be sent to the left side along with the snapshot of the live video image. The Processing event handlers mouseClicked(), mousePressed(), mouseDragged(), and mouseReleased() manage the interactive selection process. In the mouseReleased() method, you have additional code to first detect the key points from a grayscale version of the live video image; second compute the descriptors of the key points; third go through all the key points and choose only those inside the selection rectangle, drag.getRoi(); fourth prepare the trained key point list, trainKp, and descriptor, trainDc; and finally convert the selection rectangle as a MatOfPoint2f variable called trainRect.

Inside the draw() function, you just draw the temporary selection rectangle during the DRAGGING state. In the SELECTED state, you will call the matchPoints() function, which is the most complex function in the program. In this function, it first detects the key points from the live video image and computes the descriptor. When both the trained and query descriptors are not empty, it performs the key point matching. Note that the trained descriptor, trainDc, contains only the key point descriptions within the selection rectangle. After the matching, the function will go through all the matching pairs to find out the minimum and maximum distances within the MatOfDMatch object named pairs. In the subsequent loop, you process only the matching pairs with a distance less than two times the minimum distance value. After the for loop, you will have drawn the lines connecting all the matching key points and created two additional MatOfPoint2f variables, trainM and queryM, from the key point lists. When both trainM and queryM contain more than five key points each, you proceed to compute the transformation matrix (homography), hg, from the two key point lists, with the Calib3d.findHomography() method. Through the homography matrix, hg, you perform a perspective transform, Core.perspectiveTransform(), to convert the selection rectangle, which is stored in trainRect, to the queryRect. The queryRect shape consists of the four coordinates of the corners of the transformed rectangle, located on the right side of the window. Essentially, the four corners will define the rectangle of the tracked pattern. The last part of the matchPoints() function draws the four straight lines connecting the four corners found in queryRect.

Figure 7-12 shows the resulting screenshot. The quad on the right side is the region that was tracked by using the pattern detected from the static trained image on the left side. For best results, the pattern you select should contain a high-contrast visual texture. You should also avoid a similar texture in the background. In the matchPoints() function, you establish a threshold to skip the matched key points with a discrepancy larger than two times the minimum distance. You can lower the threshold to reduce noise conditions.

Figure 7-12. *Key point matching with a selection rectangle*

Besides drawing the quad's outline, the next exercise, Chapter07_12, will perform a texture mapping onto the quad drawn over the live webcam image. Instead of listing the whole source code of the exercise here, I just highlight the changes from the original version in Chapter07_11. You define a global PImage variable, photo, to keep the image that you would like to map on top of the tracked pattern. In the setup() function, you use the P3D render as size(1280, 480, P3D) and also set the texture mode to normal as textureMode(NORMAL). Toward the end of the matchPoints() function, you have the following code to draw the quad in the previous exercise, Chapter07_11:

```
if (!queryRect.empty()) {
    // Draw the transformed selection matrix.
    Point [] out = queryRect.toArray();
    stroke(255, 255, 0);
    for (int i=0; i<out.length; i++) {
      int j = (i+1) % out.length;
      Point p1 = out[i];
      Point p2 = out[j];
      line((float)p1.x+cap.width, (float)p1.y,
        (float)p2.x+cap.width, (float)p2.y);
    }
}
```

In this new version, Chapter07_12, you draw the quad by using the beginShape() and endShape() functions. Within the shape definition, you use four vertex() functions to draw the quad with the texture mapping option.

```
if (!queryRect.empty()) {
    // Draw the transformed selection matrix.
    Point [] out = queryRect.toArray();
    noStroke();
    fill(255);
    beginShape();
    texture(photo);
    vertex((float)out[0].x+cap.width, (float)out[0].y, 0, 0, 0);
    vertex((float)out[1].x+cap.width, (float)out[1].y, 0, 1, 0);
    vertex((float)out[2].x+cap.width, (float)out[2].y, 0, 1, 1);
    vertex((float)out[3].x+cap.width, (float)out[3].y, 0, 0, 1);
    endShape(CLOSE);
}
```

The resulting image will be similar to what is shown in Figure 7-13.

Figure 7-13. *Key points matching with texture mapped onto the rectangle*

You may find that the previous exercises are the foundation to build marker-less augmented reality applications. In more advanced use, the PImage variable photo will be replaced by a three-dimensional object. Nevertheless, it is outside the scope of this book to cover the details. If you're interested, you can look for *3D pose estimation* in OpenCV-related documentation.

Face Detection

In interactive media production, often artists and designers turn to OpenCV for its face detection feature. The function is one of the features in the OpenCV objdetect module. The implementation is based on the 2001 paper "Rapid Object Detection Using a Boosted Cascade of Simple Features" by Paul Viola and Michael Jones. Face detection is a machine learning process. This means that before you can perform face detection, you need to train the program to learn what valid and invalid faces are. In OpenCV, however, the distribution includes the pretrained information maintained in the data/haarcascades folder. You can use any one of the XML files to detect features such as frontal face, profile face, eye, and even expression such as smile.

In the next exercise, Chapter07_13, you will detect the frontal face of the user with the parameter file haarcascade_frontalface_default.xml. The file is located inside the OpenCV distribution folder at opencv-3.1.0/data/haarcascades. You need to copy this file from the OpenCV distribution to the data folder of the Processing sketch.

```
// Face detection
import processing.video.*;

import org.opencv.core.*;
import org.opencv.objdetect.CascadeClassifier;

// Detection image size
final int W = 320, H = 240;
Capture cap;
CVImage img;
CascadeClassifier face;
// Ratio between capture size and
// detection size
float ratio;
```

```
void setup() {
  size(640, 480);
  background(0);
  System.loadLibrary(Core.NATIVE_LIBRARY_NAME);
  println(Core.VERSION);
  cap = new Capture(this, width, height);
  cap.start();
  img = new CVImage(W, H);
  // Load the trained face information.
  face = new CascadeClassifier(dataPath("haarcascade_frontalface_default.xml"));
  ratio = float(width)/W;
}

void draw() {
  if (!cap.available())
    return;
  background(0);
  cap.read();
  img.copy(cap, 0, 0, cap.width, cap.height,
    0, 0, img.width, img.height);
  img.copyTo();
  image(cap, 0, 0);
  Mat grey = img.getGrey();
  // Perform face detction. Detection
  // result is in the faces.
  MatOfRect faces = new MatOfRect();
  face.detectMultiScale(grey, faces);
  Rect [] facesArr = faces.toArray();
  pushStyle();
  fill(255, 255, 0, 100);
  stroke(255);
  // Draw each detected face.
  for (Rect r : facesArr) {
    rect(r.x*ratio, r.y*ratio, r.width*ratio, r.height*ratio);
  }
  grey.release();
  faces.release();
  noStroke();
  fill(0);
  text(nf(round(frameRate), 2, 0), 10, 20);
  popStyle();
}
```

The parameter that you work with in face detection belongs to the CascadeClassifier class. First, you have to define an instance, face, of this class. In the setup() function, you create the new instance with the trained frontal face details from the file haarcascade_frontalface_default.xml, which you copied into the data folder. You also use the Processing function dataPath() to return the absolute path of the data folder. To optimize the performance, you use a smaller-size (320×240) grayscale image, grey, for detection in the following statement:

```
face.detectMultiScale(grey, faces);
```

The first parameter is the grayscale image that you want to detect faces. The result will be in the second parameter, which is the MatOfRect variable faces. By converting it into a Rect array, facesArr, you can use a for loop to display all the bounding rectangles. Figure 7-14 shows a sample display from the program.

Figure 7-14. *Face detection*

Once you detect a face, you can further detect the facial features within the bounding rectangle of the face. In the following exercise, Chapter07_14, you will perform a *smile* detection within a face. This program is like the last one. After you detect a face, you create a smaller image using the bounding rectangle and detect the smile facial feature within it. To test the program, you also need to copy the haarcascade_smile.xml file from the OpenCV distribution to the data folder of the Processing sketch.

```
// Smile detection
import processing.video.*;

import org.opencv.core.*;
import org.opencv.objdetect.CascadeClassifier;

// Face detection size
final int W = 320, H = 240;
Capture cap;
CVImage img;
// Two classifiers, one for face, one for smile
CascadeClassifier face, smile;
float ratio;

void setup() {
  size(640, 480);
  background(0);
  System.loadLibrary(Core.NATIVE_LIBRARY_NAME);
  println(Core.VERSION);
  cap = new Capture(this, width, height);
  cap.start();
  img = new CVImage(W, H);
  face = new CascadeClassifier(dataPath("haarcascade_frontalface_default.xml"));
  smile = new CascadeClassifier(dataPath("haarcascade_smile.xml"));
  ratio = float(width)/W;
}
```

```
void draw() {
  if (!cap.available())
    return;
  background(0);
  cap.read();
  img.copy(cap, 0, 0, cap.width, cap.height,
    0, 0, img.width, img.height);
  img.copyTo();
  noStroke();
  image(cap, 0, 0);
  Mat grey = img.getGrey();
  MatOfRect faces = new MatOfRect();
  // Detect the faces first.
  face.detectMultiScale(grey, faces, 1.15, 3,
    Objdetect.CASCADE_SCALE_IMAGE,
    new Size(60, 60), new Size(200, 200));
  Rect [] facesArr = faces.toArray();
  pushStyle();
  for (Rect r : facesArr) {
    fill(255, 255, 0, 100);
    stroke(255, 0, 0);
    float cx = r.x + r.width/2.0;
    float cy = r.y + r.height/2.0;
    ellipse(cx*ratio, cy*ratio,
      r.width*ratio, r.height*ratio);
    // For each face, obtain the image within the bounding box.
    Mat fa = grey.submat(r);
    MatOfRect m = new MatOfRect();
    // Detect smiling expression.
    smile.detectMultiScale(fa, m, 1.2, 25,
      Objdetect.CASCADE_SCALE_IMAGE,
      new Size(30, 30), new Size(80, 80));
    Rect [] mArr = m.toArray();
    stroke(0, 0, 255);
    noFill();
    // Draw the line of the mouth.
    for (Rect sm : mArr) {
      float yy = sm.y+r.y+sm.height/2.0;
      line((sm.x+r.x)*ratio, yy*ratio,
        (sm.x+r.x+sm.width)*ratio, yy*ratio);
    }
    fa.release();
    m.release();
  }
  noStroke();
  fill(0);
  text(nf(round(frameRate), 2, 0), 10, 20);
  popStyle();
  grey.release();
  faces.release();

}
```

In the setup() function, you initialize two classifiers, one for the face that you used in the former exercise. The second classifier is a new one, with the trained information in haarcascade_smile.xml. In the draw() function, you also use another version of the detectMultiScale() function. The first two parameters are the same. The third parameter is the scaling factor that the image is reduced at each scale. The larger the number, the faster the detection, but this comes at the cost of being less accurate. The fourth parameter is the minimum number of neighbors retained. A larger number will eliminate more false detection. The fifth parameter is a dummy one. The last two parameters are the minimum and maximum sizes of the objects (face or smile) you want to detect.

Within the first for loop, you display all faces with elliptical shapes. For each face, you create a submatrix (region of interest), fa, using the bounding rectangle r. Then you detect the smile within this smaller image and draw a horizontal line in the center of the detection. Figure 7-15 illustrates a successful smile detection.

Figure 7-15. *Successful smile detection*

Figure 7-16 shows another trial with an unsuccessful smile detection.

Figure 7-16. *Unsuccessful smile detection*

People Detection

In addition to regular facial feature detection, the `objdetect` module in OpenCV provides a people detection function via the `HOGDescriptor` (histogram of oriented gradients) class. You can use this class to detect the whole human body from a digital image. The following exercise, `Chapter07_15`, will demonstrate the usage of the `HOGDescriptor` function to detect a human body from a live video image. For best results, you need to detect the full body with a relatively clear background.

```
// People detection
import processing.video.*;
import org.opencv.core.*;
import org.opencv.objdetect.HOGDescriptor;

// Detection size
final int W = 320, H = 240;
Capture cap;
CVImage img;
// People detection descriptor
HOGDescriptor hog;
float ratio;

void setup() {
  size(640, 480);
  background(0);
  System.loadLibrary(Core.NATIVE_LIBRARY_NAME);
  println(Core.VERSION);
  cap = new Capture(this, width, height);
  cap.start();
  img = new CVImage(W, H);
  // Initialize the descriptor.
  hog = new HOGDescriptor();
  // User the people detector.
  hog.setSVMDetector(HOGDescriptor.getDefaultPeopleDetector());
  ratio = float(width)/W;
}

void draw() {
  if (!cap.available())
    return;
  background(0);
  cap.read();
  img.copy(cap, 0, 0, cap.width, cap.height,
    0, 0, img.width, img.height);
  img.copyTo();
  image(cap, 0, 0);
  Mat grey = img.getGrey();
  MatOfRect found = new MatOfRect();
  MatOfDouble weight = new MatOfDouble();
  // Perform the people detection.
  hog.detectMultiScale(grey, found, weight);
  Rect [] people = found.toArray();
```

```
pushStyle();
fill(255, 255, 0, 100);
stroke(255);
// Draw the bounding boxes of people detected.
for (Rect r : people) {
  rect(r.x*ratio, r.y*ratio, r.width*ratio, r.height*ratio);
}
grey.release();
found.release();
weight.release();
noStroke();
fill(0);
text(nf(round(frameRate), 2, 0), 10, 20);
popStyle();
}
```

Compared to face detection, the program is simpler. You do not need to load any trained data files. You just initialize the HOGDescriptor class instance hog and set the default people descriptor information with the following statement:

```
hog.setSVMDetector(HOGDescriptor.getDefaultPeopleDetector());
```

In the draw() function, you use the detectMultiScale() method to identify people from the grayscale image grey, and you keep the result in the MatOfRect variable found. The last parameter is a dummy one. In the for loop, you draw each bounding box, r, with a rectangle. Figure 7-17 shows a screenshot of the program.

Figure 7-17. *People detection*

Conclusion

In this chapter, you saw the different ways you can identify key points from an image. Using the key points identified from two consecutive frames, you can perform sparse optical flow analysis or general key point descriptor matching to track a visual pattern between the frames. This technique is useful for augmented reality applications. In addition to key point tracking, you explored the simple use of facial features and whole body detection in OpenCV. These methods are beneficial to artists and designers working with embodied interaction through computer vision. In the next chapter, you will learn about the professional practices of using Processing in deploying your applications.

CHAPTER 8

Application Deployment and Conclusion

This last chapter will conclude what you have learned so far when using OpenCV with the Processing programming environment. It also points out the remaining modules that were not covered in the book and where you can obtain additional resources. In addition, the chapter provides the production know-how that you can use to deploy the applications developed in Processing. This chapter will cover the following topics:

- Developing libraries in Processing

- Exporting applications from Processing

- Using system commands in Processing

- Optimizing tracking with the Kalman filter

- Other OpenCV modules

Developing Libraries in Processing

You may find that whenever you use OpenCV in Processing, you have to include the code folder along with the CVImage class definition in each Processing program or sketch. It would be much better if you could offload this process. This is where the Processing library can help. On the official Processing web site, you can find a number of community-contributed libraries at https://processing.org/reference/libraries/. Those are the third-party contributions approved by Processing. If you are interested, you can refer to the guidelines at https://github.com/processing/processing/wiki/Library-Guidelines for how to develop and distribute libraries in Processing. In this section, I will take you through the steps to prepare a temporary library named CVImage with the open source software Eclipse (http://www.eclipse.org/), a Java software development tool.

To install the centrally distributed Processing library, you can use the Processing IDE window. The installed library is located in the libraries folder within the Processing or Sketchbook folder, depending on what operating system you are using. For each library, it usually contains the following subfolders:

- examples

- library

- reference

- src

© Bryan WC Chung 2017

B. WC. Chung, *Pro Processing for Images and Computer Vision with OpenCV*,
DOI 10.1007/978-1-4842-2775-6_8

The essential one is the library folder, which contains all the Java JAR files and native libraries (.dll, .dylib, or .so files) building up the library. For the CVImage example, you will create just the library folder with the existing components that you put in the Processing code folder. You need to prepare the library only once. It can then be used on different operating systems. The following procedure will show how to use the macOS environment to prepare the library.

Install the Eclipse Software

First you install the open source Java development environment Eclipse, from http://www.eclipse.org/. At the time of this writing, the download button will take you to the download for the Eclipse Neon installer. After unzipping/decompressing the file, you can use the Eclipse installer to install the Eclipse IDE for Java Developers. Before you start the installation, you have to update the installer with the latest content, as shown in Figure 8-1.

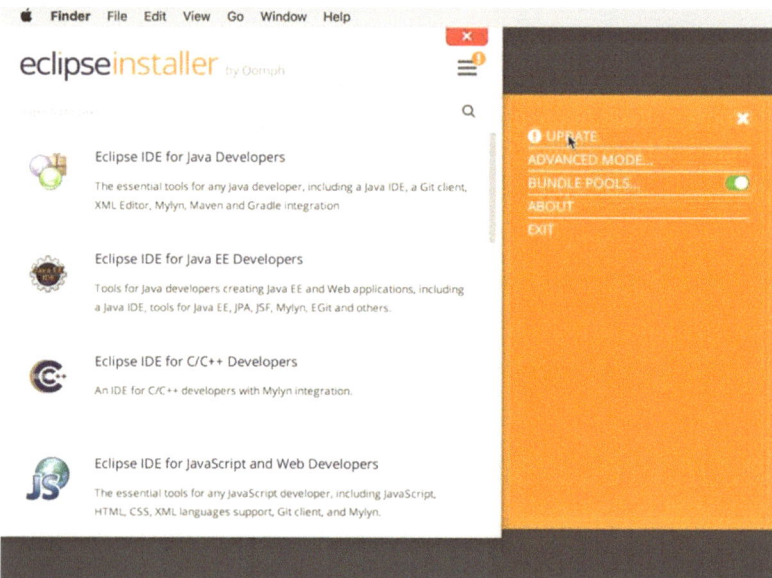

Figure 8-1. *Updating the Eclipse installer*

After the successful update, you can choose to install the Eclipse IDE for Java Developers and leave the installation folder location as the default (Figure 8-2).

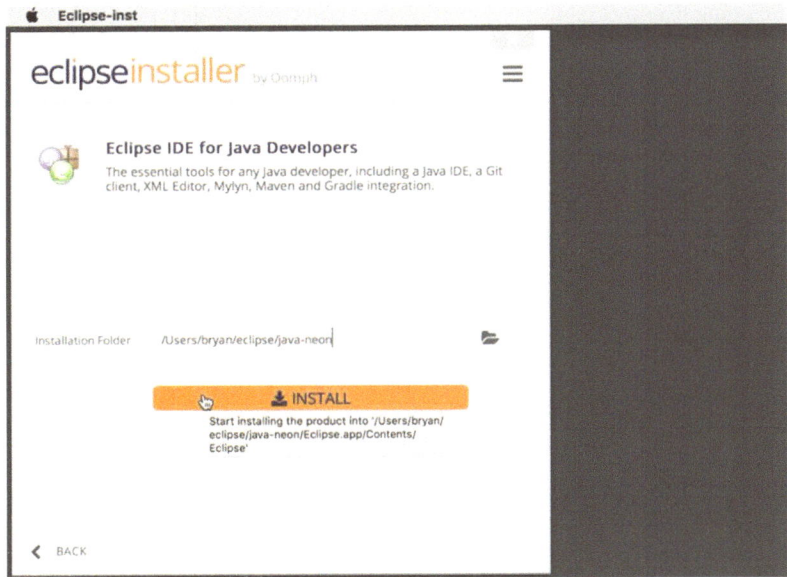

Figure 8-2. *Installing the Eclipse IDE for Java developers*

When you first launch the Eclipse IDE, it will create the default workspace for you. The location is usually in the user's default home folder or the Documents folder.

Prepare the OpenCV and Processing Libraries

In the workspace folder, you can create a new folder named libs (Figure 8-3).

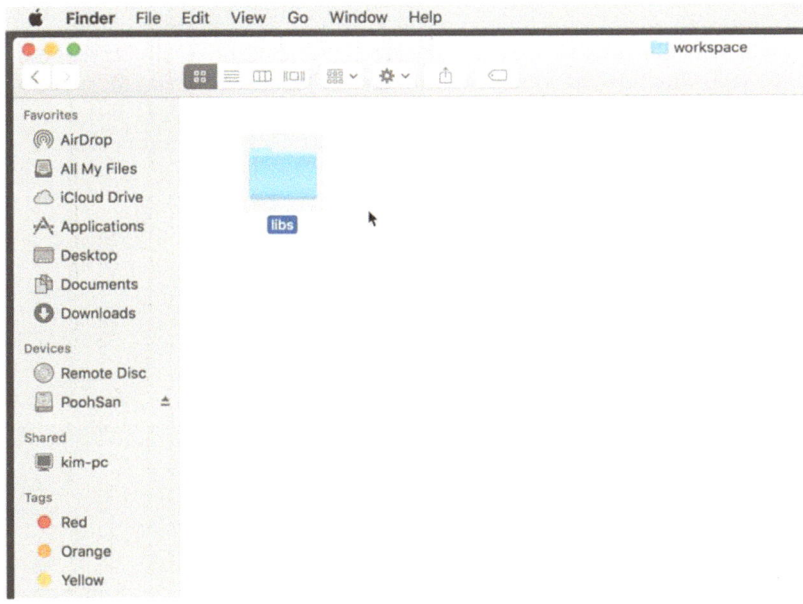

Figure 8-3. *Creating the libs folder inside the workspace folder*

Inside the `libs` folder, you are going to copy the necessary Processing and OpenCV libraries. The first one is the Processing core library. On macOS, it is a bit complex. You need to locate the Processing application. Right-click it and choose Show Package Contents, as shown in Figure 8-4.

Figure 8-4. *Searching for the macOS Processing core library*

Within the `Contents` folder, go in the `Java` folder. Locate the `core.jar` file. Copy it to the `libs` folder you just created in the previous step. At the same time, copy the OpenCV library content of the previous code folder to the `libs` folder, as shown in Figure 8-5. The `core.jar` and `opencv-310.jar` files are essential for all operating systems. The other three files are platform specific: `libopencv_java310.dylib` (macOS 64-bit), `libopencv_java310.so` (Linux 64-bit), and `opencv_java310.dll` (Windows 64-bit). For the Linux and Windows operating systems, the `core.jar` file is inside the Processing application folder at `processing-3.2.3/core/library`.

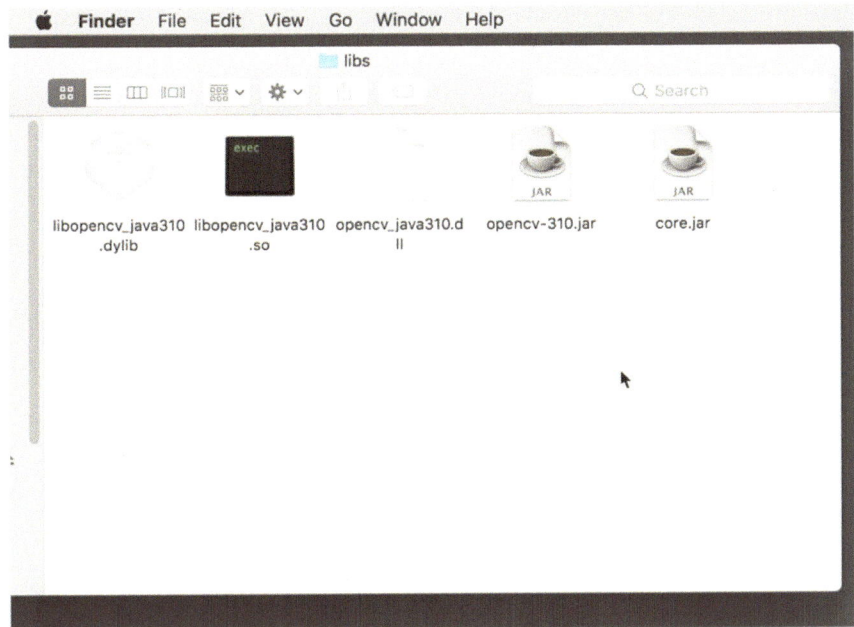

Figure 8-5. *Content of the libs folder*

Build the CVImage Library

Create a new Java project in Eclipse (Figure 8-6).

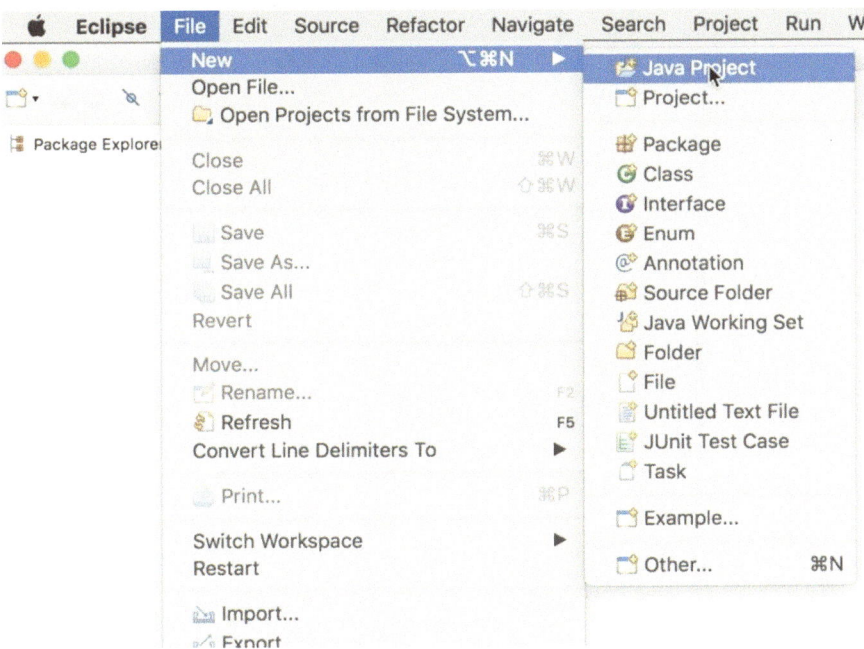

Figure 8-6. *Creating a Java project in Eclipse*

Name the project CVImage (Figure 8-7). Then click the Next button.

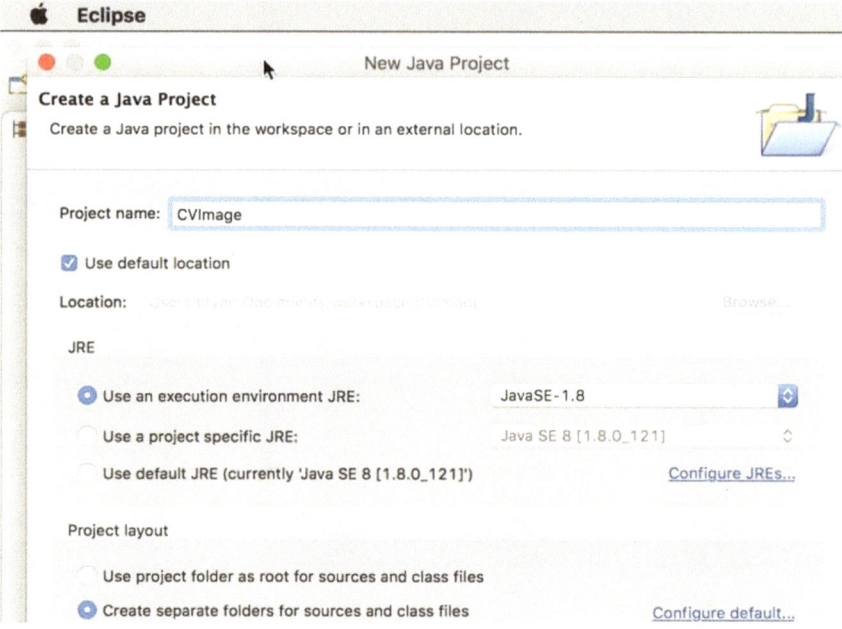

Figure 8-7. *Naming the project CVImage*

In the Java settings, add the corresponding external libraries' JAR files (Figure 8-8).

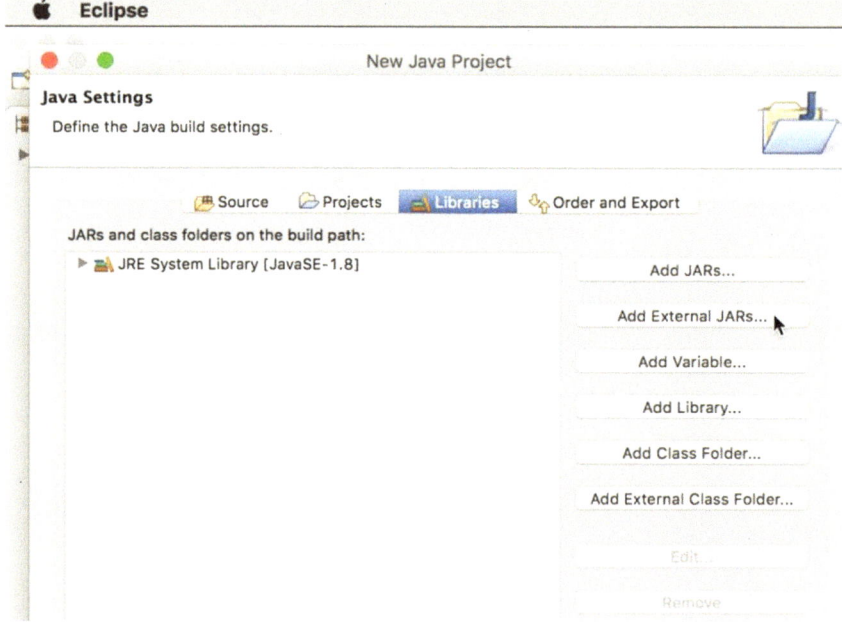

Figure 8-8. *Adding external library JAR files*

From the libs folder within the workspace, choose core.jar and opencv-310.jar (Figure 8-9).

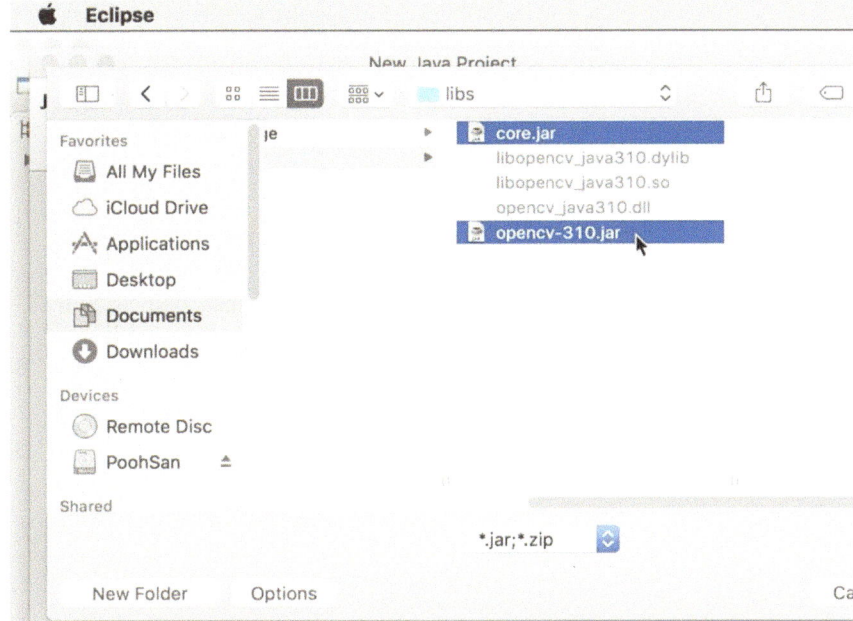

Figure 8-9. *Choosing the Processing and OpenCV JAR files*

In the library definition of opencv-310.jar, click the triangle to choose the native library location (Figure 8-10). Then click Edit and choose External Folder.

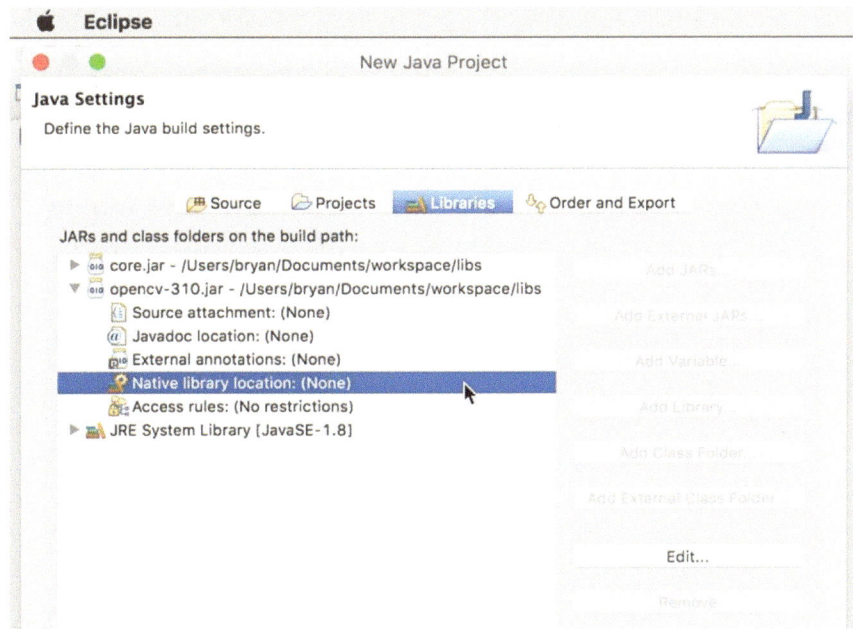

Figure 8-10. *Specifying the native library location for opencv-310.jar*

Choose the `libs` folder again for the native library location for `opencv-310.jar` because you have put all the native libraries, including for macOS, Windows, and Linux, there (Figure 8-11).

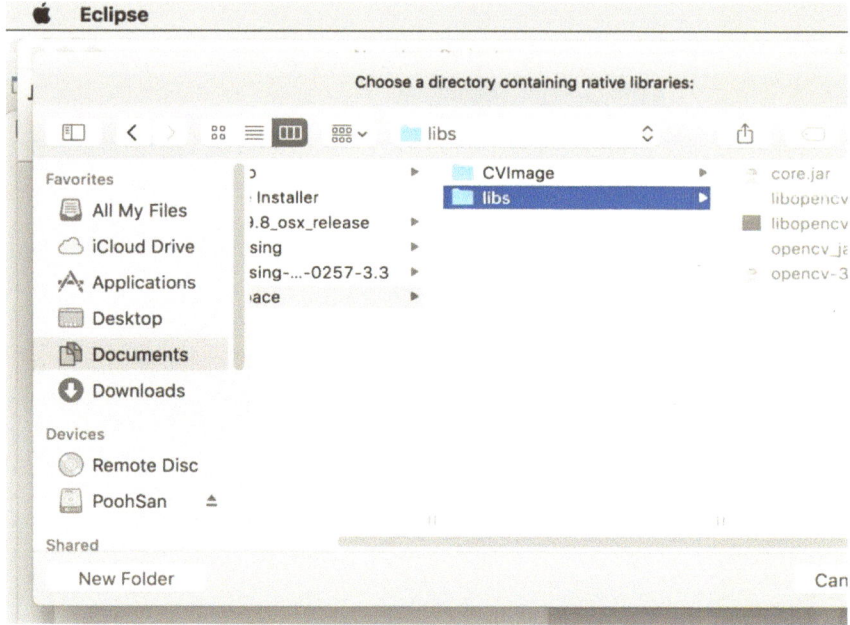

Figure 8-11. *Choosing libs for the native library location*

After clicking Finish to confirm all the information for the external libraries, you can add the new class to the project. From the Package Explorer, right-click the CVImage project to add a new package. Specify the package name, `cvimage`, for the project (Figure 8-12).

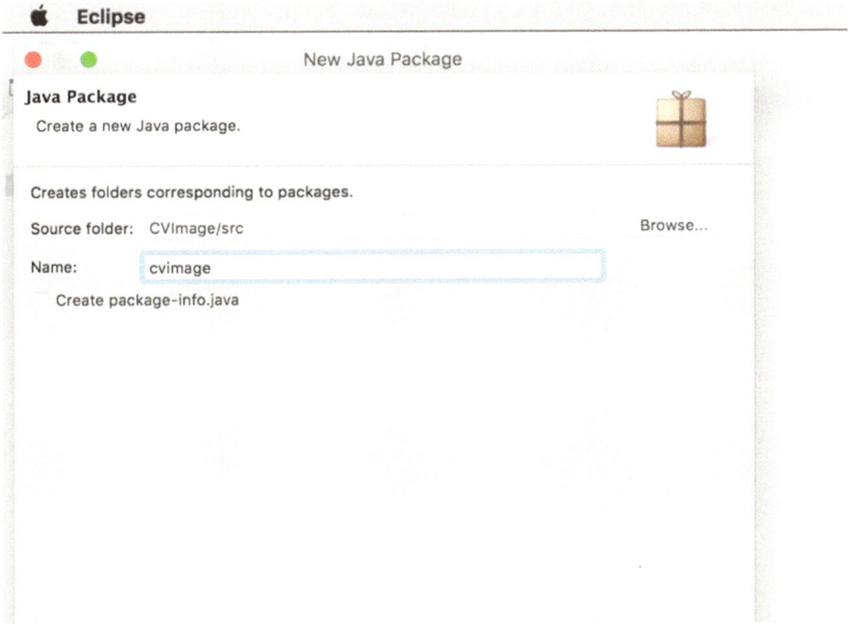

Figure 8-12. *Specifying the package name*

The next piece of information is the class name, CVImage, for the project (Figure 8-13). Again, from the Package Explorer, right-click the package cvimage to add a new class.

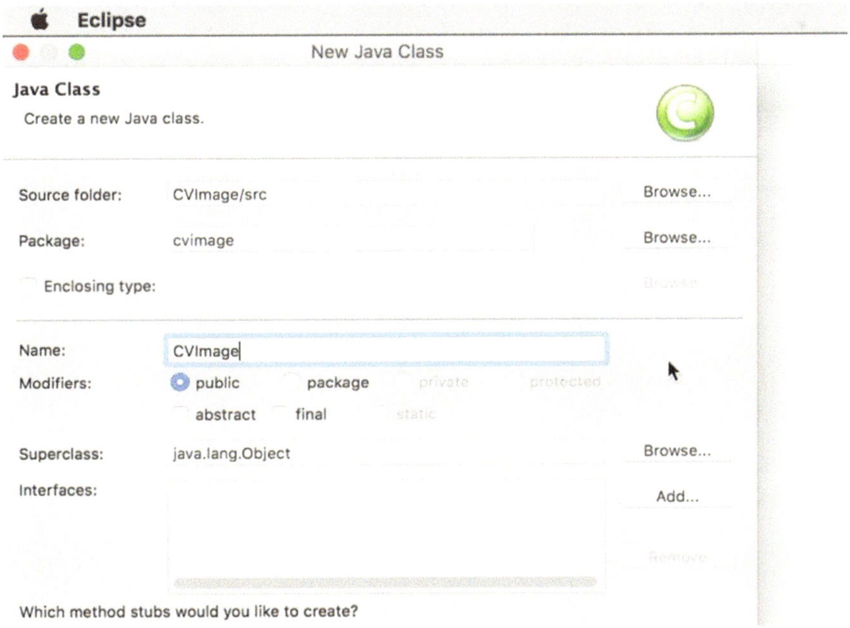

Figure 8-13. *Specifying the class name of the project*

After you fill in all the necessary information for the CVImage project, Eclipse will show you the empty file of CVImage.java. You can copy the original class definition from CVImage.pde, inside any Processing sketch folder that you have used throughout the book, to this file. Nevertheless, there are a few lines that you need to modify to cater for the Eclipse environment. The full code is as follows:

```java
package cvimage;

import processing.core.*;
import org.opencv.core.*;
import org.opencv.imgproc.*;
import java.nio.ByteBuffer;
import java.util.ArrayList;

public class CVImage extends PImage {
  final private MatOfInt BGRA2ARGB = new MatOfInt(0, 3, 1, 2, 2, 1, 3, 0);
  final private MatOfInt ARGB2BGRA = new MatOfInt(0, 3, 1, 2, 2, 1, 3, 0);
  // cvImg - OpenCV Mat in BGRA format
  // pixCnt - number of bytes in the image
  private Mat cvImg;
  private int pixCnt;

  public CVImage(int w, int h) {
    super(w, h, ARGB);
    System.loadLibrary(Core.NATIVE_LIBRARY_NAME);
    pixCnt = w*h*4;
    cvImg = new Mat(new Size(w, h), CvType.CV_8UC4, Scalar.all(0));
  }

  public void copyTo() {
    // Copy from the PImage pixels array to the Mat cvImg
    Mat tmp = new Mat(new Size(this.width, this.height), CvType.CV_8UC4, Scalar.all(0));
    ByteBuffer b = ByteBuffer.allocate(pixCnt);
    b.asIntBuffer().put(this.pixels);
    b.rewind();
    tmp.put(0, 0, b.array());
    cvImg = ARGBToBGRA(tmp);
    tmp.release();
  }

  public void copyTo(PImage i) {
    // Copy from an external PImage to here
    if (i.width != this.width || i.height != this.height) {
      System.out.println("Size not identical");
      return;
    }
    PApplet.arrayCopy(i.pixels, this.pixels);
    this.updatePixels();
    copyTo();
  }
```

```java
public void copyTo(Mat m) {
  // Copy from an external Mat to both the Mat cvImg and PImage pixels array
  if (m.rows() != this.height || m.cols() != this.width) {
    System.out.println("Size not identical");
    return;
  }
  Mat out = new Mat(cvImg.size(), cvImg.type(), Scalar.all(0));
  switch (m.channels()) {
  case 1:
    // Greyscale image
    Imgproc.cvtColor(m, cvImg, Imgproc.COLOR_GRAY2BGRA);
    break;
  case 3:
    // 3 channels colour image BGR
    Imgproc.cvtColor(m, cvImg, Imgproc.COLOR_BGR2BGRA);
    break;
  case 4:
    // 4 channels colour image BGRA
    m.copyTo(cvImg);
    break;
  default:
    System.out.println("Invalid number of channels " + m.channels());
    return;
  }
  out = BGRAToARGB(cvImg);
  ByteBuffer b = ByteBuffer.allocate(pixCnt);
  out.get(0, 0, b.array());
  b.rewind();
  b.asIntBuffer().get(this.pixels);
  this.updatePixels();
  out.release();
}

private Mat BGRAToARGB(Mat m) {
  Mat tmp = new Mat(m.size(), CvType.CV_8UC4, Scalar.all(0));
  ArrayList<Mat> in = new ArrayList<Mat>();
  ArrayList<Mat> out = new ArrayList<Mat>();
  Core.split(m, in);
  Core.split(tmp, out);
  Core.mixChannels(in, out, BGRA2ARGB);
  Core.merge(out, tmp);
  return tmp;
}
```

```
  private Mat ARGBToBGRA(Mat m) {
    Mat tmp = new Mat(m.size(), CvType.CV_8UC4, Scalar.all(0));
    ArrayList<Mat> in = new ArrayList<Mat>();
    ArrayList<Mat> out = new ArrayList<Mat>();
    Core.split(m, in);
    Core.split(tmp, out);
    Core.mixChannels(in, out, ARGB2BGRA);
    Core.merge(out, tmp);
    return tmp;
  }

  public Mat getBGRA() {
    // Get a copy of the Mat cvImg
    Mat mat = cvImg.clone();
    return mat;
  }

  public Mat getBGR() {
    // Get a 3 channels Mat in BGR
    Mat mat = new Mat(cvImg.size(), CvType.CV_8UC3, Scalar.all(0));
    Imgproc.cvtColor(cvImg, mat, Imgproc.COLOR_BGRA2BGR);
    return mat;
  }

  public Mat getGrey() {
    // Get a greyscale copy of the image
    Mat out = new Mat(cvImg.size(), CvType.CV_8UC1, Scalar.all(0));
    Imgproc.cvtColor(cvImg, out, Imgproc.COLOR_BGRA2GRAY);
    return out;
  }
}
```

In the first line, you add the package cvimage statement to specify that the class is inside this package. The other modifications are the println() functions, which are changed to System.out.println() because the class is not in the Processing environment in this case. There are three such cases in both the copyTo(PImage i) and copyTo(Mat m) methods. Build the project by choosing Project ➤ Build Project from the menu bar. After you build the project, you can export the output as a JAR file (Figure 8-14). From the Package Explorer, you can first right-click the project name CVImage and choose Export.

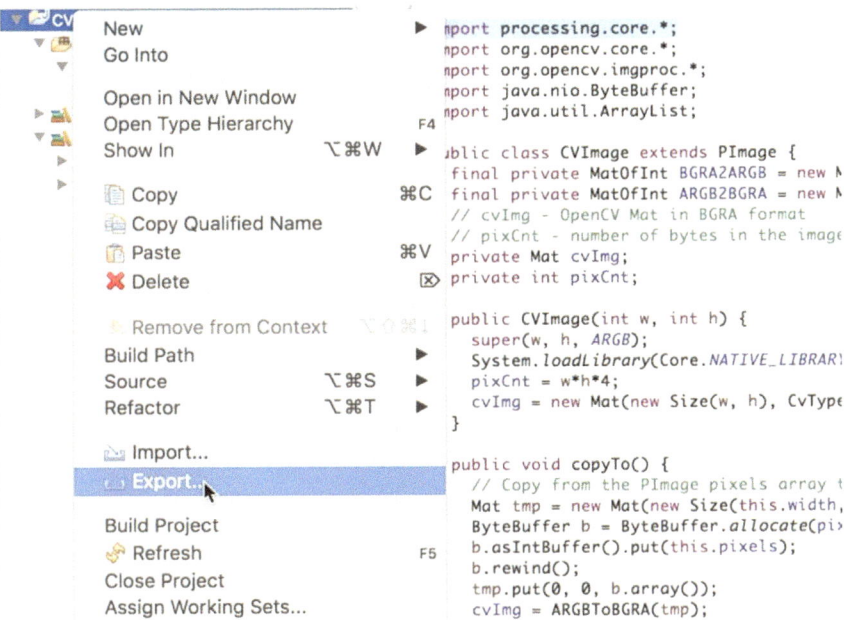

Figure 8-14. *Exporting the output JAR file*

First, you select to export the Java JAR file (Figure 8-15) and then specify where to export it (Figure 8-16).

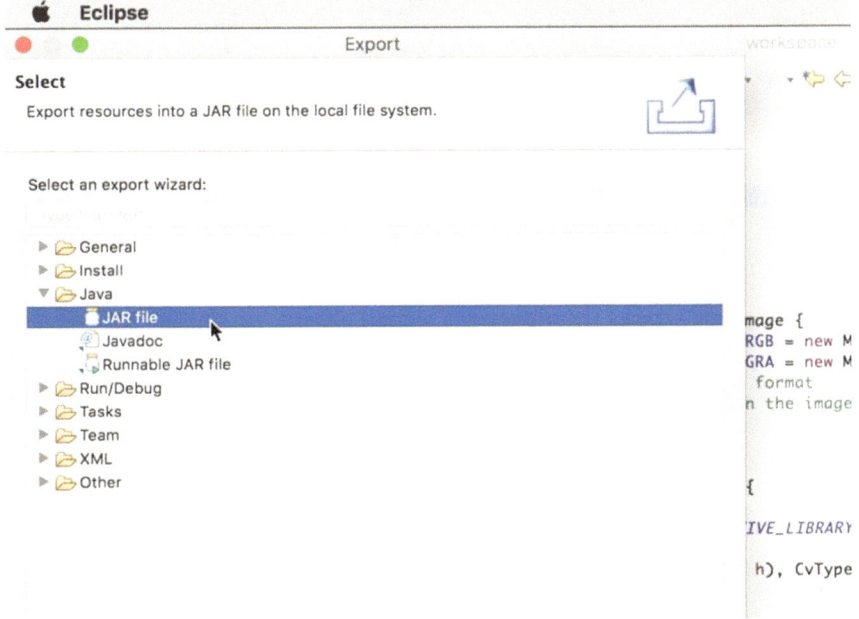

Figure 8-15. *Choosing to export the Java JAR file*

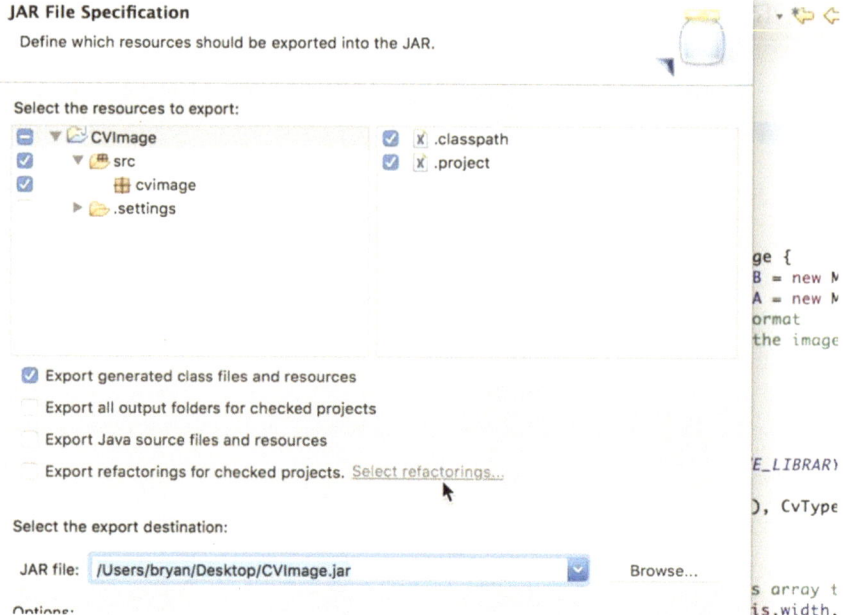

Figure 8-16. *Selecting the export destination*

To prepare your new Processing library, you need to create a folder named CVImage. Inside this folder, you create a subfolder named library. After the export action shown in the previous paragraph, copy the exported JAR file, CVImage.jar, to the library folder. Inside the library folder, copy all the files from the existing code folder there, as shown in Figure 8-17. You can also decide to copy only the native library for your own operating system.

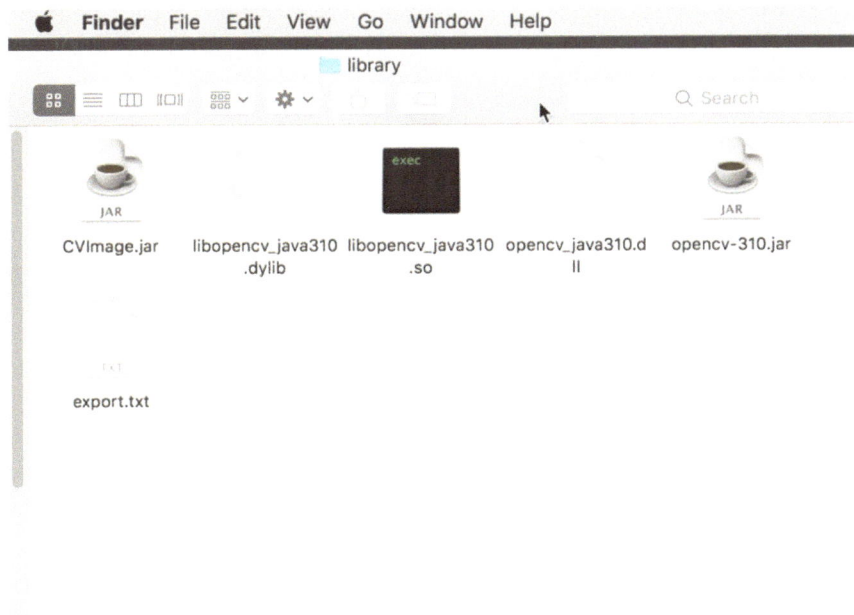

Figure 8-17. *Packaging the library content*

Inside the library folder, create a new text file, named `export.txt`, with the following content. It will instruct Processing what files it will copy to the exported application, which I will cover in the next section.

```
name = CVImage

application.macosx=CVImage.jar,opencv-310.jar,libopencv_java310.dylib
application.windows64=CVImage.jar,opencv-310.jar,opencv_java310.dll
application.linux64=CVImage.jar,opencv-310.jar,libopencv_java310.so
```

You also need to put the library folder inside another folder named `CVImage`. It will be the main folder for your newly created Processing library. You'll put the `CVImage` folder inside the `libraries` folder within your local Processing or Sketchbook folder where you keep all of your Processing sketches. From now on, you do not need to include the `code` folder and the `CVImage` class definition in your Processing programs that use the OpenCV library. In any new Processing program, you can just use the menu item Sketch ➤ Import library ➤ CVImage to include the `CVImage` library into your code (Figure 8-18).

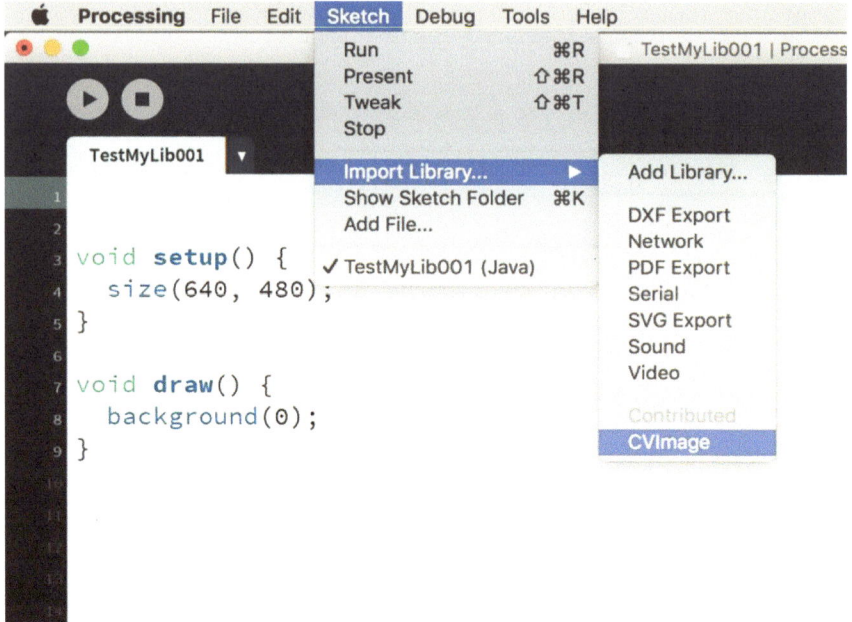

Figure 8-18. *Inserting the newly created library*

This will automatically generate the following statement:

```
import cvimage.*;
```

After the statement, you can continue to use all your code as demonstrated in previous chapters.

Exporting Applications from Processing

Until now, you have executed your Processing programs inside the IDE. In a production environment, it will be desirable to create a stand-alone native application for your program. The Processing IDE provides this function in the menu item File ➤ Export Application. By going through the options, you can choose to create the application for different platforms, such as Windows, macOS, and Linux. You can create either a full-screen application or one with a window of the size specified in your size() function. On the macOS platform, you can also choose to embed Java 8 in the application. In the following example, Chapter08_01, you can test run the export application process with an existing Processing program to display both the color and grayscale images from a webcam:

```
// Greyscale image
import processing.video.*;
import org.opencv.core.*;
import org.opencv.imgproc.Imgproc;
import cvimage.*;
```

```
Capture cap;
CVImage img;

void setup() {
  size(1280, 480);
  background(0);
  System.loadLibrary(Core.NATIVE_LIBRARY_NAME);
  println(Core.VERSION);
  cap = new Capture(this, width/2, height);
  cap.start();
  img = new CVImage(cap.width, cap.height);
  smooth();
}

void draw() {
  if (!cap.available())
    return;
  background(0);
  cap.read();
  img.copy(cap, 0, 0, cap.width, cap.height,
    0, 0, img.width, img.height);
  img.copyTo();
  Mat grey = img.getGrey();
  img.copyTo(grey);
  image(cap, 0, 0);
  image(img, cap.width, 0);
  grey.release();
}
```

Note the use of the `import cvimage.*;` statement in the program. You can proceed to export the application by choosing File ➤ Export Application in the Processing IDE. After you export the application, depending on your choice of operating system, the Processing IDE will generate these application folders:

- `application.linux64`

- `application.macosx64`

- `application.windows64`

Since you have only the 64-bit version of the library, you will not generate the 32-bit version in the export. As I am using the macOS operating system for demonstration, I can go inside the `application.macosx64` folder and double-click the icon `Chapter08_01` to start the application. Figure 8-19 shows a sample display.

Figure 8-19. *Full-screen application*

Note that I have chosen black as the background color and have placed a "stop" button.

Using System Commands in Processing

In a production environment, in addition to building a stand-alone application, it may be necessary for you to perform system tasks within your Processing application. A common task is to shut down the computer after you quit the Processing application. The next example, Chapter08_02, will attempt to call the system command to shut down the computer within the Processing application. It is the macOS version of the code.

```
// Shutdown computer
import java.lang.Process;
import java.lang.Runtime;
import java.io.*;
import java.util.Arrays;

String comm;
String pw;

void setup() {
  size(640, 480);
  // Shutdown command
  comm = "sudo -S shutdown -h now";
  pw = "password";
}
```

```
void draw() {
  background(0);
}

void mousePressed() {
  shutdown();
}

void shutdown() {
  try {
    // Execute the shutdown command.
    Process proc = Runtime.getRuntime().exec(comm);
    BufferedReader buf = new BufferedReader(
      new InputStreamReader(proc.getInputStream()));
    BufferedReader err = new BufferedReader(
      new InputStreamReader(proc.getErrorStream()));
    BufferedWriter out = new BufferedWriter(
      new OutputStreamWriter(proc.getOutputStream()));
    char [] pwc = pw.toCharArray();
    // Send out the sudo password.
    out.write(pwc);
    out.write('\n');
    out.flush();
    // Erase the password.
    Arrays.fill(pwc, '\0');
    pw = "";
    // Print out messages.
    String line;
    println("Output message");
    while ((line = buf.readLine()) != null) {
      println(line);
    }
    println("Error message");
    while ((line = err.readLine()) != null) {
      println(line);
    }
    int rc = proc.exitValue();
    println(rc);
    System.exit(0);
  }
  catch (IOException e) {
    println(e.getMessage());
    System.exit(-1);
  }
}
```

The program uses the Runtime class of Java to execute the shell command. Since it requires the sudo password to execute the command, you have to put the password in the String variable pw. For the Windows operating system, in the following example, Chapter08_03, you can simplify the code as follows:

```java
// Shutdown computer in Windows.
import java.lang.Process;
import java.lang.Runtime;
import java.io.*;

String comm;

void setup() {
  size(640, 480);
  // Command string
  comm = "shutdown -s -t 0";
}

void draw() {
  background(0);
}

void mousePressed() {
  shutdown();
}

void shutdown() {
  try {
    // Execute the shutdown command.
    Process proc = Runtime.getRuntime().exec(comm);
    BufferedReader buf = new BufferedReader(
      new InputStreamReader(proc.getInputStream()));
    BufferedReader err = new BufferedReader(
      new InputStreamReader(proc.getErrorStream()));
    // Print out the messages.
    String line;
    println("Output message");
    while ((line = buf.readLine()) != null) {
      println(line);
    }
    println("Error message");
    while ((line = err.readLine()) != null) {
      println(line);
    }
    int rc = proc.exitValue();
    println(rc);
    System.exit(0);
  }
  catch (IOException e) {
    println(e.getMessage());
    System.exit(-1);
  }
}
```

The command string is different, but you do not need to supply the password to execute the command. For Linux, it is similar to the macOS version, but again you do not need to have the sudo password part.

```
// Shutdown computer in Linux.
import java.lang.Process;
import java.lang.Runtime;
import java.io.*;
import java.util.Arrays;

String comm;

void setup() {
  size(640, 480);
  // Command string
  comm = "shutdown -h now";
}

void draw() {
  background(0);
}

void mousePressed() {
  shutdown();
}

void shutdown() {
  try {
    // Execute the shutdown command.
    Process proc = Runtime.getRuntime().exec(comm);
    BufferedReader buf = new BufferedReader(
      new InputStreamReader(proc.getInputStream()));
    BufferedReader err = new BufferedReader(
      new InputStreamReader(proc.getErrorStream()));
    // Print any messages.
    String line;
    println("Output message");
    while ((line = buf.readLine()) != null) {
      println(line);
    }
    println("Error message");
    while ((line = err.readLine()) != null) {
      println(line);
    }
    int rc = proc.exitValue();
    println(rc);
    System.exit(0);
  }
  catch (IOException e) {
    println(e.getMessage());
    System.exit(-1);
  }

}
```

Now you can export the application from the Processing IDE. Depending on the operating system, navigate inside the appropriate application folder such as `application.linux64`, `application.macosx64`, or `application.windows64`. Double-click the application `Chapter08_02`. Note that by clicking the application window, it will shut down the computer.

Optimizing Tracking with the Kalman Filter

In the previous chapter, you saw an example of face detection. In the example, you used a rectangle to indicate the region where a face is detected. If you observe the tracking result, it is easy to find that the movement of the rectangle is quite jagged. In the `video` module of OpenCV, the `KalmanFilter` class can provide the way to smoothen the tracking result. The following exercise will provide the code to smoothen the face detection tracking result. If you want an in-depth explanation of the Kalman filter, you can refer to the documentation at https://www.cs.unc.edu/~welch/media/pdf/kalman_intro.pdf. Essentially, the `KalmanFilter` class can help you to predict numeric results based on previous measurements. The exercise, `Chapter08_04`, will include a separate class, `KFilter`, that encapsulates the processing of the `KalmanFilter` class in OpenCV.

```
// Kalman filter
import org.opencv.video.KalmanFilter;

public class KFilter {
  KalmanFilter kf;
  MatOfFloat measurement;
  int numS;
  int numM;

  public KFilter(int s, int m) {
    // Initialize the Kalman filter with
    // number of states and measurements.
    // Our measurements are the x, y location of
    // the face rectangle and its width and height.
    numS = s;
    numM = m;
    kf = new KalmanFilter(numS, numM, 0, CvType.CV_32F);
    float [] tmp = new float[numM];
    for (int i=0; i<tmp.length; i++) {
      tmp[i] = 0;
    }
    measurement = new MatOfFloat(tmp);
  }

  void initFilter(int fps) {
    // Initialize the state transition matrix.
    double dt1 = 1.0/fps;
    Mat tmp = Mat.eye(numS, numS, CvType.CV_32F);
    tmp.put(0, 4, dt1);
    tmp.put(1, 5, dt1);
    tmp.put(2, 6, dt1);
    tmp.put(3, 7, dt1);
    kf.set_transitionMatrix(tmp);
```

```
  // Initialize the measurement matrix.
  tmp = kf.get_measurementMatrix();
  for (int i=0; i<numM; i++) {
    tmp.put(i, i, 1);
  }
  kf.set_measurementMatrix(tmp);

  tmp = kf.get_processNoiseCov();
  Core.setIdentity(tmp, Scalar.all(1e-5));
  kf.set_processNoiseCov(tmp);
  tmp = kf.get_measurementNoiseCov();
  Core.setIdentity(tmp, Scalar.all(1e-2));
  kf.set_measurementNoiseCov(tmp);
  tmp = kf.get_errorCovPost();
  Core.setIdentity(tmp, Scalar.all(1));
  kf.set_errorCovPost(tmp);
  tmp.release();
}


MatOfFloat updateFilter(float x, float y, float w, float h) {
  // Update the Kalman filter with latest measurements on
  // x, y locations and width, height.
  Mat prediction = kf.predict();
  measurement.fromArray(new float[]{x, y, w, h});
  MatOfFloat estimated = new MatOfFloat(kf.correct(measurement));
  prediction.release();
  // Return the estimated version of the 4 measurements.
  return estimated;
  }
}
```

The measurement that you are going to predict is the specification of the rectangle that indicates the face being tracked. It has four numbers: x position, y position, width, and height of the rectangle. For every frame, you use the method updateFilter() to update the Kalman filter with the recent information of the face rectangle and obtain an estimate of it. In the following main program, notice how you just use the information of a single face and draw the estimated position of the face rectangle:

```
// Face detection
import processing.video.*;
import cvimage.*;
import org.opencv.core.*;
import org.opencv.objdetect.CascadeClassifier;

// Detection image size
final int W = 320, H = 240;
Capture cap;
CVImage img;
CascadeClassifier face;
// Ratio between capture size and
// detection size
float ratio;
KFilter kalman;
```

```
void setup() {
  size(640, 480);
  background(0);
  System.loadLibrary(Core.NATIVE_LIBRARY_NAME);
  println(Core.VERSION);
  cap = new Capture(this, width, height);
  cap.start();
  img = new CVImage(W, H);
  // Load the trained face information.
  face = new CascadeClassifier(dataPath("haarcascade_frontalface_default.xml"));
  ratio = float(width)/W;
  kalman = new KFilter(8, 4);
  frameRate(30);
  kalman.initFilter(30);
}

void draw() {
  if (!cap.available())
    return;
  background(0);
  cap.read();
  img.copy(cap, 0, 0, cap.width, cap.height,
    0, 0, img.width, img.height);
  img.copyTo();
  image(cap, 0, 0);
  Mat grey = img.getGrey();
  // Perform face detction. Detection
  // result is in the faces.
  MatOfRect faces = new MatOfRect();
  face.detectMultiScale(grey, faces);
  Rect [] facesArr = faces.toArray();
  pushStyle();
  fill(255, 255, 0, 100);
  stroke(255);
  // Draw only one single face.
  if (facesArr.length == 1) {
    Rect r = facesArr[0];
    float [] tmp = kalman.updateFilter(r.x, r.y, r.width, r.height).toArray();
    rect(tmp[0]*ratio, tmp[1]*ratio, tmp[2]*ratio, tmp[3]*ratio);
  }
  grey.release();
  faces.release();
  noStroke();
  fill(0);
  text(nf(round(frameRate), 2, 0), 10, 20);
  popStyle();
}
```

The main program is similar to the exercise you did in the previous chapter. In the draw() function, you draws only a single face. Before drawing the rectangle, the function updates the Kalman filter with the rectangle information and obtains an estimated (smoothened) version for actual display. When you run the program, you will notice that the movement of the face rectangle will be much smoother.

Other OpenCV Modules

In this book, you have basically used the calib3d, core, features2d, imgproc, objdetect, and video modules in OpenCV. Besides these modules, there are a lot of other modules that you have not yet seen. For example, you use the Processing functionalities of image input/output and graphical display but have not used the OpenCV imgcodecs and highgui modules. Also, I have not touched on any topics related to computational photography (photo) and machine learning (ml). In 3D reconstruction, I covered only one exercise. With the use of a depth camera, such as the Microsoft Kinect, OpenCV is capable of obtaining a depth image from the videoio module using OpenNI2 (https://structure.io/openni) and also the Intel RealSense technology (www.intel.com/content/www/us/en/architecture-and-technology/realsense-overview.html). In the opencv_contrib repository, you just use the optflow module. The repository also contains modules for deep neural networks (dnn), 3D reconstruction through structure from motion (sfm), text recognition (text), and many more. In the future, it is expected that deep learning, 3D vision, and virtual and augmented reality will be areas with significant development.

Conclusion

In this chapter, I concluded the coverage of how to use OpenCV in creative application development using Processing. With this production know-how, artists and designers can deploy applications in more professional ways. Throughout this book, you learned various approaches to perform image-processing tasks and the fundamentals of object/feature detection and tracking, with the aim of enhancing the human computer interaction experience. Besides just providing a technical demonstration of OpenCV, the exercises in the book also hint at a creative thinking process that artists and designers may find helpful. With the CVImage library you built in this chapter, you can now use OpenCV without dealing with the tedious tasks of format conversion and data migration. At the same time, the library does not intend to hide every OpenCV function; feel free to explore OpenCV to better understand the essential concepts of image processing and computer vision.

Index

© Bryan WC Chung 2017
B. WC. Chung, *Pro Processing for Images and Computer Vision with OpenCV*,
DOI 10.1007/978-1-4842-2775-6

Get the eBook for only $5!

Why limit yourself?

With most of our titles available in both PDF and ePUB format, you can access your content wherever and however you wish—on your PC, phone, tablet, or reader.

Since you've purchased this print book, we are happy to offer you the eBook for just $5.

To learn more, go to http://www.apress.com/companion or contact support@apress.com.

Apress®

All Apress eBooks are subject to copyright. All rights are reserved by the Publisher, whether the whole or part of the material is concerned, specifically the rights of translation, reprinting, reuse of illustrations, recitation, broadcasting, reproduction on microfilms or in any other physical way, and transmission or information storage and retrieval, electronic adaptation, computer software, or by similar or dissimilar methodology now known or hereafter developed. Exempted from this legal reservation are brief excerpts in connection with reviews or scholarly analysis or material supplied specifically for the purpose of being entered and executed on a computer system, for exclusive use by the purchaser of the work. Duplication of this publication or parts thereof is permitted only under the provisions of the Copyright Law of the Publisher's location, in its current version, and permission for use must always be obtained from Springer. Permissions for use may be obtained through RightsLink at the Copyright Clearance Center. Violations are liable to prosecution under the respective Copyright Law.